Mamas of
DADA

Women of the European Avant-Garde

Paula K. Kamenish

Mamas of DADA

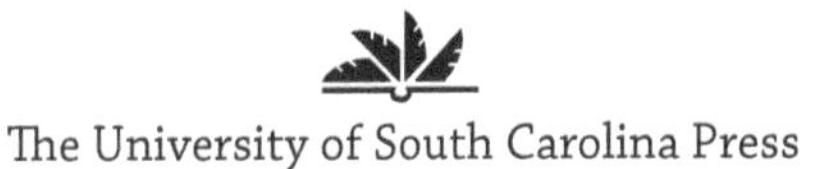

The University of South Carolina Press

Published by the University of South Carolina Press
Columbia, South Carolina 29208

www.sc.edu/uscpress

Manufactured in the United States of America

24 23 22 21 20 19 18 17 16 15 10 9 8 7 6 5 4 3 2 1

Library of Congress Cataloging-in-Publication Data

Kamenish, Paula K., 1955–
Mamas of Dada : women of the European avant-garde / Paula K. Kamenish.
pages cm
Includes bibliographical references and index.
ISBN 978-1-61117-468-7 (hardback)
1. Dadaism—Europe. 2. Women artists—Europe. 3. Women and the arts—Europe—History—20th century. I. Title.
NX456.5.D3K36 2015
700.82'09041—dc23 2014041368

Contents

Illustrations

Preface

The first thing I discovered about Dada when I mentioned the word to colleagues, students, and friends in the United States in 1996 was that the majority of them either had no idea what Dada was (giving me a blank look), or they had negative impressions of what it might be (giving me a disapproving stare). Even those who claimed to know Dada were unable to say with any accuracy what it was. They related the word to nihilism, and some vaguely alluded to antiwar and antiart activities of the early twentieth century.

I asked myself where students of literature and art should turn to learn about Dada. If they did an online search for "Dada" today, their first resource would probably be *Wikipedia,* where they would be told that Dada began as a Swiss cultural movement during World War I. They would also learn that Dadaists used multimedia to "ridicule . . . the meaninglessness of the modern world."[1] And they would be alerted to its "anarchist" spirit. The *Wikipedia* entry further offers a quick history of Dada's birth at the Cabaret Voltaire in Zurich, its growth and dissolution, complete with names of more than thirty male Dadaists and six female participants. Also included are images of Dada art by Tristan Tzara, Kurt Schwitters, Marcel Duchamp, Raoul Hausmann, and Hannah Höch. Although the reliability of *Wikipedia* entries is often questioned, the entry on Dada is unusually well documented and offers a reasonable overview of the history of the group. Nevertheless it falls short of giving a clear definition of Dada.

For information about Dada poetry, literature students would perhaps consult their *Handbook to Literature,* where they would find that Dada "was founded in Zurich in 1916 by Tristan Tzara (who then went to Paris) with the ostensibly destructive intent of demolishing art and philosophy, intending to replace them with conscious madness as a protest against the insanity of the war."[2] Besides imparting disputable information about who founded Dada, this source does not mention the wide diversity of Dada's literary products, ranging from nonsense sound poems such as "gadji beri bimba / glandridi lauli lonni cadori" (recited by Hugo Ball at the Cabaret Voltaire) to the prolific *ars poetica* manifestos of its adherents. Without references to or descriptions of types of texts, most students of literature would understandably have difficulty imagining the writings of "conscious madness" mentioned in the definition.

Met with what is at best ambiguous assistance from the most easily accessed sources for the newcomer to Dada, the student's curiosity dwindles. Dada remains a mysterious, indescribable movement of unclear origin and relevance. The problem with understanding Dada stems from difficulties encountered when defining Dada. And to some degree the lack of knowledge about many of its participants and their essential contributions to its propagation through cabarets of music, recitations and dance, its literary journals, and its art exhibits is to blame. In most histories of this avant-garde manifestation, women and their support of Dada have been overlooked and understudied.

Why should the stories of Dadaist women, their accomplishments, and their range of influence have received less attention than those of their male counterparts? Were the women of Dada merely shadows behind the men, giving technical support during performances or making the coffee? Contemporary testimony strongly suggests otherwise. Female Dadaists provided artistic components that are essential in defining the movement.

What then were their exact contributions to Dada projects? How did they define their roles as artists and writers during this period of antiwar, antibourgeois ideals? How did they live and support themselves in the era between the "new woman" and the "flapper"? Did these women choose to have partners? Children? What personal sacrifices were they willing to make to participate in Dadaist activities? Who were these women?

The following chapters answer these questions while considering six representative women who acted as mamas of Dada: Emmy Hennings, Gabrielle Buffet, Germaine Everling, Céline Arnauld, Juliette Roche, and Hannah Höch. These particular women have been selected for scrutiny because of their avant-garde pursuits in the chief centers of Dada activity and, more important, because they left behind written records of their involvement with Dada. Some were participants; others were observant and recording witnesses. All helped to chronicle Dada's European (and sometimes American) manifestations. Yet in a movement that was known for its spontaneous nature and its roots in performance art, it is quite rare to locate valuable written clues left behind by Dada women. Searching has been worth the effort, however. Their testimonies, sometimes hidden in their visual art or in their personal correspondence, reveal a new perspective on Dada, their own work, and how they viewed their contributions to the avant-garde.

This volume focuses on the women's backgrounds and confessed artistic motivations in addition to their Dadaist productions and how they were influenced by and contributed to the creative activity of the group. The result is more than simple biographies of each woman. Instead from the scattered facts of history (through a close reading of letters, memoirs, poetry, fiction, essays, and other contemporary testimony), a map of each woman's creative output, the immediacy of its influence, and the means of its survival in relation to the overall Dada enterprise emerges. Moreover each mama of Dada is given the opportunity to speak for herself and reveal her perception of the avant-garde and her role within it.

If the names Hennings, Buffet, Everling, Arnauld, Roche, Höch—and those of other women who influenced Dada or were influenced by it—seem unfamiliar to readers of Dada's early records, it is partly the fault of testimonies dating from the period. Most contemporary chronicles of the Dada era omit or note only briefly the accomplishments of female artists. Relying on the *Dada Almanach* (1920), Richard Huelsenbeck's androcentric anthology of the Dada years, which includes only one female poet (Maria d'Arezzo), one might wonder if any women were seen as significant contributors to Dada's visual arts, music, or theater. Yet women were indeed creating alongside their male counterparts. Many of these female artists and writers enjoyed success during their lifetimes, yet very few of their accomplishments are recorded in art anthologies or literary histories. To discover their contributions, one needs to search beyond such standard textbooks as H. W. Janson's *History of Art* (1962), which—before the revised edition by his son Anthony Janson (1986)—included no women among the three thousand entries. Even the 1995 edition featured only thirty-eight female artists.

Most literary histories and anthologies suffer from the same imbalance, showcasing the work of male writers at the exclusion of women's literary creations. Women writers and artists still receive little attention in dual-gendered studies of the Dada era. Noteworthy examples that provide a masculine-dominated account with a minimal representation of female writers and visual artists include histories by Hans Richter, Serge Faucherau, Georges Hugnet, Michel Sanouillet, and Marc Dachy.[3]

Even Willard Bohn's 1993 *Dada Market: An Anthology of Poetry* includes the works of thirty-seven men but only five women; yet scholars are grateful to him for these five. Between 1996 and 2006 Stephen C. Foster oversaw what became the exhaustive ten-volume *Crisis and the Arts: The History of Dada,* offering the most comprehensive study of the movement to date. The essays introduce readers to (mostly male) individual artists and poets in their geographical, historical, and political contexts. In 2006 Dafydd Jones, a contributor to *Crisis and the Arts,* edited a collection of essays titled *Dada Culture: Critical Texts on the Avant-Garde.* Its focus is the theoretical and philosophical framework for interpreting Dada, and it features an all-male cast. Also in 2006, Tom Sandqvist published a well-supported and convincing argument in *Dada East: The Romanians of Cabaret Voltaire* that Zurich Dada was preformed in Bucharest with Tzara, Arthur Segal, and the Janco brothers. Matthew Biro's 2009 study, *The Dada Cyborg,* commendably devotes two chapters to Höch's construction of hybrid bodies and goes so far as to suggest that Höch's montages predict Donna Haraway's feminist interpretation of the cyborg. These are all welcomed studies of Dada; however, they still leave a blank to be filled.

Before the 1970s only the stories of women of the stature of Cleopatra or Catherine the Great made it into the body of general knowledge taught in schools and discussed in intellectual circles. Even Mary Ann Caws, presently one of the strongest contributors to the study of women in the arts, focused on the works of four men and no women in her 1970 *The Poetry of Dada and Surrealism: Aragon, Breton, Tzara, Eluard, Desnos*. In the past forty years, the women's movement has had a pervasive influence on reviewing, revising, and sometimes rewriting world history and culture. Nevertheless even today, women's history remains a marginalized and specialized discipline, often relegated to women's studies programs rather than routinely integrated into mainstream courses and texts.

Fortunately in the past fifteen years, scholars have begun to examine gender identity and production in the avant-garde and to pose questions about the roles of individual female Dadaists. Since the early 1990s feminist scholars have been publishing excellent volumes on individual women artists and writers of the period (including Mina Loy, Florine Stettheimer, Elsa Freytag-Loringhoven, and Sophie Täuber) and assembled informative collections of essays on Dadaist women (notably by Britta Jürgs and Naomi Sawelson-Gorse). The view of the public role of women in literary and art history has changed even since 1996, when I began seeking out the women who contributed to the European Dada movement. In the final years of the twentieth century, scholars such as Sawelson-Gorse and Jürgs noticed the vacuum in Dada studies and began to fill it with Sawelson-Gorse's 1998 *Women in Dada: Essays on Sex, Gender, and Identity* and the Jürgs's 1999 *Etwas Wasser in der Seife: Portraits dadistischer Künstlerinnen und Schriftstellerinnen* (Some Water in the Soap: Portraits of Female Dada Artists and Writers). These collections began the work in Dada studies that a group of landmark texts on women had already begun for Surrealism.[4] While *Women in Dada* with its affirmative title provides a comprehensive collection of essays on individual women (and some men)—mostly involved in New York Dada,[5] *Etwas Wasser in der Seife* has a primarily European focus in its choice of subjects and is accessible only to readers of German. Both collections emphasize biography and cultural history, but provide little analysis of the women's writings. In fact most recent studies of women connected with Dada deal with those who were principally visual artists (Stettheimer, Täuber, and Höch) and neglect the poetry, essays, memoirs, and novels of their sisters.[6] The exceptions are Carolyn Burke's *Becoming Modern: The Life of Mina Loy* (1996), which provides a highly readable cultural biography as well as analysis of Loy's poetry and assemblages, and Irene Gammel's *Baroness Elsa: Gender, Dada, and Everyday Modernity* (2002), a comprehensive study of the life and works of Freytag-Loringhoven. René Gass and Bärbel Reetz have contributed

German biographies of Hennings's life and times, while Bernhard Echte's 1999 *Emmy Ball Hennings 1885-1948* provides us with the scholarly background to the artist's work.

In one of the largest Dada projects ever undertaken, Leah Dickerman edited *Dada: Zurich, Berlin, Hannover, Cologne, New York, Paris* (2005) to accompany the three-location pedagogical exhibition titled Dada at the Centre Pompidou in Paris, the National Gallery of Art in Washington, and the Museum of Modern Art in New York. Essays by Brigid Doherty, Dorothea Dietrich, Sabine Kriebel, Michael Taylor, Janine Mileaf, and Matthew Witkovsky are richly inclusive, giving information about both male and female Dadaists. Photographs of artists and vibrant color plates of their work illustrate the volume. The geographically organized sections, along with Amanda Hockensmith and Kriebel's biographies of artists and Witkovsky's chronology, invite easy access.

In 2009 Ruth Hemus brought attention to five significant female Dadaists in *Dada's Women*. Her biographical-historical study, interspersed with close readings and high quality color reproductions, links Hennings, Täuber, Höch, Suzanne Duchamp, and Arnauld with the three centers of Dada activity: Zurich, Berlin, and Paris. Most important, Hemus includes a study of the Dadaist poet Arnauld, who drew attention when her poetry first appeared in Bohn's anthology.

All the women involved in the multimedia manifestations of Dada merit further study, but most especially those who "mothered" the movement. These mamas of Dada include those who were instrumental in birthing new techniques, nurturing and sustaining the movement both financially and aesthetically, challenging it with self-reflection, and recording its everyday life. Instead of relying merely on the male-dominated perspective of historical records, this book looks to the women themselves, to allow them to tell their stories, which are embedded in the visual and verbal texts they left behind.

Even a decade into a new millennium, art and literary historians, both in the United States and Europe, invariably raise their eyebrows and say, "Women in Dada? Were there women involved?" This is because the contributions of some key female figures have not received the close attention they are due. Hennings is a case in point. Despite her role as the cofounder of Dada's Cabaret Voltaire, which housed Zurich Dada, and despite her avant-garde performances, which drew the first unsuspecting audiences to Dada soirees, her work receives scholarly attention almost exclusively in relation to her memoir of her life with her husband, Hugo Ball. Further study reveals her serious and sometimes conflicted commitment to all Dada activities in Zurich, even after she was forced by family circumstances to flee to the Swiss countryside. During the Dada years, she alternatively abandoned and returned to her career as a performance artist to support her family and satisfy her own desire for the stage.

In any study of Dada personalities, their interactions, and their production, Everling's memoirs of the period are essential. Because her apartment provided a refuge for Parisian Dadaists, she became privy to crucial information about Francis Picabia's circle. She wrote with bittersweet emotion from the point of view of a former lover, at times sympathetic to him, but often critical of the painter-poet and his artistic companions.

Buffet also deserves to be moved from behind the shadow of her more famous provocateur husband. Her remarkable intellect made her an exceptionally capable and formidable woman, who became Picabia's anchor, both artistically and emotionally. Her own works lead readers to a clearer understanding not only of her husband's art but also of the broader meaning of the European avant-garde and her part in it.

Another apt example is Arnauld. There has been woefully little discussion of Arnauld's poetry and its role in furthering Parisian Dada. Although her writings influenced the poetic vision of Tzara and Paul Dermée and although she was responsible for founding at least one Dada journal to publish her colleagues' works, her voice has until recently been unheard by scholars and publishers. Her avant-garde symbolism, which illustrates the metamorphosing of the Dadaist rebellion into the Surrealist aesthetic, led other writers to praise and follow her.

Another inexcusable omission is Roche. In Dada histories the works of the articulate Roche are mostly neglected in favor of the controversy surrounding her husband, Cubist painter Albert Gleizes. In her literary and artistic career, Roche moved with grace and ease among the Nabis, the Cubists, Jean Cocteau's group, and the Dadaists. Her greatest contributions to the avant-garde are to be found in her typographically innovative poetry, her unpublished memoir, and her satiric novella, which reveals the behind-the-scenes adventures of thinly disguised versions of Arthur Cravan, Marcel Duchamp, and Picabia.

Finally the pioneering Höch deserves further study in the context of women who mothered Dada. This artist once claimed that she would rather work like a dog in Berlin, where she was the only female member of the Dada group, than live a quiet, comfortable, and wasted life at home in Gotha with her family. Her networking capabilities and her international travels spread her influence to many artists and writers, including Hans Arp, Kurt Schwitters, and poet Til Brugman during their nine-year lesbian relationship. The influence of these artists on each other cannot be overlooked. The case of Höch's extensive influence also serves as an example of Dada's method of embracing multiple disciplines, a feature of Dada that contributed to its survival.

Each of the six women chosen for this study deserves to tell her story. Luckily, they left behind evidence in their own words and in the works of their contemporaries. Most of their poems, novels, memoirs, and testimonies are well hidden, out of print, stored in remote archives, or even lost from library shelves. But they must be taken into account if one wishes to draw a complete picture of Dada, especially as a source of, but distinct from, later manifestations of the avant-garde.

Acknowledgments

This text presents the findings of my research between 1996 and 2003 on the subject of women who influenced the development of Dada, conducted at the following locations: the Dada Archive at the University of Iowa; the archives of the Berlinische Galerie; the Kunsthaus Zürich; the Musée et jardin de sculpture de la Fondation Jean Arp at Clamart; the Bibliothèque Marguerite Durand (Paris); the Musée d'Art Moderne de la Ville de Paris; the Bibliothèque Sainte Geneviève (Paris); the Bibliothèque de l'Arsenal (Paris); the Bibliothèque Kandinsky (Paris), the Bibliothèque Administrative de la Ville de Paris; Humboldt Universitätsbibliothek (Berlin); the Staatsbibliothek at Potsdamer Platz (Berlin); the de Pury & Luxembourg Art Gallery (Geneva); and the Musée d'art et d'histoire Genève.

Many thanks are owed to my sponsors, sources, and supporters during this project: the University of North Carolina at Wilmington Cahill Grants and Semester Research Reassignment Award, the UNCW College of Arts and Sciences Summer Research Grant, the UNCW Office of International Programs Travel Grants, the National Endowment for the Humanities 1997 Seminar in Paris, and the Maison des Sciences de l'Homme and Maison Suger (Paris). Special thanks to Ralf Burmeister, Gunda Luyken, Greta Stroh, Timothy Shipe, Guido Magnaguagno, and Rudolf Kuenzli, who graciously answered my questions. Thanks also to John O'Hara, Mari H. O'Brien, Jesse Waters, Liliane DeFant, and Debra Niven for their support. Thank you to Gail Kamenish for readying several images, and to Béa Aarronson for her *Hasard ou Destinée*. Finally, heartfelt thanks go to Peter Nierychlo, Elke Bickert, Hans Kreutzjans, Chantal Vidil, and Olivier Rateau for making my research possible by welcoming me into their homes.

Introduction

The Problem with Dada

Of all forms of twentieth-century avant-garde, Dada is the most international in its adherents, the most interdisciplinary in its mediums, and for its short duration the most widely spread geographically. Nevertheless, despite its pervasive and diverse nature, it remains incomprehensible and unappetizing to most palates. For many, Dada is a bad taste in the mouth, a goalless, nihilist revolt situated among many avant-garde "-isms." For some, however, Dada stands as a captivating marker in the history of literature and art.

Although there are some variations in the recorded history of the genesis of the Dada movement with conflicting stories about how the movement got its name, it began in earnest in 1916 and flourished in Western Europe through 1924. The first group called "Dada" formed in Zurich at Emmy Hennings and Hugo Ball's Cabaret Voltaire in February 1916. During the war-ravaged years, Dadaists proclaimed to seek authentic reality through the abolition of traditional culture and aesthetic forms. Stephen C. Foster has summarized the commonly accepted goals of the Dadaists: "Mounted out of a setting that no one could measure and that defied conventional contextualization—World War I, the 'war of wars'—Dada committed itself to the deconstruction of lethal culture and its reconstruction according to more humane principles. Its success was constituted in the intensity and scope of its critique. Its efforts to organize and network itself were designed to guarantee, as best Dada could, the dissemination of its critique."[1]

Dada's method of deconstruction took the form of provocative acts of rebellion through theater, dance, poetry recitations, and musical performances with elaborate stage settings and costumes, as well as paintings, sculptures, drawings, puppets, collages, and an array of poetry journals, flyers, posters, and manifestos.

The War Orphan

At the beginning of the twentieth century, nations were redefining their borders in Europe and in their colonies. Living in close proximity to their adversaries, Europeans were dramatically touched by the conflicts that arose and were fought on their soil. During a war that ultimately left ten million dead and some twenty million wounded or mutilated, the expatriate group who settled in Zurich in 1915 and 1916 was composed of young writers and artists, both male and female. They came from an assortment of national, linguistic, economic, and cultural backgrounds, driven by a strong urge to revolt and to create.

Dada had some early manifestations in New York before 1915 with Duchamp, Picabia, Man Ray, and the Arensberg circle. (Duchamp's first ready-made *Bicycle Wheel* dates from 1913). Yet the movement was a child of pure European blood, born of Germanic-Latin ancestry. Its supporters sought an escape from the military, political, or societal restrictions of their European homes, and New York offered this freedom to those who could afford the voyage. Others found the neutrality of a Swiss wartime refuge necessary, and so they formed the first official Dada center in Zurich, featuring a lively cabaret, gallery, and literary journal.

This 1914–16 immigration caused great personal and financial loss for many in the generation born during the 1890s. One can only admire their initiative and resolve to desert the familiarity of one's country at a time of war and strong nationalistic sentiment to establish a new home in a "neutral land." This uprooting of intense young artists and writers, combined with the disappointment and disillusionment of their generation, inspired acts of revolt against the established authority and set the stage for Dada events.

The Dadaists of Zurich's Cabaret Voltaire expressed their angst as well as their periodic joie de vivre through evenings of cabaret performances that incorporated their varied talents in music, dance, singing, and acting. Hennings, a noted German singer and diseuse, and Ball, a reputable German dramaturge, were joined in their performances by Tzara, Hans Arp, Täuber, Marcel Janco, Huelsenbeck, Adya Van Rees Dutilh, and Otto Van Rees. On a typical evening crazed audiences protested the loud jangling of piano keys; marionettes and hats recited poems; performers screamed simultaneous verses to the beat of a kettledrum; dancers demonstrated endless gymnastic exercises; chairs with words attached to them were arranged and rearranged to form static, visual poems.[2] Artistic expression had crossed over into a realm that defied the reliable rules of decorum, logic, and order.

These antiaesthetic, antiform, antibourgeois artists and war protesters spread the rebellious spirit of Dada as they left Zurich after the war. Eventually Dada groups formed in Berlin, Cologne, Hannover, Paris, Madrid, Barcelona, Rome, Prague, the Netherlands, and beyond during the early years of the twentieth century. Each location cultivated its own flavor despite often sharing its participants with Dada groups in other places.

Berliner Dada formed with a certain anarchical flare driven by Huelsenbeck, Richter, Raoul Hausmann, Johannes Baader, George Grosz, John Heartfield, Wieland Herzfelde, and Otto Dix, among others. The group was known for the political radicalism of its publications, the militant satire of its paintings or collages, and events of brutal monstrosity such as the First International Dada Fair of 1920, which included a suspended effigy of a "Prussian Archangel" set against Höch's photomontages featuring the faces of actual government and military leaders clipped from the daily newspapers.[3]

The Cologne Dada group was inspired by the less acerbic spirit of Arp, coming from Zurich to meet at the home of the more radicalized Heinrich and Angelika Hoerle with "Dadamax" Max Ernst and Communist activist Johannes Theodor Baargeld. At the same time, Hannover Dada gathered around Schwitters, known for his sound poetry and Merzbau assemblages. Both groups interacted heavily with the Berliner Dadaists and excelled at producing collage pieces of political and cultural critique.

Meanwhile Parisian Dada, held firmly together by poets, was a literary Dada. Key figures (who later favored Surrealism) were André Breton, Philippe Soupault, Louis Aragon, Paul Eluard, Georges Ribemont-Dessaignes, and Arnauld. When Tzara and Picabia united the group under an umbrella of proliferating journals, Dada exploded in iconoclastic displays of exhibitions, stage shows of music and drama, competing manifestos, and new poetry publications. Dada soirees featured such absurdist plays as Tzara's *Gas Heart* with actors playing the roles of Eye, Mouth, Nose, Ear, Neck, and Eyebrow and audience members calling the police.

Individual Dadaists were constantly on the move in wartime Europe, forming subgroups in Barcelona and New York. Dada proved portable and adaptable. It traveled light, going on tour in the Netherlands and Czechoslovakia. It borrowed whatever elements it desired from other forms of the avant-garde (such as Cubism, Expressionism, Constructivism, and Futurism) and transformed them according to its needs and perspective. It was open, inviting, and nondogmatic. Dada by definition was an experiment, unstable, without rules, and constantly reshaping itself. Having survived the war, Dada followed more individualized paths to MERZ or De Stijl[4] or was transforming into other movements such as Surrealism by 1924.

When studying the origins of Dada, some scholars emphasize the historical period and the significance of Zurich as a geographical crossroads. The prevailing opinion on the genesis of the movement implies that Dada activities began in Zurich because it became the meeting place of artists with a common sentiment against World War I. It is true that without the attitude of revolt against rising militarism and against the bourgeois values the war represented, there would have been no spark to ignite the Dada movement. The atmosphere of Zurich in 1916 certainly did create a politically neutral haven that encouraged a nonconformist display of artistic expression through its cabaret and gallery life. However, one must question how a supposedly antiwar protest movement could outlive the actual military conflict by at least four years.

There was at work a broader revolt against a way of life, a form of government, and the sustaining values of the dominant classes. A generation's exasperation was brewing against society at large. It took the form of behaviors that shocked and sometimes provoked riots. Its creative products were labeled irreverent, dangerous, and degenerate. Although Hamid Dabashi refers to the recent protests of Aliaa Magda Elmahdy and Golshifteh Farahani,[5] his 2012 description of such defiance equally defines Dadaist acts of rebellion when he points out the "staged formal destruction that disrupts the 'normality' of socializing norms for a deliberate pause."[6] There must be a public platform, a tangible display forced on the eye of society in order to startle and affect the viewer. Zurich performances of nonsensical sound poems emitted from anonymously masked faces and punctuated by heavy drums accompanying incomprehensible dance movements challenged the eye, the ear, and (for some) the stomach. Revulsion is a response, and physical reaction forces the mind's attention. Just because the frustration results in "art," the element of danger in the political and cultural protest is not reduced. When taking a stand against a regime that espouses the mechanized consumerism of war and uses the bodies of the young as its currency, the transgression of the rebellious act necessarily exposes and attacks the governing culture. More than any previous manifestation of the avant-garde, Dada remained offensively antagonistic to society, and that was enough to draw condemnation or attempts at obliteration.[7]

But clearly Dada relied on more than hostile acts to voice its war protests and political stances. Its identifiable sarcastic tone is built on the humor, irony, audacity, and youth of its participants, who nourished each other's imaginations. One outlandish joke in "DADA—Dialogue Between a Coachman and a Swallow," mocks the entire enterprise while it simultaneously advertises one of its publications. In the dialogue Huelsenbeck (the German-speaking coachman) and Tzara (the French-speaking swallow) feed off each other's words to poke fun at those who would nail down a definition of Dada:

Huelsenbeck (coachman): The sky is bursting open into little scraps of cotton wool. The trees are walking about with swollen bellies.

Tzara (swallow): Because the first edition of the *Dada Review* comes out on 1 August 1916. Cost 1Fr. Editorial and administration: Spiegelgasse 1, Zurich. It has nothing to do with the war and is an attempt at a modern international activity hi hi hi hi.

Huelsenbeck (coachman): Oh yes, I saw that . . . Dada emerged from the body of a horse as a basket of flowers. Dada bust like a boil from the chimney of a skyscraper, oh yes, I saw Dada . . . as the embryo of the purple crocodile flew his cinnabar tail.[8]

What, then, is the definition Dada? Is it what makes the spring arrive? Is it a new international experiment organized by a coachman and a swallow with acute linguistic challenges? Does it have more to do with fanciful flowers, skyscrapers, and a purple crocodile than it does with the cold reality of a world war?

By looking at the products of the Dadaists it is clear that the distinctive artistic qualities of Dada—the irreverent, provocative, nonsensical language and images evidenced in the movement's multidisciplinary manifestations—result from something other than just the political neutrality of its birthplace. Dada's birth, shaping, and reshaping are indebted to the outrageously inventive imaginations of the individual men and women who conceived, nurtured, and sustained the movement in a tumultuous world climate. The particular talents offered by the members of the ever-expanding group and the mixture of their personalities made possible the spontaneous and varied forms of Dada expression.

The Hole in the Middle of Dada

In their unifying goal to tear down a "lethal culture" that was found lacking and create a platform on which to test the accumulating and competing voices of the avant-garde, Dadaists relied on their unique abilities and followed their personal inclinations. Some painted and exhibited, others wrote, danced, acted, made collages, or music. Each talent contributed to Dada's objectives.

Involved in these endeavors were the most recognizable participants:

Tristan Tzara	Man Ray
Hugo Ball	Richard Huelsenbeck
Raoul Hausmann	Marcel Janco
Paul Dermée	Christian Schad
Paul Eluard	Hans Richter
Arthur Cravan	Marcel Duchamp

Otto van Rees
Walter Mehring
Wieland Herzfelde
Jean Crotti
Philippe Soupault
John Heartfield
Rudolf Schlichter
Max Ernst
Georg Scholz
Heinrich Hoerle
Louis Aragon
El Lissitzky
Johannes Baargeld
Kurt Schwitter
Hans Arp
Francis Picabia
George Grosz
Otto Dix
Walter Serner
André Breton
Johannes Baader
Georges Ribemont-Dessaignes

A generous list of less known contributors includes

Alice Bailly
Marietta di Monaco
Greta Knutson
Maria d'Arezzo
Katherine Dreier
Jane Heap
Renée Dunan
Valeska Gert
Claire Walther
Hannah Höch
Katharine Nash Rhoades
Juliette Roche
Agnes Ernst Meyer
Louise Stevens Arensberg
Alexandra Exter
Sophie Täuber
Marie Laurencin
Mary Wigman
Gabrielle Buffet
Marthe Tour-Donas
Bernice Abbott
Adrienne Monnier
Clara Tice
Nina Naj
Céline Arnauld
Florence Henri
Natalia Goncharova
Käthe Wulff
Ella Bergmann
Käte Steinitz
Suzanne Duchamp
Gala Eluard
Mabel Dodge
Isadora Duncan
Emmy Hennings
Käthe Brodnitz
Germaine Everling
Florine Stettheimer
Adya van Rees Dutilh
Margaret Anderson
Germaine Albert-Birot
Erika Deetjen
Maya Chrusecz
Angelika Hoerle
Meret Oppenheim
Til Brugman
Liubov Popova
Louise Norton
Marguerite Buffet
Varvara Stepanova
Mina Loy
Sonia Delaunay
Nelly van Doesburg
Djuna Barnes

Edith Olivié
Olga Rosanowa
and Else Von Freytag-Loringhoven
Beatrice Wood
Claire Goll

In one contemporary directory of Dadaists, "Quelques Présidents et Présidentes" (composed by male members of the group and printed in the February 1920 issue of the journal *Dada*) there are seventy-five names arranged alphabetically. This roll represents a liberal grouping of individuals who were in some way involved in or supportive of the Dada philosophy. The presence of most names is predictable: Duchamp, Hausmann, Ribemont-Dessaignes, and Tzara. Others, such as Igor Stravinsky, are surprising. Yet all these male affiliates are easily recognizable to avant-garde scholars. Few art and literary scholars, however, will know all fifteen women listed in the roster: d'Arezzo, Arnauld, Bailly, Gabrielle and Marguerite Buffet, Chrusecz, Dodge, Duchamp, Everling, "Mina Lloyd" (Loy), "Miss Norton" (Louise), Olivié, Rhoades, Täuber, and Wigman.

Despite their documented participation in Dada events, most of the "Présidentes" are less easily identified than their male counterparts. Even such a well-edited contemporary source as *Dada*, either cannot spell correctly or manage to list Loy under her published name instead of a name used by her husband (Arthur Cravan, also known as Fabian Avenarius Lloyd). Misspelling of their names was a problem suffered by other female Dadaists. Höch's was spelled incorrectly at the Berlin International Dada Fair and the 1921 Vortragsabend, and Arnauld's is misspelled in volume 7 of *Dada*. In one history of Dada, Arnauld's name is misspelled "Arnaud" and mistakenly identified as a pseudonym for her husband, leading unsuspecting readers to doubt her actual existence.[9] Duchamp's name is perhaps recognized because of her brother Marcel's reputation, and a few people recall her work in conjunction with her husband, Jean Crotti, with whom she created the Dada offshoot called TABU; yet her own daring work made her a crucial link between New York and Parisian Dada, especially among visual artists. Until recently Täuber's reputation was tied to her husband's, but with her distinctive talents in sculpture, textiles, and dance, she helped solidify the establishment of Zurich Dada, even at the risk of losing her teaching position at the School of Applied Arts. Neglecting to note the many contributions of female Dadaists when compiling a history of this manifestation of the European avant-garde only muddles the picture. The works and words of the other half of Dada's participants, their essential contributions to the propagation of this literary and artistic movement through its cabarets of music, poetry and dance, its literary journals, and its art exhibitions, are the missing pieces in the story of Dada.

Dada's Missing Pieces

While many male artists and poets produced easily retrievable records in the form of manifestos, letters, poetry, plays, posters, canvases, or histories of Dada, many female contributors to Dada expressed themselves through the visual or performing arts, leaving behind relatively few physical objects to mark their participation. Looking merely at what men published in the form of personal manifestos, for example, one finds a profusion of confrontational and contradictory texts that document the period from their perspectives. Between the founding of the Cabaret Voltaire on February 5, 1916, and the closing of the second great forum at Zurich's Galerie Dada on June 1, 1917, there were at least four published manifestos by Ball, Tzara, and Huelsenbeck. In Berlin, Dada debuted with Huelsenbeck's 1918 manifesto and the 1919 publication of *Der Dada,* and in Paris one need only look at 1920 for a surge of theories and declarations appearing in every French Dada publication. Among these, one is hard pressed to uncover a manifesto or history penned by a female Dadaist. This fact accounts for the single-gendered recording of the group's activities that has biased history. Relying on the male-authored discourses of Ball, Huelsenbeck, Tzara, Breton, and Richter to tell the story of Dada reveals only half the picture. The only way to present a fair and accurate record of Dada activity, its products, and its contributors is to take into account the testimony and products of all parties. Perhaps then the puzzle of Dada will be more easily deciphered.

Zurich Laban dancer Suzanne Perrottet's testimony "Ich war auch dabei" (I Was Also Around) is emblematic of the long-accepted state of affairs. This unpublished memoir, alongside Roche's, holds keys to defining Dada. Clearly women's renditions of the Dada years add a new dimension to the extensive body of contemporary male-authored texts that tell the story from a (more often than not) jealously competitive perspective. Huelsenbeck, Richter, Mehring, Tzara, Breton, Ball, Arp, Picabia and their intentional histories of the period do not supply the missing pieces of Dada. These records mention the contributions of the female members of Dada briefly, but usually do not provide details on their lives, works, or networking methods that led to the spread of Dada.

The women's narrations of events confirm that Dada was a collaborative and gender inclusive movement that grew through contacts between individuals. In Zurich, Dada owed a great deal to the painting and tapestry work of Bailly and van Rees-Dutilh; it relied on Hennings's voice and seductive presence; it was enriched by Täuber's and Hennings's marionettes and their dances with members of the Laban school, Mary Wigman, Maya Chrusecz, Suzanne Perrottet, Claire Walther, and Jeanne Rigaud. In Germany Dada was enriched by the photomontages and marionettes of Höch; it exhibited the paintings and drawings of Henri and Hoerle; and it collaborated and traveled with Höch and Brugman to Holland. In France, Dada was costumed by Delaunay and satirized by Roche; it was analyzed by Everling and Knutson, painted by Duchamp, and published by Buffet and Arnauld.

Dada was more than a brief and irreverent revolt against the war, the bourgeoisie, and existing moral and artistic codes. For eight years Dadaists remained true to their goals: to question, to tear down, and to rebuild art in every form.

Dada was neither steeped in theory, nor directed by a single individual. Perhaps the lack of a dominant manifesto expressing a unified declaration of intent and a strong central leadership to enforce its goals caused Dada to be short-lived compared to, for example, the more strictly structured Surrealist movement. But Dada by its nature was a paroxysm, a quick and spontaneous act. Too much deliberation, too clear a strategy, and the spirit of Dada would be destroyed, as both Ball and Picabia warned their colleagues. Dada offered to its unusually diverse and collaborative members new ways of creating via live performances and open soirees. By employing cabaret and theater, the most interactive forms of artistic expression, in addition to provocative and subversive exhibitions, Dada artists immediately reached a curious public that was shocked, exasperated, and even insulted, but at times it was attracted to and gradually seduced by Dada's irreverent creations.

1. Emmy Hennings

From Cabaret Singer to the First Mama of Dada

Emmy Hennings (1885–1948) has been acknowledged by most revisionist scholars today as the cofounder of Dada's first home: the Cabaret Voltaire. But it is important to see this accomplishment and her further nurturing of Dada in a larger context. To understand Hennings and her involvement with Zurich Dada, one must first recognize her paradoxical nature, one that caused her to vacillate between two contradictory lives: the criminal and the pious. Hennings was forced to see herself as both sinner and penitent, and she showed unease with both roles. She was the ultimate nightclub performer, spending half her life in smoke-filled cabarets, captivating male audiences both on and off stage with her body and her voice. But her later autobiographical records of her earlier years are so deeply imprinted with her religious conversion that catching a glimpse of Hennings during the Dada period can be challenging. For a true portrait of the Dadaist Hennings, researchers must rely on a combination of sources and read behind her writings. Clues to her bohemian life appear in her early poetry; the chilling prose piece *Gefängnis* (Prison), which describes her stay in prison; her autobiographical *Ruf und Echo* (Call and Echo); and the accounts of other

Dadaists, such as Ball, Arp, Perrottet, and Huelsenbeck, who bore witness to her avant-garde performances and lifestyle.

The Lure of the Cabaret

Emma Cordsen was born in Flensburg, on the German border with Denmark, on January 17, 1885. Her German-Danish parents, Ernst Friedrich Matthias and Anna Dorothea, were fifty and forty-two years old when their only child was born. Her father had been a helmsman on a sailing ship but later worked as a wharf-side rig maker. From his daughter's memoir it is known that he used to build model boats in his free time and that young Emmy used to hem the sails. The imagery of ships and of the wandering life at sea recurs in Hennings's writing and seems to prophesy the instability of her itinerant life.

> I love the white, loose
> Like sun, sea and wind,
> Because to the homeless
> They're sisters and angels[1]
>
> Ich liebe die Weißen, losen
> Wie Sonne, Meer und Wind,
> Weil sie der Heimatlosen
> Schwestern und Engel sind . . .

Emmy became one of these "homeless" early in her life. She left her parents' household and, at the age of fifteen, began to earn her living as a maid, kitchen helper, and washwoman. At the same time, she made her first amateur stage appearances. At age seventeen she married a typesetter named Josef Paul Hennings and gave birth to a son. Leaving the baby with her mother in Flensburg, Hennings joined an itinerant theater troupe and traveled alongside her husband, who abandoned her after a few weeks. Soon afterward, she learned of the death of her child and that she was again pregnant. She chose not to look for her husband, but to go instead with a theater troupe to Schlesien, where her daughter, Annemarie, was born in Penzig. Once again Hennings left the baby with her mother and returned to the theater, where, according to her daughter's memoir, Hennings felt in her element.[2] By age twenty-three she had become a cabaret performer (Vortragskünstlerin), usually singing ballads and songs on request from seven in the evening to three in the morning. A stanza of her poem "Nach dem Kabarett" (After the Cabaret) describes how she saw her life at the time:

> I go home in the early morning.
> The clock strikes five, it's already brightening,

But the light still burns at the inn.
The cabaret is finally over.
In a corner children cower,
To the market farmers already ride,
To the church go the quiet and old,
From the belfry solemnly ring the bells,
And a whore with wild curls
Still wanders, sleepless and cold.[3]

Ich gehe morgens früh nach Haus.
Die Uhr schlägt fünf, es wird schon hell,
Doch brennt das Licht noch im Hotel.
Das Cabaret ist endlich aus.
In einer Ecke Kinder kauern,
Zum Markte fahren schon die Bauern,
Zur Kirche geht man still und alt.
Vom Turme läuten ernst die Glocken,
Und eine Dirne mit wilden Locken
Irrt noch umher, übernächtig und kalt.

The poem is descriptive of her life as a cabaret entertainer, not judgmental. Nevertheless her tone is clearly somber and uninviting. The poem suggests that loneliness results from living on a schedule that isolates the poet from the activities of the world around her. She sacrifices much to try to find success as a performer. In her autobiographical poetry Hennings often reflected on the costs, both physical and moral. In fact Hennings supplemented her meager music-hall earnings with work as peddler, nightclub hostess, and occasional prostitute as she traveled in Munster, Cologne, Frankfurt, and Hannover. "Nach dem Kabarett" alludes to her underworld occupations as it contrasts women of the night with workers and worshippers of the morning.

Still earning her living in cabarets and honkytonks, Hennings is said to have traveled as far as Russia, according to her daughter. She settled for a while in Berlin, where she entered the underworld through her acquaintance with artist and writer John Höxter. Through him she met Ferdinand Hardekopf, described by Höxter as the darkest of all morphine addicts. In 1910 Hennings traveled with Hardekopf to France, where she contracted typhus and turned to Catholicism. Returning to Germany, the young cabaret artist worked at the Simplicissimus nightclub in Munich and came into contact with poets Georg Heym, Frank Wedekind, and Franz Werfel, as well as other members of the Expressionist movement. Hennings continued to work on stage in Berlin and came to be known as the Danish Futurist. In what seems to be an action inconsistent with her previous life choices, Hennings was then baptized in the Catholic church of St. Ludwig on July 14, 1910.

Wavering again between her religious conversion and the lure of the criminal world, Hennings returned to Paris with Hardekopf in 1913. She had just published her first poem, which suggests the difficulties she faced in her relationship with him and the life he represented. Hennings's layered imagery evokes a theme of drug-induced abandon in the poem "Aether" (Ether),[4] which was published in the August 14, 1912, issue of *Aktion* and then again in her 1913 collection *Die Letze Freude* (The Last Joy).

Hennings's early poetry is full of expressionistic imagery that reflects the events (imagined or real) of her life and times. For example the short poem "Aether" produces complex hallucinogenic aural, visual, and tactile images. The word "schlägt" in the first line "An die Scheiben schlägt der Regen" (rain strikes the windowpanes) effectively uses sound imagery to capture a quotidian slapping sound that might awaken a sleeper, while "Eine Blume leuchtet rot" (A flower lights up red) evokes otherworldly characteristics by its ambiguity, as a red blossom is lit by an unknown source, be it from within or without. Awakened by a cool draft, the speaker is disoriented, seeing the outside world through rain-smeared glass that is unnaturally tinted by the diffused red light. Her exhaustion and confusion cause the sleeper to ask: "Wach ich, oder bin ich tot?" (Am I awake or dead?). Such an ontological question in the middle of the night suggests a drugged state. Meanwhile, the fifth line, "Eine Welt liegt weit, ganz weit" (A world lies far, far away) underlines the isolation of the speaker as "Eine Uhr schlägt langsam vier" (A clock strikes slowly four). The word "schlägt" connects the sound of rain from the first line to the tolling of bells, but the measuring of time is perceived in unsettling slow motion. The sleeper is suspended in her etherized trance. Ironically the slow ringing of the hour draws the sleeper from her hallucination so that she can return to comforting dreams, implied by falling back into the security and oblivion of her lover's arms.

This poem, a kind of waking dream, ends with her descent back to earth, as "aether" can mean either the narcotic that causes sleep or an ethereal realm. In its Greek origin, "aither" refers to the upper skies, where the stars are suspended and the gods live. In the poem the narrator's moment of wakefulness paradoxically brings the sleeper to a higher, "etherized" dream state, to an unconventional moment of salvation. Hennings's life of contradictions is encapsulated in this poem, which combines drug-induced hallucination with heavenly deliverance.

In 1913 Hennings published more poems, appeared in Berlin cabarets, and sang and danced in productions at Budapest's Royal Orfeum. While in Munich she met her future partner and husband, Hugo Ball, at the Café Simplicissimus in the autumn of 1913. One of Ball's biographers suggests that Hennings had a mysterious past that included a suspected homicide, but the basis of this accusation remains unclear.[5] Rumors frequently spread through the World War I emigrant community to which Ball and Hennings belonged, and people's pasts were often embroidered with questionable adventures that they seemed reluctant to deny. In Hennings's case, she probably benefited from and thus cultivated a mysterious air as part of her stage persona. There is no doubt, however, that the young nightclub singer lived on the fringes of society and was frequently on the wrong side of the law as evidenced in her later arrests and incarcerations.

Ball frequented the Café Simplicissimus because of his interest in the lively Hennings, who was ten years younger than her future husband. He begged her to repeat certain songs for him, such as "Liebe ist Leben" (Love Is Life), and he asked for some of her poetry. By this time she had produced several hand-copied volumes with her own watercolor illustrations, bound in silk.

As seen in her handcrafted books and in her published 1913 collection, *Die Letzte Freude,* Hennings's early writing already uses the dark imagery for which she became known. In an excerpt of a poem dedicated to Hardekopf, the speaker wanders through the night and thinks of her missing lover:

> Alone I wander through the nights and think of you
> Sometimes I see a coat that resembles yours.
> And then I softly call your name.
> My heart stands still with grief.[6]
>
> Einsam irr ich durch die Nächte und denke an dich.
> Manchmal sehe ich einen Mantel, der deinem gleicht.
> Und dann rufe ich dich leise beim Namen.
> Mein Herz steht still vor Trauer.

The sense of loss and its resultant loneliness in these words are held together by the simple image of the overcoat, which is then strengthened by the recurring image of the speaker walking alone each night and whispering the name of the one she longs for. A heart that stands still with the grief of loss suggests her torment with the double meaning of the German "still" as "stopped" and "quiet." The choice of "Trauer" suggests that the loved one could have been lost through death, misfortune, or abandonment, while "Mein Herz steht still" allows the ambiguity of a resigned acceptance of one's grief, or the implication of the narrator following her lover in death, perhaps metaphorically. The theme of loss echoes throughout Hennings's work; her focus perpetually comes to rest on what is missing, what is lost to her, the emptied space, and her isolation. This kind of loneliness that haunted her for years made her search out and welcome the community of artists she later found in the Dada group.

The poetic excerpt, chosen for inclusion in Gisela Brinker-Gabler's two-volume encyclopedic study of women in German literature (*Deutsche Literature von Frauen*) by the chapter's editor, Ruth Wolf, is poetically richer than Wolf's commentary suggests. She merely credited the verses with illustrating the freer feelings about love that many women shared through poetry during this period. Wolf's commentary misses the mark, however; Ball reported in his diary, *Flucht aus der Zeit* (Flight Out of Time), that the bilingual Hennings thought the German language was poor in words of tenderness and love. She found Danish to be infinitely richer, and so she would presumably not choose to compose love poems in German. By seeing the verse purely as a love poem, Wolf has overlooked Hennings's artistic skill in capturing an everyday image (a familiar overcoat in the distance) and transforming it into a universally understood symbol of torment. The poem provides concise, stark, and personal images that evoke an unmistakably somber tone and an enigmatic theme of loss in what would otherwise be a simple sentimental verse. Hennings's dark and secret poetry is a personal expression of a kind of solitude that seems in contrast to, but is actually a consequence of, the extroverted life she found in the theaters and nightclubs.

Owing in part to Hennings's extensive experience and alluring stage presence, Ball found himself offering her the leading female role in the play he was to direct for the Munich Kammerspiele, saying "I knew it from the beginning. No one else can be considered for the role. Only you, you are it."[7] The young couple arranged to meet in Munich's Englischen Garten to read Leonid Andrejew's *Das Leben des Menschen* (The Life of Men); Ball took the role of the man while Hennings read the role of the woman. Hennings's autobiographical commentary on the dramatic discourse of the woman offers a glimpse into how she viewed her role as Ball's life partner and as a member of the avant-garde. It also gave her the title of her autobiography, *Ruf und Echo: Mein Leben mit Hugo Ball*, published in 1953: "She speaks as if she has no words of her own, often repeats the words of the man, without seeming monotone. It is like a call and echo. If the echo were not there, then the man would hardly hear his own voice. It's as if he hears himself only through the woman, and so his words flow pleasurably back to him. It is like music in a still night. The play of the man is transformed into that of the woman, the melody of the two beings flows through each other like one sound embracing the other, and the flowing harmony of the play is indescribably beautiful."[8]

Couples who collaborate on successful artistic projects often share a "call and echo" relationship. Hennings longed to regard her aesthetic relationship with Ball in such terms, perhaps as an alternative to the chaotic, itinerant life she was living. It remains to be seen if this was indeed a valid description of her role as an artist. Was her primary function to allow Ball to "hear his own voice" through hers? Her writings and her role in the Dada group reveal the answer.

Hennings's description of herself as Ball's echo also makes a point that can be applied to the Dadaists in Zurich and to other aesthetic movements in general. In each group, there are outspoken members (such as Tzara, Huelsenbeck, or Breton) who animate the activities and provide the much-needed publicity that brings the movement to the eyes and ears of its spectators. There are also the less commanding collaborators (such as Hennings) who actively participate without leading. Without the important "echo" that the quieter members of an artistic or literary group provide, the more verbose partners would be speaking to themselves, without the benefit of the reflective gaze and echoing voice within the group that allows them to see, hear, critique, find direction, and put into context their artistic and literary products. Hennings's insightful commentary is applicable to the role played by many of the women and the less garrulous men of the avant-garde. They served as important echoes to the louder members, and their "echoes" often took the form of their own art and poetry, or valuable records and reviews of events.

As a dancer, poet, and cabaret singer in prewar Munich, Hennings participated in several Expressionist theatrical and cabaret evenings. She was friends with Expressionist poets and collaborated on publications such as *Die Aktion* and *Revolution.* One of her poems appeared in *Der Mistral* (1913), an anthology of lyric poetry, and several of her new poems were published in the October 1913 issue of *Die Neue Kunst* alongside works by Jakob van Hoddis, member of the "New Club" circle of early Expressionists. During this time Hennings also met and worked with Huelsenbeck, a future Berlin Dadaist.

Hennings's acting career and Ball's theatrical projects were soon abandoned when the outbreak of war closed the Kammerspiele. In 1914 Ball volunteered for military service but was refused for medical reasons. After a short visit to the war in Belgium, he moved to Berlin to work as an editor for the illustrated newspaper *Zeit im Bild.* Hennings joined him in the capital just after her release from a six-week prison sentence, allegedly for forging passports. It is possible that she was involved, along with fellow writer and future Dadaist Walter Serner, in the military desertion of Expressionist Franz Jung in December 1914. There is evidence of Hennings's other imprisonments, before and after this incident. In a letter to pacifist journalist Kurt Tucholsky, theater critic Siegfried Jacobsohn wrote that Hennings received a six-month sentence because, out of love for Hardekopf, "she walked the streets, and, at his suggestion, stole from clients."[9] An August 6, 1914, journal entry by Erich Mühsam, the anarchist poet who himself was not a stranger to prison sentences, supports this hypothesis, saying that he went to visit Hennings in prison, where she was being held on larceny charges.[10] Munich registration documents record that Hennings was again imprisoned for about a month (September 20 to October 19, 1914). It is believed that Hennings was returned to prison at the end of the year and at the beginning of 1915 for small infractions. These periods of incarceration had a lasting effect on her health and her writing.

Moving away from her Expressionist friends and their frequently harmful influence, Hennings left Germany with Ball to live in Zurich in May 1915. At first the couple lived in abject poverty as unregistered aliens, selling all their possessions and scavenging for food. Hennings returned to drug use and prostitution. In despair Ball attempted to commit suicide. An October 1915 entry in Ball's *Flucht aus der Zeit* refers to the vaudeville troupe Flamingo, which he and Hennings joined to avoid starvation. According to Hennings's memoir, Ball sent her into the club Hirschen because they thought that a performer there might be willing to purchase Ball's tuxedo jacket. He waited outside for her to call him if the entertainers were interested in buying it. When she did not return, he walked inside and found her in a silver lamé dress and feeling quite at home, auditioning for a cabaret job.

With Flamingo the couple traveled to Basel but soon returned to Zurich. Hennings moved into the Goldenen Stern in Bellevueplatz, where she found time to read and write. It was at this time that she might have begun work on *Gefängnis,* her autobiographical account of her imprisonment. After December 1915 Hennings began working with Ball at the Cabaret Maxim in Zurich; she sang, and he played piano.

When Henning's mother died in March 1916, Hennings's nine-year-old daughter joined her in Zurich. This was the first time she was able or obliged to take on the role of parent. With the added responsibility of looking after her child came the stress and guilt associated with combining motherhood and a professional life. Hennings found escape through performance, poetry, and possibly drug use.

Ball's journals reveal that he had also been experimenting with narcotics just prior to 1916. During this period Hennings published a bleak poem titled "Morfin" (Morphine), which describes how she and Ball "float groundless through life." It is possible that her poems record her own narcotic-induced visions or those of Ball, who often told Hennings his dreams and asked her for explanations of them. Curiously enough Hennings reported in *Ruf und Echo* that, as a child, she was not allowed to tell her dreams in her parents' house, but "Hugo and I sometimes dreamed so vividly that we often told each other our dreams, like two people who are so close that they share with each other all their experiences."[11] She wondered, however, if telling dreams was healthy, because some dreams were better not shared when they could hurt someone. Perhaps they, like drug hallucinations, were better turned into poems.

During this pre-Dada phase of her life as Hennings strove to be a stage artist and poet, she was already part of the counterculture. But the threatening life choices she made led to chaos, despair, and misery. She lived perilously close to the edge of illness and incarceration. Soon wartime Zurich allowed her to find herself among new artistic influences as young, like-minded artists joined the exiled and marginalized immigrants at a new cabaret.

The Lean Dada Years

Although some sources neglect to mention Hennings's contribution to its foundation, the Cabaret Voltaire is certainly the child of both Ball and Hennings. In

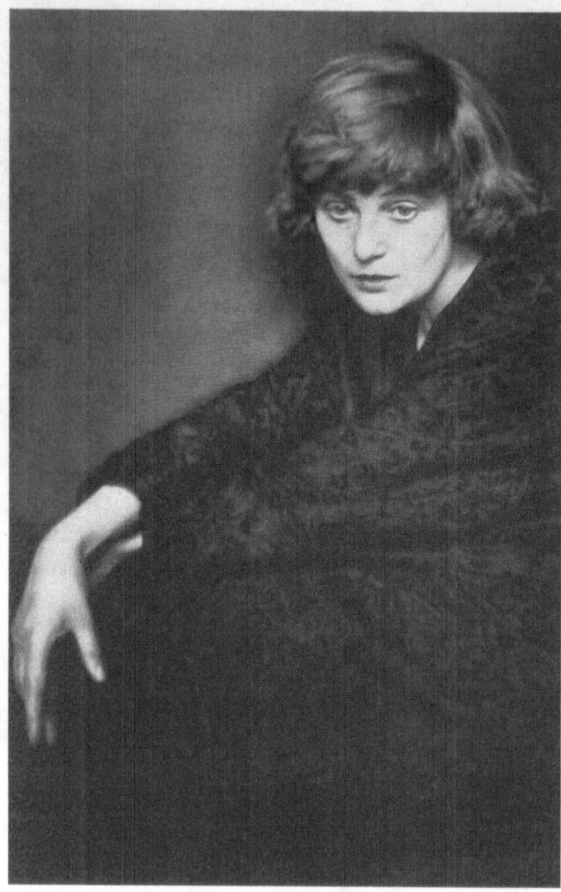

Emmy Hennings. Photograph courtesy of the Benziger Archiv, Museum Fram, Einsiedeln, Switzerland.

February 1916 the pair began the cabaret in the Holländischen Meierei at Spiegelgasse 1, the address of the first center of European Dada. Ball recorded in his journal that among those present were Tzara, Janco, and Arp. A few days later Huelsenbeck, who had worked with Hennings and Ball on the revue *Die Aktion*, joined the group. Not long after came Friedrich Glauser and Serner, who had been actively involved with the Expressionist publication *Die Aktion* and with *Sirius*, which had featured the work of Arp. This group was joined in their Dada activities by the dancer and multimedia artist Sophie Täuber, artists Otto Van Rees and Adya Van Rees Dutilh, and poet-painter Francis Picabia during his brief Swiss sojourn. A network of avant-garde artists was forming around the talented cabaret couple.

Despite Huelsenbeck's assertion "There were almost no women in the cabaret. It was too wild, too smoky, too way out,"[12] women's contributions were fundamental to Dada stage entertainment. The implication is that the cabaret nightlife was morally corrupting and no place for women, but Hennings, Dutilh, Täuber, and a company of Laban dancers[13] were active and important participants in Dada soirees. Dutilh's feminine reputation was safe because of her status as a married woman and the ever-constant presence of her husband. Täuber was respected because she was an art professor and one of the only legally and gainfully employed of the bunch, while the Laban dancers participated as a group. Hennings would have been seen as the only morally suspect woman of the cabaret—a financially unstable immigrant and unmarried mother who had served several prison sentences and made a living off pleasing men, both on and off stage. In spite of these shortcomings, or perhaps because of them, Hennings was able to draw audiences to the unorthodox performances of the Dada group.

To these avant-garde adventures, Hennings contributed her charming dancing and singing talents, made costumes and hand puppets, and recited her poems and the works of other writers. For example Hennings is listed in the program for the first public Dada soiree, the July 14, 1916, Autoren-Abend at the Zunfthaus zur Waag, as reciting a prose piece, "Zwei Frauen" (Two Women), and four of her poems (including "Aether") and performing three Dada dances to the music of Ball with masks made by Marcel Janco. She also took part in a "Cubistischer Tanz" (Cubist dance) with Ball, Huelsenbeck, and Tzara. Arp's description of the evening in his "Dadaland" gives us a glimpse of Hennings: "On the stage of a gaudy, motley, overcrowded tavern there are several weird and peculiar figures representing Tzara, Janco, Ball, Huelsenbeck, Madame Hennings, and your humble servant. Total pandemonium. The people around us are shouting, laughing, and gesticulating. Our replies are sighs of love, volleys of hiccups, poems, moos, and miaowing of medieval Bruitists. Tzara is wiggling his behind like the belly of an Oriental dancer. Janco is playing an invisible violin and bowing and scraping. Madame Hennings, with a Madonna face, is doing the splits. Huelsenbeck is playing away nonstop on the great drum, with Ball accompanying him on the piano, pale as a chalky ghost. We were given the honorary title of Nihilists."[14]

Hennings was very much a part of this circuslike atmosphere and, with her many years of professional cabaret experience, she was decidedly a great asset to the entertainment value of the Dada programs, attracting the praise of newspaper reviewers. Her small physical appearance contrasted with her strong artistic gifts and assertive personality. She was described by her contemporaries, including Hermann Hesse, as original and bold.[15] Even Huelsenbeck admitted in *Memoirs of a Dada Drummer* that she recited aggressive poems powerfully, something he did not think her capable of.[16] Laban dancer Suzanne Perrottet recorded the following memory of Hennings at the Cabaret Voltaire: "I had never seen anything like it and was immediately won over by the Dadaists. Emmy Hennings stood there dressed in a roll of cardboard, from head to foot, her face was a ghastly mask, the mouth open, the nose off to one side, the arms lengthened in thin cardboard rolls, with long stylized fingers. The only living part that could be seen was her feet, naked, all by themselves at the bottom; it was so terse and impressive. That's how she danced. She could do nothing else but clatter her feet and bend the whole thing like a chimney. While doing that she spoke now and then, but no one could understand it, they could feel it. And sometimes she let out cry, a cry. . . ."[17]

Hennings's place in the center of the Dada group is further confirmed by one of its most sexist members: in the great debate over the invention of the word *Dada,* Huelsenbeck named Hennings as a witness to validate his version of the story, a version that demonstrates his jealousy of Tzara. Huelsenbeck insisted that he and Ball (not Tzara) chose the word *dada* by chance from a German-French dictionary. Saying that only Ball, Hennings, and himself were in the room at the time, Huelsenbeck recalled suggesting they adopt the word as it conveyed the primitiveness of a child's first sounds and the newness of this avant-garde art. He claimed that Hennings was at that moment erecting an altar in a corner of the room and that she agreed with the men that *Dada* would be an excellent word.[18]

Hennings's own words add to the testimonies of Arp, Perrottet, and Huelsenbeck. Her *Ruf und Echo: Mein Leben mit Hugo Ball* is important to the study of Dada because it provides a behind-the-scenes perspective on the Dada events taking place in Zurich. It likewise defines her as a witness to and analyst of the personalities surrounding her. In the chapter "Der Dadaismus," Hennings claimed that Dada began quite innocently at the literary Cabaret Voltaire, when Ball, Arp, Huelsenbeck, and Tzara founded the movement. She did not spend as much time describing specific Dada events as one would hope. In fact, writing decades later, she seemed reluctant or ashamed to delve into her memories of the avant-garde, perhaps associating it with her illicit past, but she admitted that she could not skip over this tumultuous episode in her life.

Hennings was compelled to look back to 1917, when Dada was vital and new. Its proponents opened the first Galerie Dada in the Sprünglihause (chocolate manufacturers) on the fashionable Bahnhofstraße, where, according to Hennings, Cubist and Expressionist paintings were first exhibited. The expositions at the Galerie Dada were well attended despite what Hennings considered as a high entrance fee. The inaugural celebration was held on March 29, followed by the April 14 Dada Abend. Meanwhile, with an increasingly critical attitude, Ball described the gallery as having three faces: one is that of a "teaching body for schoolgirls and upper-class ladies"; a second is a candlelit Kandinsky room for esoteric philosophy; and the third is the face of lively soirees that "have a brilliance and a frenzy such as Zurich has never seen before."[19] Hennings initiated a political puppet show at the Galerie Dada with her Czar and Czarina marionettes. This project allowed her to work with Täuber, who also created many Dada puppets in Zurich. Later Hannah Höch continued the marionette or doll-making tradition in Berlin and, like Täuber with her wooden sculptures, developed it into abstract Dada heads in her paintings.

Hennings appreciated the excitement and the intellectual stimulation of her fellow poets, also in exile during the war. Above all, however, Hennings was a performer and loved the stage. She took an active part in the April 14 Sturm-Soiree at the Galerie Dada: not only did she recite poems by Jakob van Hoddis, but she played the role of the "weibliche Seele" (Female Soul) Anima in Oskar Kokoschka's *Sphinx und Strohmann* (Sphinx and Straw Man). Ball described the alluring Hennings: "Emmy was the only one not wearing a mask. She appeared half sylph, half angel, lilac and light blue."[20]

At the third Dada Abend, on April 28, 1917, at the Galerie Dada at Bahnhofstrasse 19, Hennings contributed "Kritik der Leiche" (Critique of the Corpse) and "Notizen" (Notes). At the fourth Dada Abend, on old and new art, held on May 12, she recited her poem "O ihr Heiligen" (O You Saints), read from three texts of medieval literature, and presented her "Legende." "O ihr Heiligen" shows a break from her earlier style:

O you saints with the precious names,
All who over the crossroads came,
I lost my way,
Went silently through thorny hedges
Of most painful annihilation.

I am in the dark,
And no stars spark
In my dusk.
My face turned toward the wall,
The fire of my hearth is out.
I am worth nothing now. [21]

O ihr Heiligen mit dem kostbaren Namen,
Die alle über den Kreuzweg kamen,
Ich vergaß meine Wege,
Ging still durchs Dornengehege
Schmerzlichster Abtötung.

Ich bin im Dunkeln,
Und keine Sterne funkeln
In meine Dämmerung.
Das Gesicht zur Wand gekehrt,
Verlöscht mein Feuer auf dem Herd.
Ich bin jetzt nichts mehr wert.

This poem differs noticeably from those previously quoted. Although rich in imagery and resorting to rhyme, the poem remains obscure in its narration and takes the form of an intimate prayer or confession. With a sacred-sounding title and first stanza, the poem begins much like a hymn or biblical text. Nonetheless a more secular allusion can be found in the mention of holy ones coming together at a crossroads (or emigrants meeting in Zurich). Though the others have arrived at their destination, the narrator's way still lies through thorny and painful annihilation, which are the obstacles that have always threatened her art and her survival. The second stanza continues the use of the first-person pronoun, while it begins the dark/light imagery that causally connects the first stanza to the third. The speaker finds herself in darkness where no stars give direction or hope. She is isolated, even confined, in the final stanza. Her face seems voluntarily turned toward the wall, suggesting her lack of concern when the fire goes out in the hearth. The choices she has made and the situation in which she finds herself lead her to conclude that she no longer has any worth, a feeling she revealed in a lamenting letter she wrote to Tzara, also in the spring of 1917.

In some ways, this poem tells the story of Hennings's desire to be part of the cultural dynamism in Zurich, but she hesitated and questioned her role. It is important to notice that it is not her poetic light that dies out in the poem but the fire in her hearth. She seems to be unwillingly connected to the household fireside and what it represents: a reminder of the hardships of daily life and a type of domestic servitude that embodies traditional female tasks. These prevent her from taking a fuller part in the stimulating artistic activities that attract and complete her. The hearth can be seen as a symbol of obligations that come with motherhood, constant household financial concerns, and her emotional partnership with Ball. Her frustration takes the form of feelings of self-doubt and worthlessness. Again she faces the tension that lies between her bohemian and her domestic selves, between the lure of her errant ways and her moral conscience.

Hennings's poems of this period often reveal an ominous or even suicidal side to the cabaret performer. Ball noted her serious tone in his diary entry for December 21, 1917. Mentioning her "Brief einer Leiche" (Letter from a Corpse), he said that in the poem she "talks about the corpse's instinct for self-preservation in a mordantly humorless way."[22] Hennings's personal dilemmas undoubtedly influenced her poetry and how she was perceived by her fellow Dadaists.

Hennings was not only a founding participant in Dada soirees and responsible for opening the Galerie Dada with Ball and Tzara in 1917, but she served as a valuable eyewitness to much Dada history. For example, according to her *Ruf und Echo*, Tzara's arrival made a singular impression on her and others: when he recited his French poem "Adieu, ma mère; adieu, mon père" (Farewell, my mother, farewell, my father), he was generally mistaken for a young homesick Romanian. Later Hennings described Arp in his unforgettable pyramid skirt, which made him resemble a native of Mars or the constellation Orion, on this planet only on a stopover to somewhere else. She also provided a portrait of Ball at work, reciting his *Lautgedichte:* "He wore a kind of knight's armor made of blue glazed paper, and his long, narrow, abysmally earnest face looked just like that of Don Quixote, like one imagines the Knight of the Sorrowful Countenance, and how Goya would have painted him."[23] Just such a serious and melancholic face appears in many photographs of Ball.

Hennings recorded her impressions of the Dada years in her journal, then converted them into a memoir of her life with Ball. Although she and Ball are principally known today because of their initiation of Zurich Dada, based on the slight number of pages she devoted to the period in *Ruf und Echo,* Hennings seems to have assigned this chapter of her life relatively little importance. Instead of revealing details about her life as a Zurich Dadaist, she intentionally withheld information. At the time she wrote her autobiography, the mother of Zurich Dada preferred to concentrate on her personal life with Ball and the more scholarly or theological accomplishments of his career in an effort to distance herself from a past that she viewed as morally contradictory to her later life. Throughout *Ruf und Echo* she nevertheless provided valuable insight into the events that affected her life with her husband by recalling specific incidents and often quoting Ball or including excerpts from his and other writers' poetry. She inserted letters exchanged between her and Ball, in addition to Hesse's effusive praise of her husband's work, praise she considered significant. Periodically she offered analyses of the episodes she recorded, and she described her role as similar to that of a spiritual medium, an intermediary between the event and its documentation in the memoir: "I am not writing a novel, it must truly be my life that I disclose and that haunts me. The more one wants to push it away, the more it flows through. I'm not the one who decides what I write, I have no choice, and I would like once to have a choice."[24] Overall Hennings had a special understanding—and dread—of the task of recording her history, and she recognized the responsibility of her text as a truthful witness of its era, despite its faults.

In addition to telling the truth, Hennings also took on the task of reconciling art and politics. Her discussion of the role of art in *Ruf und Echo* reveals yet another aspect of her personality: her antiwar stance. In her opinion art was purely a symbol of the times. Thus Dada art, according to Hennings, should not astonish anyone because it was the poetic transformation of actual events and experiences that were disturbing and puzzling. The chaotic artistic production of the Zurich Dadaists merely reflects the uncertain times. Hennings claimed that Dada was created as a reaction to the events of the period, to the atmosphere of madness and tumult in which "there is no longer any perspective in the moral world. Up is down and down is up."[25] With the advent of the war, the whole world had become monstrous and frightening. She elaborated: "The artist must be at peace to work, if he wants to get to the center, to the heart of the matter. He is thrown off his track; his space will be taken from him in such an unpeaceful time when he is no longer the heart of the world. Where everything leads to annihilation, we see the violation of the soul. Where cannons thunder, where chaos reigns, harmony cannot be created. The voice of the poet dies out. There was so much desperation in Dada, at least in the beginning when it was not yet a fashion, not yet renowned, when it was still genuine."[26]

In her reflections on the period, Hennings asserted that Dada truly was a necessary, spontaneous, and desperate response to the war and its destruction, to the loss of peace and the resulting violence against the soul of the artist; the irreverent and provocative artistic manifestations of Dada clearly do reflect the uncertainty of the times. The notion of Dada as a spontaneous act was echoed by other Dadaists, namely Ball and Picabia. Avant-garde performance art, so common in the early Dada years in Zurich, was by its nature chaotic and ephemeral. Nevertheless, Hennings pointed out, as time went on and Dada became more widespread, it lost its original form and meaning: "Dadaism was pushed on further and further, and not only by the Dadaists. It was there, and yet it was somehow already gone. I don't mean that it was 'outmoded.' As soon as it was taken seriously by the press and the public it became recognized. The success was inevitable, and right before it became stamped into a mold, before the success, Hugo had an instinctive revulsion. He began to call Dadaism a whim that one should not make into an art movement. Everything should stay suspended, as suspended as possible."[27] For Hennings, the later manifestations of Zurich Dada were not truly "Dada" because they lacked the necessary initial spontaneous impetus. They no longer responded to the war and its perpetrators with impulsive desperation but became instead calculated and well publicized.

When Ball became disillusioned with the new commercialized form of Dadaism and physically exhausted by the overwhelming duties he took on in organizing the Zurich events, he distanced himself from the group by going to Magadino (in Tessin) with Hennings's daughter, Annemarie. Hennings joined them a few weeks later. In the meantime he wrote to her: "My dear little Emmy, I am so thankful that I am here and that you have helped me so much in my 'flight.'"[28] He mentioned to her that his voice, eyes, and heart were completely worn out, and he asked if Tzara was upset to have been left running the gallery. During this time Hennings served as Ball's intermediary in his dealings with the Dada group, and she seemed to take on this task willingly in order to stay in the city.

Hennings and Ball moved to the Swiss village Vira-Magadino in 1916 but were forced to abandon their plans to live in the countryside for lack of funds. Financial problems plagued the couple for the rest of their lives. Hennings stayed with her daughter in Ascona while Ball went to Bern to seek employment. By the end of November, Hennings and Ball were back in Zurich, in time for the January 1917 first public Dada exhibition at the Galerie Corray at Bahnhofstraße 19. Hennings's chaotic lifestyle began to take a toll on her health. On February 1, 1917, Ball noted in his diary: "Emmy fainted in the street. We were waiting under a streetlamp for the tram. She leaned against the wall, staggered, and gently collapsed. I got help from passers-by, and we carried her to the first-aid post in the nearby police station. Her little head was resting so peacefully and comfortably on my shoulder as I was carrying her. A strange scene in the police station: the two of us on and by the bed, and six or seven worried policemen's faces around us, giving her some water and stroking her blond hair. On the way home she smiled and said, 'Why is your mouth so bitter.'"[29]

Family responsibilities, lack of sleep, an unhealthy lifestyle, and poor nutrition probably contributed to Hennings's collapse. But Hennings, drawn by her love of performance and, more important, their financial need seemed fully engaged in activities several days later. In a letter she wrote to Ball on February 6, 1917, Hennings recounted her fruitful meetings with Hardekopf and Richter in Zurich, reporting (and perhaps bragging) that they had discussed all kinds of literary and political topics.

On May 12, 1917, Hennings again participated in a soiree on "Alte und Neue Kunst Dada," the fourth private soiree. She translated and read poems along with Janco, Ball, and some of the other Dadaists at the Galerie Dada. Around this time Ball was asking in his diary if Dadaism were "a game in fancy dress, a laughingstock? And behind it a synthesis of the romantic, dandyistic, and demonic theories of the nineteenth century?"[30] By June 1917 Ball was rephrasing biblical scripture in his diary: "'Take the child and his mother and flee,' the angel said to Joseph. And Joseph fled to Egypt, to the land of magic. What we have experienced is more than a Bethlehem infanticide."[31] Ball felt that he again needed to distance himself from the Zurich Dada group, and Hennings and her daughter followed him to Ascona.

From there she wrote to Tzara that she was so separated from Zurich she felt like a picture fallen from the frame or like a silly little bad-timbered excursion boat that could not weather the storm at sea.[32] In the letter she wished him good luck on the opening, "as much as a woman can." The letter is disturbingly full of self-effacement, yearning, melancholy, and loss of hope in phrases such as "es ist das einzige, was ich kann" (it's the only thing I can do) and "Ich empfinde in mir etwas schwer und suche den Grund, sei dieser Grund selbst die unergründliche Unendlichkeit" (I feel something heavy in me and look for the reason, be this reason the unfathomable endlessness). In this second statement, Hennings played with the words "schwer" (difficult or heavy) and "Grund" (reason, basis, or ground): she found no stable ground, only an abyss. She said she was ready for a change and looked for a place for herself, the self-described naïve child in love. "You are right to live the way you do," she said to Tzara, "and I will always be glad to see you, as much as I am able to." Her letter makes it clear that she longed to return to Zurich and take part in Dada events, while it underlines her feeling of helplessness, loss, confusion, and isolation in the countryside.

From the village of Vira-Magadino on May 19, 1917, Hennings again wrote to the "Tzara-Dada" and reaffirmed her allegiance to Dada and its manifestations. She mentioned that she would send Tzara a delicate silk picture and the czar puppets, because the others he requested had been promised to Hugo. Her concern for and support of Dada are clear: "Tonight you have your soiree, and I wish you much luck, and that our beloved gallery, our child of joy and sorrow will be well treated and entrusted to you to the end. And if I must, I will come."[33] Hennings showed more than a passing interest in the Galerie Dada. There is a maternal possessiveness in her words, but she entrusted the gallery to Tzara, almost as if she were leaving a child in his care. She seems saddened that she could not take part in the events, perhaps feeling obliged to stay in Vira-Magadino with Ball. She signed the letter, "Ihre Hennings-Dada" (Your Hennings-Dada), again asserting her membership in the group, while demonstrating her fondness for Tzara.

When Ball's poor health finally influenced him to retire permanently from Dada activities and lead a calmer life, he sent Hennings at the end of May 1917 to collect his belongings from Zurich and settle financial accounts with Tzara. In June he sent her a letter with detailed instructions for paying debts and packing his personal effects. He signed it, "I send my love, my darling, and a thousand thanks for your true help, your Hugo."[34] In September 1917, Ball moved to Bern, where he worked for *Die Freie Zeitung* for more than two years. He and Hennings married in Bern nearly three years later.

By this time the couple's direct involvement with Dada events was coming to an end, and Zurich was giving birth to new centers of Dada in Germany and France. Hennings's name still appears on the April 11, 1919, "Radical Artists' Manifesto," suggesting that she signed alongside Richter, Arp, Janco, and others. Nevertheless what remained for Hennings and Ball of their Dada years were their memories (to be recorded later, in the case of Hennings), their continued contact and friendship with Dadaist colleagues, and the influence of their cabaret years, an influence that they often tried to veil beneath their growing religious zeal. Hennings's spiritual struggle played out in her works, beginning with *Gefängnis* (Prison). For the rest of her life she was engaged in a battle between the lure of the artist's world of rebellion and the striving for a pious and peaceful, though perhaps less stimulating, existence.

A Memoir of Prison

During the hectic days of 1917, Hennings was readying her first major prose work, the autobiographical novella *Gefängnis* for its 1919 publication. Under two hundred pages in length, the text is divided into two parts: from her arrest to her trial and her subsequent prison sentence and release. The events she recounted take place during the winter of 1914–15. *Gefängnis* is an important work in that it represents some of Hennings's most personal and tonally richest writing. It also marks the cabaret performer's first public success as a writer.

Hennings's text begins by revealing the confusion the narrator feels with the unsettling statement that "in the meantime three months passed" and she still has not received a summons for a trial.[35] Readers immediately seek a time frame for the action of this in medias res tale and thereby share her doubts and uncertainty. She reveals that she has returned to "M" (one assumes Munich) and that she dares not take a job abroad. She worries about the effect of a jail sentence on her ability to find work and about who would bother to ask after her if she were to disappear. Although she continues to receive compliments on her voice and acclaim for her performances, she feels a lack of personal, human connection. She dwells on her uncertain future, on being misunderstood and alone.

The text then offers a flashback to explain that when she wanted to accept a four-week job in Paris, she wrote a letter, requesting to know if she could have her court appearance scheduled in the next few days or after her return from France. The message is politely phrased but clearly makes the assumption that she is free to travel.

As a result of this short straightforward note, new problems arise, and a nightmarish plot begins to unfold. There is a knock on her door one morning around eight o'clock. When she does not answer, a man enters. He announces he is from the police and that she should appear for questioning at ten o'clock. At the police station she is kept waiting by a man writing at a desk. Finally he addresses her with one question, "Is this your letter?" When she answers yes, he studies her file, claps it shut, makes a quick phone call, and then ignores her for more than twenty minutes. The ominous mood of the text conveys her growing discomfort.

Suddenly a huge guard enters, startling her. The desk man declares, "Also Sie sind verhaftet" (Well, you are arrested). She protests, claiming there must be some mistake and asking where this is guard taking her. She receives no reply. Finally she is told she is being arrested for "Fluchverdacht," contemplating flight. She complains that she is being done an injustice, that she came of her own free will and that now they want to arrest her. She cries and tries to run to the corner of the office but is led down endless corridors and through doorways, sandwiched between the guard and the police officer who appeared earlier in her room. Finally, she writes, "I stay still . . . I cannot breathe. What is wrong? Now I know, I know forever: There is no space, there is no time, there is no air."[36]

Thus begins Hennings's story of hopeless imprisonment. The novella records daily routines, conversations with characters who move through the text without offering hope, and the narrator's methods of counting the seemingly endless days. The prose is direct, unencumbered, and honest in tone. Through her barely concealed narrator, Hennings captured her own self-doubt and vulnerability.

The story of her arrest and trial, the confusion and helplessness she felt, reminds readers of Kafka's tale of accusation and guilt, *Der Prozeß* (*The Trial*), published in 1925. Clearly not indebted to Kafka's text, since her book appeared in 1919, Hennings, like Kafka, reworked her life experiences with psychological insights to bear witness to the impersonal and inscrutable power of an unassailable wartime authority. The regime her novella evokes seems to compensate for its loss of control over the new age of technological progress by imposing its authority without reason or explanation on the weakest of its citizens. This short autobiographical work brilliantly conveys the traumatic psychological results of incarceration on those who believe themselves innocent.

Hennings's writing illustrates the reconstruction of the self that her main character must undertake in order to compensate for a gradual loss of mental balance. In a scene in her jail cell, the narrator strives to remain steady and focused but finds it difficult: "I lay my mouth in this little curve. The iron bars are cool. The glass is so smooth and cold! My lips move on the black glass that remains still. And I speak, whisper, so no one will hear us: 'Stay true to me. You will not disappoint me. Be smooth under my eyes. Submit to my will. Be merciful and let me seduce you until I dominate you. Be the reflection for my soul's picture. I need your echo. Sound it back, long: I love you, quietly, quietly, love you.' What spoke? Was I speaking?"[37]

All she seeks is some hope in the feeling that someone cares about her, but she has realized from the beginning of her incarceration that no one will know to look for her. Alone in her prison cell, she creates a comforting partner: the cell itself, with its iron bars and cold glass, becomes her secret lover that she will seduce and master. All she asks is that it return her words of love in an echo. This scene is the most startling of part 1, a section that captures images from the prisoner's wandering mind and sets them in precise language that appeals to the senses. The text begins to make a strong statement about the harsh reality of imprisonment and its accompanying loneliness and despair, which affected Hennings for a lifetime.

The second part of *Gefängnis* begins with the narrator's dreamlike vision, again foreshadowing Kafka's *Prozeß:* "I stand before a high iron gate that I try to open."[38] As the narrator describes her reconstructed past from the safety of her present, she wonders who now stands before that gate. In an accusatory tone she demands to know how many must stand before it, raped by its iron authority. With the opinion that the sooner she goes in the sooner she will be let out, she relinquishes her freedom to the power beyond the walls.

Six weeks after her arrest, she is released. Freedom is foreign to her and she is unsure of her way. But somehow it does not matter. In a memorable image, the protagonist moves across a wide snow-covered field, her eyes focused on an image of home: "The longer I go, the freer I feel."[39]

The final lines of the text are full of poetry and peace: "Slowly it becomes darker. I don't get frightened. The snow shines. I am so alone. And I pass no one.

No one sees me. I spread my arms wide out of happiness. I haven't yet reached the city, and the people."[40] Again she feels alone, but this time without the constraints and observing gazes imposed by her prison. She walks across the snow with arms outstretched. The solitary walk through the dark causes no fear. Her final puzzling remark about not yet reaching the city and the people shows both an excited anticipation of a life to recommence among others and an anxiety of what the future might hold for her.

Throughout the text, *Gefängnis* depicts a character who candidly reveals her confusions and fears but who has the will to withstand the deprivations and isolation of prison. Although her spirit will be battered, it will not be crushed. Though written early in her career, this depiction of a heroine who will not concede defeat perfectly describes Hennings during her entire lifetime of deprivation and loss. She was consistently uprooted and replanted throughout her cabaret career, as well as during her marriage with Ball. Every time she found herself in unfamiliar circumstances, Hennings took up the challenge, living by her wits, her talents, or her charms. She was always the consummate survivor. But what was the cost of her survival?

In his diary entry of June 9, 1919, Ball recorded his opinion of Hennings's *Gefängnis* and that of the press in a revealing excerpt: "People are beginning to be interested in Emmy's *Gefängnis*. The book expresses the character of the age and its sufferings. A Berlin critic calls it 'modern memoirs from a charnel house' and can compare his impressions only to those he received from Hamsun's *Hunger*. A Munich journal writes: 'One-third child, one-third woman, one-third gamin, the author of this book stands out from the many similar to her because the archetypal human element in her sympathetic, gentle hands glows like a red ruby, compared to which everything else disintegrates into gray ash.' The book is stylistically an incessant filing and gnawing at iron bars. It knows no capitulation, no compromise. It is unshakable in its precise honesty."[41]

Among these favorable reviews lies a reference to the "woman-child," a revealing description of Hennings that recurs in the texts of Ball and his colleagues, as well as that of a literary critic from Munich. Hennings was ten years younger than Ball, with a tiny frame and small, nearly pixielike features. Her physical appearance seemed to inspire in those around her a sense of protectiveness. But the critic leads us to believe that her writing itself reflects these physical characteristics. Certainly *Gefängnis* is precise, economical, and unpretentious in its style. It is never lofty, flamboyant, or verbose. Nor is it indifferent or aloof. Such a style suits a naïve and bewildered young narrator who feels unjustly imprisoned. Hennings was often stereotyped by those who limited their initial observations to her physical traits. Although petite, she proved to be hardy and enduring.

Nevertheless the six months that Hennings spent in jail certainly affected her emotional and physical well-being. Family members affirmed that the experience had a lasting effect on the writer. After the demanding Dada years in Zurich, as she began to settle into a calmer life with Ball, Hennings felt the need to write about earlier experiences that made her who she was. Her days of being tagged a criminal, of living on the edge, separated from the bourgeois society of predictable routines and obeyed laws, led her to prison. Releasing the story of what she underwent as an accused woman and prisoner allowed her a cherished sense of freedom. Later in her life, Hennings showed a great interest in court trials and often attended them as a spectator, making sketches of court scenes.

Muse and Mother

Soon after the successful publication of *Gefängnis*, a series of entries in Ball's diary reveals that his wife suffered from a serious case of pneumonia. His February 12, 1919, entry notes that he gave Hennings the first copy of his *Zur Kritik der deutschen Intelligenz* (Towards a Critique of German Intelligence) in the hospital on her birthday. He wrote that "she had a high fever, barely recognized me, but caressed the book I brought her and smiled in a sad way as if she were saying good-bye forever. It was a few days before the crisis. The doctor really did not want to let me go into the room for a few minutes."[42] Although Hennings was suffering from a life-threatening case of the Spanish flu compounded by pneumonia, a week later Ball's diary offers a glimpse of her performing domestic tasks at home: "With Emmy, tired and drained, on the deck chair. It is nice to fall asleep slowly while she attends to her little jobs. She puts a lighted cigarette in my mouth; gives me an ashtray, and taps the ash into it herself. There is a cold draft through the crack in the door, so she covers me with her brown coat and makes pancakes. That is very nice."[43] Hennings's physical strength seemed to rally when she was given the task to care for Ball, who elicited her maternal persona.

A few days later Ball recorded in his diary a dream he had about Hennings: "In my dream I see Emmy with raised hands being carried down the aisle of the Munich Frauenkirche to the altar. I am in the crowd of people pushing forward in excitement. She stands with her back to the altar. I see grace, joy, and vigorous life; lovers sacrificing themselves; the dead leaving the requiem offered them with a smile."[44] This image of Hennings glorifies her as a saint or the Virgin Mary carried like a statue in a procession on Assumption Day. She represents a mixture of holiness, vitality, and joy that evokes excitement and rejuvenating hope in the admiring onlooker. Just like the woman-child figure mentioned in the Munich newspaper review, this depiction of Hennings as a holy vision also distorts her value as a thinking, productive artist and writer. Instead she becomes a kind of sacrificial virgin marched to the altar.

Again that month, Ball recorded: "I usually spend the evenings now with Emmy in her Marzilli room. She tells stories or reads to me. . . ."[45] It seems obvious from the testimony of Ball's diary that he viewed Hennings as a composite muse and maternal figure in his life. She was the lively and motivating spirit who drove his work, while her roles as housekeeper and domestic partner made his research and writing time possible. But what was the effect of these traditionally female roles on her and her art? Usually Hennings accepted the tasks foisted on her. There were times, however, when she felt the need for some independence through writing, travel, or a return to cabaret performance.

While Ball often recorded Hennings's domestic contributions, his diaries also provide insights into her professional life as a writer. For example Ball mentioned that Hennings was preparing a new book, *Das Brandmal* (The Brand), which was published in Berlin in 1920. He recorded that he had read the first sixty pages and predicted that this book too would become a sign of the times: "The beginning, in which a small company of actors disbands and scatters to the ends of the earth; the useless prayer in the cathedral, hunger, disgrace—what is that if not abandonment? But then the heavens divide and the stars shine softly. A young bird sings . . . it whistles so white. A child walks at night and cries. . . . A ray of light over the child! A smile over the singing child! The soul wants to rise up out of decay and woe. . . ."[46] *Das Brandmal,* praised by both Hardekopf and Rilke, is rich in disturbing imagery, conveying a heaviness of tone that makes a strong personal statement about modern malaise. It draws on Hennings's experiences as a prostitute during World War I and the lean Dada years in Zurich.

After sharing years of poverty and hardship, Hennings married Ball on February 22, 1920. She finished *Das Brandmal* the day before her wedding. Soon thereafter, Hennings and Ball returned to Germany, stopping for a short visit in Ball's hometown of Pirmasens. According to Hennings's *Ruf und Echo,* they came upon some angry men who menaced them with stones in protest against Ball's *Zur Kritik der deutschen Intelligenz.* They called him "Landesverräter" (a traitor to his country) and encircled the couple. Hennings said she tossed a stone up from under her arm as she had learned to do in a juggling act for vaudeville, and made a comment about stoning. The antagonists might have thought she was ready to throw rocks at them, she reported, and so they dispersed.[47] Although Hennings was able to make a joke to lighten the situation, Ball was devastated by the attitude of the citizens of his hometown.

The newlywed couple and Annemarie soon moved to Hennings's family home in Flensburg, where she played the role of landlady in the house she had inherited at her mother's death. The couple was now living a life completely divorced from their Dada past. In fact Dada had moved out of Zurich and was on its way to Berlin and beyond. Meanwhile Hennings found her artistic outlet in her writing instead. *Das Brandmal* was published in November. Ball noted that there was no debate over its success in Europe. Everyone could identify with the text: "Here is this age, experienced and suffered physically."[48]

The couple sold the house in Flensburg and returned to live in Switzerland, in the Tecino village of Agnuzzo, in September 1920. Hennings said that they immediately fell in love with the place, its isolation, and its beauty, especially an old country palazzo that had not been inhabited for years. They stayed there for four years, except for the twelve months that they spent in Munich (October 1921–October 1922) so that Ball could be near a library for his research. It was in Agnuzzo that Ball pursued his intense reading for his *Byzantinisches Christentum,* and Hennings became more committed to Catholicism. According to Ball, she was also working on a new book at this time, though he did not mention which one. She could have been writing her 1922 collection of religious-inspired poems, *Helle Nacht* (Luminous Night) or beginning *Das Ewige Lied* (The Eternal Song), published in 1923.

During the winter of 1923–24, Hennings left Ball in Agnuzzo and traveled to Italy. She wrote that "we wanted to try to work independently from each other. I have to admit here that for my part, I wasn't completely thinking of work. I wasn't convinced that work was the main or near to the most important thing in our life."[49] During her time away from Ball, she visited Pisa, Florence, and Milan, and her *Ruf und Echo* includes letters that she and her husband exchanged during this time of separation. The letters reveal that she often went without adequate food or lodging during the trip. When he found out she went to bed hungry, Ball scolded her for not asking for more money. Her daughter remembered that, when Hennings rented a room in Florence, she paid for it by cleaning. This left her hardly any opportunities to see the city. One can also imagine that her labor left her little time for writing, reading, or relaxing. Even so, Hennings managed to draft a second novel on a recurring and haunting topic: her time in prison. The manuscript of "Das graue Haus" remains unpublished.

In one letter, she wrote from Italy about her despair and desire for Ball: "I am tired, very tired, and I would like to come home. I don't know if I'll send this letter. Maybe I'll throw it in the Arno and then the waves will take my words, the gentle supporting waves."[50] And in the same letter she noted, "I would like to speak to people unseen. I love them and I don't want to see them. A dark glow is often in your words, Hugo, a burning beautiful thing like a fire that I cannot get enough of. I am addicted to your words and flame."[51] Her letter shows her reluctance to write to her husband, fearing her level of energy and her mood would not match the task. At the same time she clearly hungered for Hugo's written words more than his physical presence. Even when they felt inclined to live apart, Hugo and Emmy seemed to thirst for each other's support and inspiration.

In October 1924 Hennings and Ball attempted to establish a residence together in Rome. She described their motives: "Maybe in Rome we were not seeking peace, not the ultimate peace, but only a little rest, a calm in the darkness of the days."[52] But after six months they had exhausted their funds and settled instead in the southern Italian village of Vietri-Marina, where former Zurich Dadaists Arp and Täuber visited them. During the hot summer in Albori, Ball worked on his *Flucht aus der Zeit* while Hennings did some research for his work on exorcism. Hennings was Ball's devoted helpmate, often collecting excerpts for his research and discussing theories with him. Although she respected his space and methods

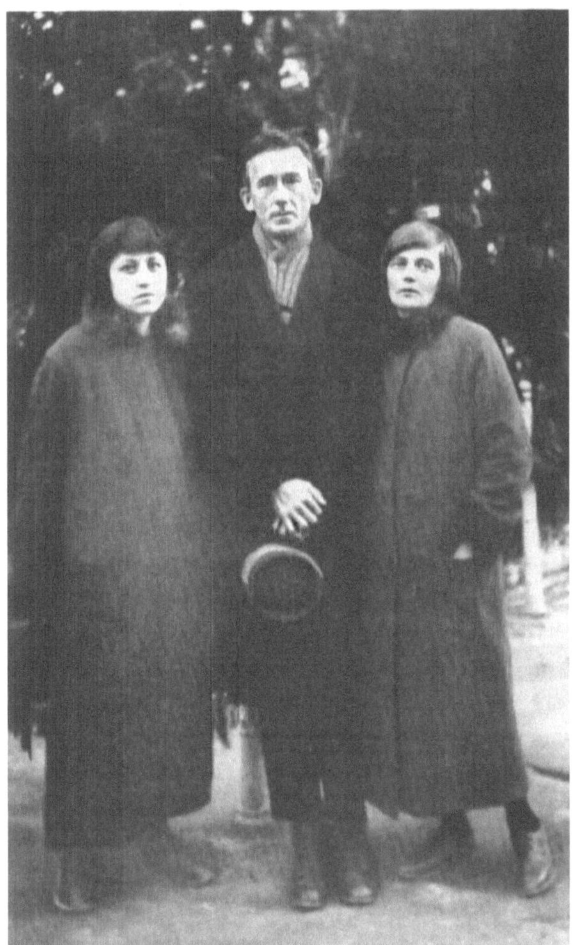

Hugo and Emmy Ball with her daughter, Annemarie, in Sorengo, 1926. Photograph courtesy of the Benziger Archiv, Museum Fram, Einsiedeln, Switzerland.

of work, she worried about his tendency to write without adequate light or air, reporting that she found his office and sleeping room unhealthy.

Ball and Hennings stayed in southern Italy for approximately one year with financial support from their close friend Hermann Hesse. At one point Hennings made a trip to Rome, trying to sell artists' ceramics, but she had little luck. In May 1926 the couple returned to Switzerland. A photograph taken that same year of them with Annemarie in Sorengo shows a thin, pale Ball and a tired but determined Hennings, her body slightly tilted towards his and dwarfed by his height. All three subjects appear serious and express no joy before the camera.

In order to earn a little money, Hennings returned for a while to Germany when she was invited to perform in Berlin, Stuttgart, Frankfurt, and Munich. Ball wrote to her that her book *Der Gang zur Liebe* (The Way to Love) had just been published. The work is Hennings's record of her Italian trip. Meanwhile her daughter came down with typhus, and Hennings was anxious for news of her welfare. Ball told Hennings that she should stay in Berlin, because in Sorengo she could do nothing but wait for Annemarie's recovery: "we must realize, Emmy, that the child is in God's hands. So, you can stay calm."[53] When she received the letter, Hennings ignored Ball's advice and rushed to Tessin, obeying her maternal instincts, which told her she should be with her ailing daughter rather than on stage.

In May 1927 Ball wrote in his diary a list of plans for the year, which included Hennings's returning to work in Germany, Ball's writing the exorcism book, Annemarie's attending art school in Zurich, Ball and Hennings's moving to Heidelberg or Freiburg, and later their taking a trip to Paris. All these plans were abandoned when Ball was diagnosed with stomach cancer and underwent surgery in Zurich on July 2, 1927. The couple moved instead to the village of Sant' Abbondio, thirty minutes from Hesse's residence, for Ball's convalescence, but he died on September 14.

Afterward Emmy traveled to Rome, Assisi, Paris, Stuttgart, Frankfurt, Cologne, Berlin, and Zurich, while she wrote and published poetry, biographical works about Ball, and novels. She professed one of her goals in the foreword to her 1940 *Flüchtige Spiel* (Fleeting Play): "Already for many years I've followed a plan to lay down a written confession of my life."[54] Although *Ruf und Echo* partially fulfilled this goal, not many details are known about Hennings's later years. She eventually settled in Tessin, rented out rooms to vacationers, did factory work, and continued a devoted friendship with Hesse. Her *Briefe an Hermann Hesse,* published in 1956, includes letters from 1920 until the month before her death. They remain the only readily available autobiographical records of her later years. She died of pneumonia on August 10, 1948, in the Clinica S. Anna at Sorengo/Lugano and was buried in Sant' Abbondio beside her husband.

The number of published works by Hennings illustrates how consistently committed she was to writing throughout her life. While her early poems allude to her bohemian lifestyle, her later works appear as acts of penance and affirmations of her faith. Her books include the poetry collection *Die Letzte Freude* (1913); the novella *Gefängnis* (1919); the autobiographical *Das Brandmal* (1920), which Ball mentioned by name in his journal; the poetry collection *Helle Nacht* (1922); the prose work *Das Ewige Lied* (1923); the prose work *Der Gang zur Liebe* (1926); the biographies *Hugo Ball: Sein Leben in Briefen und Gedichten* (1929) and *Hugo Balls Weg zu Gott* (1931); the prose work *Blume und Flamme: Geschichte einer Jugend,* with a foreword by Hesse (1938); the volume of poetry *Der Kranz* (1939); the prose work *Das Flüchtige Spiel: Wege und Umwege einer Frau* (1940); tales *Märchen am Kamin* (1943); and short stories *Das Irdische Paradies und andere Legenden* (1945). Finished just before her death, the posthumously published *Ruf und Echo: Mein Leben mit Hugo Ball* (1953) recounts her life but chiefly in relation to Ball's.

This extensive list of accomplishments does not mention her many Expressionist and Dadaist performances in dance, music, and poetic recitations—all ephemeral arts, unrecorded and easily overlooked. Hennings's contributions to the avant-garde and specifically to Dada were many and varied, as were her talents. Moreover, her courage, persistence, and attractive presence were essential to the founding and success of Zurich Dada. In honor of her work, the Museo Hermann Hesse at Montagnola, Switzerland, hosted the retrospective Ich bin da. Pardon (I'm here. Excuse me) from April 15 to September 10, 2006. The exhibition featured three months of cultural and educational activities and the catalog *Emmy Ball-Hennings: Musa, Diseuse, Poetessa.*

Two biographies of Emmy Hennings have come out in German: René Gass's 1998 *Emmy Ball-Hennings: Wege und Umweg zum Paradies* (Emmy Ball-Hennings: Paths and Detours to Paradise) and journalist Bärbel Reetz's 2001 *Emmy Ball-Hennings: Leben im Vielleicht* (Emmy Ball-Hennings: Life in Perhaps). Although both works shed light on Hennings's life, neither studies Hennings in one of her most important roles in literary and art history—as the mother of the Dada movement, as an instigator of Dada performance, or as a model for the group through her stage talent and sometimes disreputable lifestyle. What Hennings witnessed and recorded in her autobiographical writings about this era outlasts her initial and ephemeral theatrical contributions to Dada. Her antibourgeois perspective is historically significant because it provides another glimpse of early Dada and its proponents from a female participant and observer whose background and life experiences differed remarkably from those of the other women featured in this study.

Because of her initiative and support, Hennings was a motivating force behind the founding and success of Zurich Dada. She was an experienced and seductive actor and singer who drew clients to the cabaret. Without an audience, who would notice the Dadaists' antics? Nevertheless her intense involvement in Dada events lasted only a few years, primarily because of her relationship with Ball, who drew her away from her central Dadaist contribution: performance. One can see that her preoccupation with the avant-garde seemed to wane soon after Ball distanced himself from Dada activities in favor of the more scholarly life of a writer.

As her involvement with the outlandish behavior of Zurich Dada diminished, Hennings's poetry became more traditional in rhyme, phrasing, and imagery. Her dark doubts, so closely linked to her years of prostitution, illness, drug use, prison, and nightclub work were replaced with declarations of faith. Her prose continued to retain her early candor, but became increasingly influenced by religious thought. Even so, her impact on the members of the Dada group was deep and lasting. As the only entertainer with cabaret experience, she modeled a rebellious lifestyle in her choice of profession. In fact she was one of the few participants who had truly lived the daring bohemian life of the itinerant artist instead of a comfortable and stable middle-class existence that was conveniently shed to indulge in artistic expression. Her life was a reexamination and reinvention of the self as she moved through the stages of singer, dancer, puppet maker, poet, essayist, novelist, and memoirist.

Ball's isolation and intense concentration on religion, history, and philosophy had a tremendous effect on Hennings and her choice of artistic medium. But her writings, personality, and energy affected him and his production just as much, especially during the couple's years in Zurich. Despite what Hennings herself might have suggested, she was not merely Hugo Ball's "echo" in their artistic relationship. Her many performances and publications—at least half of the latter dating from after his death—are witness to the fact that she was a worthy artist in her own right.

Nevertheless Ball's influence on Hennings's career choices foregrounds which part of herself as a woman she had to sacrifice for an intimate relationship and a family. In the case of Hennings, there is evidence that she reluctantly chose to relinquish her active and stimulating life, her devotion to Dada, and her love of performance for a partnership with Ball. When she made this commitment to her partner, she made it for the rest of her life in that she kept Ball's reputation alive through her biographical writings and by editing his works. However, if one wishes to discover the Hennings who was the mother of Dada, one must look beyond her self-effacing role as Ball's muse and nurturer and instead approach her through the impressions she made on her co-Dadaists. Additionally one must read deeply in her guarded poetry, memoirs, letters, and other prose works. As a result, one will uncover the most remarkable paradox surrounding Hennings: her presence was clearly compatible with and appropriate to each stage of her life, even when she remained incongruous within herself. As such, she emerges as one of the avant-garde's most enigmatic women.

2. Gabrielle Buffet and Germaine Everling

Picabia's Cacodylic Eyes

Gabrielle Buffet (1881–1985) and Germaine Everling (1887–1975) had several things in common: they were intelligent, attractive, and articulate women who witnessed the explosion of Dada in Paris. But their most obvious connection stems from their simultaneous relationships with Francis Picabia, the Spanish-French painter and poet, who dabbled in Impressionism and Cubism on his way to Dada. In 1921 he began the controversial autograph painting *L'Oeil cacodylate.*[1] The canvas includes the prominent drawing of a single eye, photo collage, postcards, découpé, and approximately fifty signatures and messages from those who visited his Paris studio. Among the autographs and messages are one from his wife, Buffet, and another from his mistress, Everling. This was not the only document the two women signed together: letters addressed from Picabia to Tzara and the Zurich Dadaists often carried friendly greetings from both Buffet and Everling.

It is not solely the intersection of their lives with Picabia, however, that make Buffet and Everling noteworthy. Buffet's writings demonstrate her early involvement with and evaluation of the avant-garde through her Dadaist poetry, her "Petit Manifeste" of 1919, and her essay collection *Aires abstraites* (Abstract

Surfaces). On the other hand, Everling's frank 1970 memoir, *L'Anneau de Saturne* (Saturn's Ring), preserves her personal recollections of Dada's personalities as well as her reflections on the movement.

These two women, talented in their own right, witnessed and recorded the birth, evolution, and demise of Parisian Dada. They were able to observe and evaluate the subject of their study from an intimate perspective because, in the company of the overwhelmingly flamboyant Picabia, they were often not noticed and thus not scrutinized. Buffet and Everling both used this innocent anonymity to their advantage. Thanks to their privileged and respected positions within the Parisian Dada group (at least until 1921 when Picabia renounced Dada), they were able to interact with the major figures of the movement, all the while negotiating their own relationship with one another as women laying claim to the same man. Thus, for the early years of Parisian Dada, Buffet and Everling served as a pair of *yeux cacodylates,* eyewitnesses who wavered between aesthetic goals and the discords caused by amorous and sexual betrayals. Further examination will tell whether their commentary on Picabia and Dada proves to be laudatory or as poisonous as the cacodylic eye.

Gabrielle Buffet: Playing the Dada Game

In his October 1955 introduction to Buffet's *Rencontres* (Meetings), Arp offered an assessment of his friend: "Her truly French gifts are intellect, spirit, judgment, understanding, finesse."[2] All these so-called French qualities can indeed be seen in Buffet in character testimonies left behind by other writers and through her many published works. She repeatedly demonstrated gifts of insight, learning, humor, and analysis, which help put modernism—and more important the Dada events of New York, Barcelona, Zurich, and Paris—into a human context. Buffet was an astute and capable cultural critic who took advantage of her travels and encounters to compose a coherent and lucid account of the evolution of an array of modernisms.

Owing in part to the urging of her friend Guillaume Apollinaire, whom she met in July 1912, Buffet left behind a considerable collection of writings on art, music, and figures such as Marie Laurencin, Alexander "Sandy" Calder, Duchamp, Apollinaire, Cravan, Arp, Täuber, Alberto Magnelli, and of course Picabia. She also published Dadaist poetry—"Portrait dédié à l'Espagnol" (Portrait Dedicated to the Spaniard) and "Gambit de la reine" (Queen's Gambit)—a "Petit Manifeste" of Dada, as well as the preface to Picabia's 1920 *Jésus-Christ Rastaquouère.* Her essays on topics such as the Section d'or, the introduction of modernist art in the United States, the birth of the journal *391*,[3] and the pre-Dada and Dada eras contain invaluable reflections on the rise and spread of the avant-garde on both continents. She also published various small and, in her consideration, unimportant articles, mostly in U.S. newspapers. Buffet's writings on art and literature deserve critical attention; her firsthand observations and stylistically precise prose resulted in valuable historical and literary documents in the study of the avant-garde, while her experiments in Dadaist poetry and manifestos deliver the group's daring antiaesthetic stance, but from a new and differently formed perspective.

Buffet's background and education as the granddaughter of the well-known botanist Antoine Laurent de Jussieu prepared her well for a life among literary, music, and art figures. Born in 1881, she was admitted to the Schola Cantorum, which, under the direction of Vincent d'Indy, became the most liberal and most controversial center of music in France. As a nineteen-year-old student, Gabrielle was strongly influenced by d'Indy and also by his curriculum, which exposed students to the links between music and the other arts—painting, sculpture, and architecture.

Eventually her independent and ambitious character made the young Gabrielle determined to study music in Berlin, the center of musical studies at the time, where she encountered the latest ideas in music, politics, and philosophy. With Edgard Varèse, a former Schola Cantorum student, Buffet explored new, liberated musical forms under the influence of composer and theorist Ferruccio Busoni. She summed up their common goal: "we wanted to liberate ourselves and release ourselves from all traditional technique, from all the old syntaxes and grammars, to explore what we called pure music."[4] The nature of this "absolute music" did not derive from representation and description but from originality in the form of expression.

Not surprisingly Gabrielle's intentions of establishing a musical career ended when she met the dynamic and seductive Picabia during her winter 1908 vacation in France. Nevertheless her musical background, especially in pure and antiacademic styles, did not go unappreciated. Buffet's studies in absolute music, which eschews traditional tonality and convention, influenced Apollinaire's and Picabia's theories on abstract painting and poetry.

Early in 1914 Apollinaire published Buffet's article "Musique d'aujourd'hui" (Today's Music) in *Soirées de Paris*. In it she compared unconventional music to nonrepresentational painting that liberates itself into the domain of pure speculation. In a letter dated July 21, 1915, Apollinaire suggested that she submit some of her writings on German music to the *Revue Hebdomadaire*. Clearly Apollinaire, the seminal figure in the formation of European Modernism, saw Buffet's talent and encouraged it. By 1915 Picabia's paintings were showing evidence of the new trend: he had moved from creating a representation of nature to rendering a consciousness of nature driven by the senses. In imitation of pure music, he strove to paint pure art, an abstract reality of form and color.

Early in 1913, during Apollinaire's preparation of his collection of poems *Alcools*, he spent an evening at Buffet's family home at Etival, a village in the Jura Mountains, alongside a border area called "la zone," where Picabia had brought the poet and Duchamp during torrential rains. Buffet captured the scene in her

1937 essay "Rencontre avec Apollinaire." After dinner Buffet's mother begged Apollinaire to recite a few of his poems. The description of the scene is so precise that it allows an uncommon glimpse of the poet testing out the last additions to one of his masterpieces: "He recited [the poems] with a certain amount of pomp, in a restrained voice, putting emphasis on the rhymes. His Roman profile was lit by the flame and all this romantic atmosphere suited him marvelously, I admit. Thus, he recited several poems from the collection *Alcools* that was not yet published at the time, and one of them that retraced his life, his childhood, and his disappointments made a big impression on my mother. . . . She asked him the title of this poem. 'It is not yet finished, he responded, and does not yet have a name.' Then, suddenly he turned nicely to her and said: 'I will call it *zone*,' which was done."[5] Buffet's anecdote about the "petite cérémonie poétique" at her mother's house places Apollinaire's hymn to modernity in context: "How far we were that evening from the Esprit Nouveau, from the differentiations between Cubism and Orphism!"[6] What Buffet witnessed revealed to her the great poet's unique location within a perplexing and multifaceted Modernism: "between a certain attachment to the romantic and conservative tradition and a just as imperative desire that pushed him toward the avant-gardes of dawning Surrealism."[7] Buffet's "Rencontre avec Apollinaire" records a moment of creation and Apollinaire's ability to open the door, through the language of a poet, to a newly industrialized century with its themes of alienation, technology, and urban life.

Just as her link with Apollinaire was instrumental in her writing, Buffet's relationship with her energetic husband also inspired her work. In her essay "Dada," which first appeared in a 1950 issue of *Art d'aujourd'hui,* she stated: "For me, the dada era began the day I met Picabia."[8] She equated the onset of the Dadaist period with an awareness of a new conception of forms and colors. Furthermore she considered Picabia and Duchamp the primary innovators of this art, labeling the New York circle of artists "pre-Dada." Supported by the avant-garde works of this circle that were exhibited in the 1913 Armory Show, Buffet was able to argue that Picabia drove the wave of early Dadaist activities as they washed from New York to Barcelona and back. She further traced Dada's movement through Picabia's invitation to Tzara, which, she claimed, initiated a true Dada flood from Zurich to Paris. In all Dada's locations and manifestations, Buffet kept an alert eye on her husband, his colleagues, and their activities. She observed, participated, analyzed, and recorded. Unlike the self-interested recollections of Picabia, Breton, or Tzara, who jealously fought for dominance of the group in Paris, her essays provide refreshingly unprejudiced analyses of the period.

In her "Introduction de l'art moderne aux Etats-Unis" she detailed her trip with Picabia to America and his collaboration with Duchamp in the Armory Show. According to Buffet, a voyage "outre-Atlantique" was considered audacious at the time, and their families were not easily convinced. She related that on arrival after a twelve-day crossing on the ship *La Lorraine,* Buffet was immediately assailed by a man identifying himself as a journalist and soliciting an interview with her on the topic of American women, who were, as she reflected later in her essay, "free and responsible before the law" (unlike French women at the time, who were "eternal minors who could not sign a check or withdraw money without conjugal authorization"). She surprised her interrogator when she wisely responded that she could not speak about American women without knowing them. The interview came to an abrupt halt when the journalist addressed a question to Picabia, who did not understand a word of English.[9]

The couple took up residence in the Brevoort Hotel on Fifth Avenue between East Eighth and Ninth Streets, "one of the French hotels of New York," where they encountered four or five more journalists representing various newspapers and seeking an explication of "futurist painting." When she discovered the next day that the interview had been published, along with a photograph taken during a clandestine trip the couple had made to Cassis before their marriage, she understandably referred to the American press as "a dangerous thousand-tentacle hydra."[10] The intrusions and subsequent embarrassment caused by the widespread popularity of a mass press could not be underestimated.

Through porcelain exporter and modern art enthusiast Paul Haviland, Buffet and Picabia met Alfred Stieglitz and Agnes Ernst Mayer, who ran Gallery 291 on Fifth Avenue. Through this connection to 291, Buffet met American painter John Marin, Mexican-born artist Marius de Zayas, art patron Mabel Dodge, American painter Marsden Hartley, and *Little Review* directors Jane Heap and Margaret Anderson, whom she described as real heroes, ready to defend their right to print censored materials such as forbidden texts by James Joyce.[11] Many of the figures she encountered at 291 became involved to varying degrees in Dada activities. Through Duchamp, whose 1912 *Nu descendant un escalier* (*Nude Descending a Staircase*) was exhibited beside Picabia's canvases at the 1913 Armory Show, the couple later came into contact with Cubist Albert Gleizes, poet and painter Juliette Roche, French artist Jean Crotti, painter Suzanne Duchamp, photographer Man Ray, Italian-born painter Joseph Stella, American painter Morton Schamberg, and the entire avant-garde group that gathered around patrons Louise and Walter Arensberg. Buffet wrote that "we were, from the time of our arrival, incorporated into a heteroclite and international group in which night was made day, where conscientious objectors of all kinds and all nationalities kept close in an unimaginable outburst of sexuality, jazz, and alcohol."[12] Her descriptions are supported by similar accounts penned by her neighbor at the Brevoort, Juliette Roche.

Meanwhile, surrounded by a curious American press who pressured her into interviews that tested her spoken English, Buffet turned to writing lively and entertaining newspaper articles, offering her impressions of the city and certain American character traits. While Picabia scandalized curious interviewers by professing that what interested him the most in New York was "jazz, the cinema, and bridges made of iron,"[13] Buffet wrote in "Impressions of a French Woman on

New York and Certain American Characteristics" about how her visit to the city had destroyed the illusions she had previously held of America. On first arriving in New York, she said, it was the filth and dust that immediately shocked her. Surprising also was the temporary look of the homes and buildings, as well as their uncleanness and lack of decoration.[14] Possibly what she was noting is the difference between the utilitarian edifices of a growing, industrialized city such as New York with its increasingly crowded immigrant neighborhoods and the solidly constructed, ornate, and historically significant structures found in, for example, the wealthy neighborhoods of Paris that she frequented.

In the same article she also remarks on the ironic differences and contradictions in the treatment of women in the United States. Her discovery of the subtle controls placed on her sex reveals degrees of puritanism and hypocrisy in American behavior never evidenced in Europe. For example she was surprised to learn that a single woman in a hotel room did not have the right to receive a male visitor, but, if she were in a suite with a sitting room, she might entertain whomever she wished, at whatever hour she desired. This discovery implies that such gender restrictions were allied to class and economic status. Buffet concluded that in the so-called land of liberty, citizens were probably the most controlled, monitored, and treated like children.[15]

As part of her cultural commentary, Buffet identified what she saw as the main goal of Americans: "having a good time," or "avoir du bon temps," and this they did by mixing money, love, and sports, three separate occupations for the French.[16] Her frank observations about Americans reveal the lifestyle of the first decades of the twentieth century in New York, an era also captured in the writings of her compatriot Roche. One wonders how American newspaper readers reacted to Buffet's judgmental article. The New York press obviously valued her opinion, no matter how controversial, since they published her writings often.

Buffet felt she was generally well received in New York, where she was flooded with attention by the American media. In her records she expressed some embarrassment that she was forced to do all the speaking for the famous couple because Picabia could speak only two words in English: "railroad" and "Broadway." Her biggest regret was what she referred to as her "last exploit" in New York, that is, agreeing to address a particular group of American women in 1918.

Stieglitz had persuaded her to give a lecture on modern art before a club of female "anarchists," who were, surprisingly, adorned with ostrich-feathered hats, furs, and jewels. These women seemed far from any European notion Buffet held of anarchists. Never had she seen so much elegance at nine in the morning and so many beautiful automobiles—which she recognized as yet another surprise of the New World.[17] Her memorized speech, which she had originally written in French and then had translated into English by the staff of Stieglitz's literary and art journal *291*, met with an unexpected response. When Buffet explained that one should not look for representational meaning in abstract art because it represents nothing objective, the group exploded in uncontrollable laughter. A flustered Buffet wondered if it was her ideas or her French accent that was so hilarious, so much so that she was forced to let the club president finish reading her speech to the unruly audience. Looking back on the incident with humor, she admitted in 1957 that she never understood how the event had anything at all to do with anarchy.[18] Nevertheless her message on modern art remains: Stieglitz eventually published her lecture, "Introduction de l'art moderne aux Etats-Unis," in *291*.

Between 1915 and 1918 Buffet and Picabia spent most of their time in New York, except for a brief trip to Panama and several months in Spain. These years in the United States left Buffet with memories of a time rich in experiences and happiness despite the shadow of war. She developed her observant eye, witnessing and recording scandals such as that involving boxer, future Dadaist, and anarchist Cravan's outrageous behavior when asked to lecture at New York's Grand Central Gallery in 1917. According to Buffet, he was arrested after addressing the audience with "one of the most insulting epithets in the English language."[19]

In the summer of 1916 Buffet and Picabia traveled to Barcelona to join another colony of international artists who were seeking refuge from the war in neutral Spain. In the hospitable Catalonian city, the couple met artists Hélène Grunhoff and Serge Charchoune, who had been in Barcelona since the outbreak of the war. Buffet and Picabia also came into contact again with some of the exiles they had met in New York: the artistic couple Roche and Gleizes, as well as Cravan, whose poetry Buffet later studied in the essay "Arthur Cravan and American Dada," published in *transition* in 1938. Laurencin, about whom Buffet wrote a poetic and personal essay for the May 1917 issue of the *Blind Man*, also welcomed the couple to the Mediterranean. Buffet's portrayal of Laurencin differs considerably from her husband's *Portrait de Marie Laurencin, Four in Hand*, of the same year. The mecanomorphic picture of his former fellow student of the Ecole des Arts Décoratifs is an ink and watercolor fanciful machine of gears, chains, and a ventilator, punctuated with scattered inscriptions about Laurencin's dog Coco and her German husband. Picabia created a similar mechanical portrait of another female member of his artistic circle, Juliette Roche, during this same period in Barcelona.

Instead of using gears and wheels, Buffet constructed her portrait of Laurencin with verse. Her appreciative portrayal begins with the structural repetition of the pronoun "Elle," as Buffet lists the eight most defining attributes of her subject: "She is near-sighted, nevertheless not a single detail of life escapes her. She is sentimental, however, she possesses an acute sense of irony and ridicule. She is bourgeois and respectful of social conventions, but recognizes no law other than that of her own imagination. . . . She gives herself, reveals herself, opens her life like a book, but remains elusive. . . ." Each indented descriptive phrase sets up a contrast, suggesting the contrary states of an artist whose adaptability to her environment was essential. Buffet assessed Laurencin, the female artist who "loves her own femininity that she exalts and cultivates, and from where she draws the best of her imagination." Her charm and attention to detail can be seen, said Buffet in a kind of recommendation or advertisement, in the watercolors on display at the Modern Gallery of de Zayas.[20]

Also in 1917 came the birth of Picabia's journal *391*, of which, according to Arp, Buffet was a founding member. Evoking Stieglitz's New York journal *291* (named after the street number of the art promoter's Photo Secession Gallery on Fifth Avenue), the controversial *391* was published between January 1917 and November 1924 wherever the editor was residing at the time: Barçelona, New York, Zurich, or Paris. Each issue documents the group of artists and writers with whom he was associated at the time of publication, and so contributors range from Tzara, Ribbemont-Dessaignes, Apollinaire, Breton, and Walter Serner to Philippe Soupault, Louis Aragon, Paul Dermée, and the only female Dada poet of Paris, Céline Arnauld. Of course Picabia's own poetry and drawings figure prominently.

Buffet described the inception of *391* as Picabia's utopian attempt to unite the diverse and war-isolated group of avant-gardists in Barcelona by creating a small publication. Unlike its New York cousin, Picabia's first issue was modest, featuring "mediocre texts" and the founder's mechanical drawings with frequently subversive labels.[21] Buffet—whose daughters, Marie and Janine, had contributed a portrait of Laurencin to the issue—pointed out the teasing and sometimes antagonistic spirit of subsequent issues, calling the journal's attitude increasingly "aggressive."[22] The tone of the New York issues (March–July 1917) proved to be even more cruel and destructive despite their joking nature, making them, according to Buffet, "a flagrant witness to the revolt of the spirit."[23] In her article "Pourquoi *391*?" she seemed to defend Picabia's boldness by suggesting that it was only through such a combination of humor and scathing attacks that one could deal with the most vital and difficult questions during the war.

Even when she was called away by the needs of her growing family, Buffet remained connected to the publication in one way or another. A teasing note in the first issue of *391*, in a section titled "Whispers from Abroad," mentions that a musical composition by Buffet was to have been printed in the edition but that she was instead learning to ski in Switzerland. In fact Buffet had rejoined their children in Switzerland while Picabia was sharing a house in Spain with painters Otto Lloyd and Olga Sacharoff. Household matters had to be attended to, and Picabia usually expended his energies elsewhere.

Buffet's essay "Cinématographe," with a title that recognizes the motion-picture camera and film projector first created by Auguste and Louis Lumière in the 1890s, appeared in the third issue of *391*, offering a critical overview of European and American cinema with a sharp and sarcastic timbre. Buffet's short 1917 study examines the appeal of cinema across classes and national borders. Each culture, she claimed, produces its distinct version of film.

In her estimation, Italian and Spanish films were generally exaggerated in sentiment, costuming, and tragedy, and, while Italian film was fatal to the genius of cinematography, Spanish film evoked for her the mood of the Inquisition. Buffet noted that Scandinavian cinema seemed to draw its characters directly from Henrik Ibsen's plays, while a Swiss detective film was characterized by its photographic boredom. Using figurative language, she joked that, although French films were deemed shallow and lacking in innovation, they did "serve up" a dénouement that was "well done" (bien cuit). American cinema was singled out as creative and new, giving free rein to fantasy and the prodigiously active imagination of American genius.[24]

According to Buffet, the success of film lies in the fact that it does not languish in useless representations or pantomime where the audience is forced to use its powers of deduction to understand. It is an immediate and direct interaction. Buffet clearly foresaw the significance of what was becoming the almost universal accessibility of film and its wide-reaching cultural implications. In its projection of instant and intense images, it has the power to grip and hold the attention of a large number of spectators. Some of Buffet's observations on this increasingly popular public entertainment were later explored in the poetry of Arnauld and Tzara, and her commentary adds to the conversation about a cultural medium that continued to be acknowledged and manipulated by the Dadaists through their soirees, fairs, and experimental films.

After another trip to New York, where Picabia published numbers five through seven of *391*, Buffet and her husband returned to a Paris at war. On May 2, 1918, she served as a witness at Apollinaire's wedding. According to Buffet, Picabia's health caused them to move to Switzerland that same year. When his *Poèmes et dessins de la fille née sans mère* (Poems and Drawings of the Girl Born without a Mother) appeared in Lausanne, it was distributed among the avant-garde war exiles in Zurich. Soon afterward, Picabia received an invitation from Tzara ("au nom du Comité directeur") to join the Dadaists. Buffet recalled: "Very amused by the name 'dada' that we had never heard before and the enthusiastic tone of the letter, he answers the invitation and we go to Zurich at the beginning of 1919."[25] No one could have realized at the time that this decision would ultimately lead to Dada's explosion in Paris in 1920.

For Buffet, the time spent in Zurich was "one of the best stages of all our journeys"[26] because of the warm reception of Arp, Richter, Tzara, Ball, Hennings, Täuber, Huelsenbeck, Serner, and the Janco brothers, among others. As she analyzed the Swiss-based group and compared it to avant-gardists she had encountered earlier, Buffet remarked an obvious contrast between the humorous Zurich Dadaists and the "ferocious" egoists of *391* in New York and Barcelona. The former she described as moralists, the latter as immoralists. Speaking of the good-natured Dadaists while implying a comparison with the vice-driven *391* community, Buffet concluded: "Their poisoned arrows are for fun and they're more for play than for massacre."[27] She also appreciated that the Zurich Dadaists incorporated the mystical and the naïve into their work. She preferred their leanings toward common, primitive, and automatic experiences instead of *391*'s individualist endeavors.[28]

As a participant and observer of Dada activities through the years, Buffet was in a different position from one in an enviable leadership role, such as Picabia, Tzara, or Breton. She could stay on the sidelines, avoid the backbiting of the competing leaders, and work undisturbed. Arp described Buffet among the Dadaists as "a beaming prominence of every color of the rainbow" and "a whimsical and seductive woman"[29] who proved to have exceptional talent as a writer. Contemporary photographs show an alert, self-assured, and graceful woman, posed with her husband or reclining contentedly in a wicker lounge chair. In each view she projects intellectual and social self-confidence.

From her privileged vantage point, Buffet witnessed a moment of paramount importance in the dissemination of Dada: the fusion of the two representative journals—*Dada* and *391*—when a special edition of each periodical was published in Zurich. She, Arp, Picabia, and Tzara collaborated on the project. After this point of intersection and "cross-contamination," *Dada* began with issue 4/5 to exhibit the sarcasm and bitterness characteristic of *391*.

The 1919 issue of *391*, printed in Zurich, features on the second page the "Petit Manifeste" penned by Buffet and recognized as "as much an anti-manifesto as Tzara's own 'Dada Manifesto 1918.'"[30] Tzara published Buffet's manifesto as well in the May 15 Zurich "French edition" of *Dada* 4/5.

The "Little Manifesto" begins with a gentle warning to "you" who solicited explanations, saying that you shall have them, even though they fill your ears with humming. Buffet depicted the alarming state of mankind, which has jumped through history by leaps and bounds and is now hanging on to the leftover heroism of Friedrich Nietzsche or Jesus, numbed by today's mechanized life. She adopted the language of the technoscientific age to confront the poets she addressed. They were alone in the world, "fermented" in their "hygroscopic sinecure affirmation," creating their "hyperbolic asphyxia" and "hygienic hymns." She accused them of being unable to do anything on their own, even make love. Her continued use of the second-person pronoun suits the Dadaist confrontational attitude as it allowed her to face off against her audience, implicating and provoking the *391* or *Dada* reader.

In the same paragraph, Buffet tempered accusations of deterioration and paranoia with playfulness, joining in the jovial, teasing spirit of Dada that characterized the Zurich Dadaists:

> Don't be afraid: what's scaring you right now is the shadow of your navel—it can only hold a drop of water—that frightening noise is the beating of your heart. Approach the monster it doesn't bite—its coat is like silk plush and reflects fools, its eyes roll to the right and to the left forward backward like

chameleon's eyes, in its belly hums the sound of a motor, see its feet, they move. . . . it's going to pounce. . . . it pounces ah! ah! ah! ah!—

But of course—it's simply a toy."[31]

This excerpt illustrates the informal tone, disjointed syntax, erratic punctuation, and harshness of tone mixed with joking that are characteristic of Swiss Dada writings of the time, hardly the kind of academic prose Buffet was accustomed to publishing. In 1919, during her time spent among the Zurich Dadaists, there was a visible shift in Buffet's writing. From her scholarly analyses of contemporary music and art, she moved to an experimental prose and verse that suggest the influence of Tzara, Janco, and Pierre Albert-Birot in subject matter and structure.

While her earlier modernist writings such as "Cinématographe" incorporate humor or satire, they still adhere to rules that clarify, not complicate, meaning. In the Dadaist spirit Buffet's manifesto's most distinguishing feature is its innovative use of nonsequential and obscure allusions. Her reference to "le vieux monsieur," or the old man, who is offended and does not want to admit that his game of red and black pebbles is just as pointless as a game of bridge, hints at her longtime admirer Duchamp at his chessboard. Meanwhile nonsensical sentences layer one upon another, combining beautiful living patterns of cells with virgins who are judged not in the least guilty for the incomplete organization of their genitals.

Buffet described such discourse in her essay "L'Epoque 'pré-dada' à New York" as "anarchic language but not hermetic, where words lose their direct meaning and trade the exigencies of syntax for those of a rhythm and an image, and become themselves plastic art."[32] In the manifesto repetitions of sounds "asphyxié hyperbole, hymne hygiénique" and "ah! ah! ah! ah!" suggest a panting breath, highlighted by spondaically accented syllables. The language of the text has become radicalized, but it is still recognizable, understandable, and even pleasurable.

Buffet's Dadaist writing of the period clearly mixes well with the tangible and assaulting language found in issues of *391*, but the "Petit Manifeste" also mimics the playful satire associated especially with the Zurich Dadaist performances and manifestos that Buffet was discovering at the time of the writing. The manifesto also shows a marked resemblance to Arnauld's Parisian manifesto of May 1920 in that both pieces instruct their skeptical audiences while mocking them. In addition both poets refuted previous poetic traditions by their rejection of logical associations.

An example of Buffet's Dadaist poetry, her "Gambit de la reine," which appears on page 19 of *Dada* 4/5 (February 1919), moves abruptly from one nonsensical image to another. There is an unpunctuated jumble of prison bars shining like stars, a tool colored with the pleasure of muscles, and a priesthood of illusions near houses of ill repute. After the jolting and shifting of purposefully incomprehensible sequences, the poem concludes that it is "impossible to avoid the symbolism" when "hypnotized by the saccharine sweetness of chocolate candies."[33]

Since the subtext of the poem, suggested by its title, is a game of chess with "gambit dame" as one of its most famous openings, what overture was Buffet making here and to whom? It seems that her first published Dadaist poem takes the form of an opening move toward the New York group that she identified with chess master Duchamp.

Her experiences among the Dadaists in Zurich undoubtedly shaped Buffet's poetic experiments. While "Gambit de la reine" alludes to the chess-obsessed Duchamp, "Portrait dédié à l'Espagnol" (Portrait Dedicated to the Spaniard), which was printed in the December 1919 issue of *391*, seems, by its title, directed at Picabia. The poem outlines wartime domestic duties and their physical and emotional effects on the narrator through a type of balance sheet:

Here is the balance sheet for three days.
N° 1 the fountain gone
    too much fat
    or too little
    busts of unknown people
    lifeless
    playing heads or tails
    time passes
N° 2 eye of blue glass
    the other has the shape of microscopic mushrooms
    sentimental syntax
    of the wife who cries between gramophone records
    and culinary odors,
    she cries out with you yes,
    but why not speak more clearly
    am I not ready to receive the groceries; I'm thinking
N° 3 the painful cracks get larger
    in contact with tender looks
    the polar heliotrope star
    to force the occasion
    to go beyond its limits
    from where pressure and regular destruction
    in the joy of symmetrical simulacra.[34]

Voici donc le bilan de trois journées.
N° 1 le jet d'eau disparu
    trop de graisse
    ou trop peu
    bustes de gens inconnus

sans entrain
pour jouer à pile ou face
le temps passe
N° 2 oeil de verre bleu
l'autre a la forme des champignons
microscopiques syntaxe sentimentale
de la mariée qui pleure entre les disques de gramophones
et les odeurs culinaires,
elle s'écrie avec vous oui,
mais pourquoi ne pas parler plus clairement
ne suis-je pas prête à recevoir les provisions; je pense
aux biscuits en forme de sphère
N° 3 les fissures douloureuses s'élargissent
au contact des regards tendres
Etoile polaire héliotrope
forcer l'occasion
dépasser ses limites
par où pression et destruction régulière
dans la joie des simulacres symétriques.

Is the poet's accounting of assets and liabilities for her own records, or, as the title suggests, does she feel the need to account for household supplies and her behavior to an overseeing power, the subject of her "portrait," her "Spanish" husband of the title? The list for day one is straightforward: it suggests a state of affairs in an unpredictable time. The circumstances of one's life have changed, and all one can do is pass the time, toss the coin, and wait. The second day's inventory begins more fancifully with a blue glass eye but soon dissolves into an image of a weeping wife surrounded by kitchen odors, domestic disagreements, and groceries. By the third day the catalog of complaints enlarges and forces a resolution: a tearing down to achieve joy through harmonious substitutes that will take the place of the unpleasantness of real life.

Just as Hennings employed domestic metaphors to signify the stifling and trivial work needed for survival of herself and her family, Buffet recorded the physical and emotional tedium of life on the home front in the form of a poetic list of incongruous images. For both women the stimulating and public life of art and fellow artists was sometimes postponed by the mundane work of organizing the home. Despite the pretense at justifying expenses with "Here is the balance sheet for three days," the mocking Dadaist mood of the poem allows a playful, absurdist tone to frame any complaint. In the final analysis, the poem morphs from a practical list of tangible items and common domestic sights and sounds to a make-believe, conceptual solution.

In his manifestos Tzara had called for poetry to disorder meaning. Buffet's "Portrait dédié à l'Espagnol" does so in defiance of its first line's promise of an organized balance sheet. An additional ironic twist is found in the structure of the poem. The numbered items—missing fountain, glass eye, enlarging cracks—do not constitute a list of comparable objects, nor do they represent a logical sequence as the numbered ranking might propose.

As part of her ongoing contribution to the avant-garde and Dada, Buffet wrote the preface for Picabia's *Jésus-Christ Rastaquouère*, published in 1920. Even her husband's mistress praised Buffet's study in "C'était hier: DADA" by saying: "She defined with great sensitivity the philosophy of Picabia and what he held as solid in the game of his paradoxes."[35]

In the preface Buffet went beyond a mere introduction to Picabia's work and covertly delivered another Dada manifesto, demanding a new form of art because previous forms had lost their value in the postwar world. She called for an unconventional way of thinking, again using the provocative second-person pronoun: "You have the habit of arranging ideas, feelings, like objects in an apartment." Instead of bourgeois habits, there will be "new games, new rules."[36] The overhaul of language begins by suppressing the verb "être," then sucking everything out, creating a void with an air pump, a fitting mechanical touch for a Dadaist. Anticipating her critics, the introduction maintains that getting rid of the old principles will not destroy the foundations of life. Everything depends, Buffet explained, on refocusing one's vision with a kind of lorgnette. She employed the elaborate eyeglasses to symbolize any method that would allow a new way of perceiving the world. The essential, according to Buffet, is to have the means to see. This is what Dada as a manifestation of the avant-garde attempted to do: destroy the former rules and then provide a new way of looking, a new way of seeing. Dada's performances, paintings, poems, and exhibitions forcefully carry out the duties of Buffet's "air pump" (clearing out the old) and "lorgnette" (seeing differently).

The Picabias had returned to postwar Paris by February 1919. Soon thereafter Picabia invited Tzara to come from Zurich and organize "a Dada season" with him. Tzara complied most willingly. According to Buffet, it was in Paris that Tzara discovered "the blossoming of his gifts as a poet and a polemicist and that of his ambitions."[37] As it turned out, Tzara encountered a group of poets who welcomed him with enthusiasm, stimulated him as a writer, and finally considered him a rival.

It is important to note Buffet's continued participation in and commentary on the French manifestations of the movement. She accounted for Dada's immense success in Paris by pointing out that its nihilism corresponded perfectly with the general feeling of skepticism and disillusionment of the period. The physical and moral costs of the war had been devastating. Parisian Dada gave artists an outlet for free expression. Moreover, according to Buffet, the city attracted talents from an exceptional surplus gathered around Paris at the time.[38]

Alongside Paul Eluard, Breton, Soupault, Tzara, Ribemont-Dessaignes, Aragon, and Théodore Fraenkel, Buffet took part in one of the controversial high points of Parisian Dada, the May 26, 1920, Festival Dada at the Salle Gaveau, where the public threw tomatoes and cutlets at the performers as they recited incoherent texts while disguised in cylinders, blackface, or as women. The more one knows about the maternal Buffet, her socially connected upbringing and her controlled demeanor, the more difficult it is to imagine her involved in such an unruly scene. The seeming contradiction of her background and her involvement in Dada manifestations can be explained by her continuing intellectual curiosity and boldness to explore new forms of expression.

Even at a time when Picabia was beginning to reject Dada, Buffet was still considered its supporter and was included in the group-sponsored events. On the April 1921 posters advertising "Excursions & Visites DADA 1ère visite: Eglise Saint Julien le Pauvre," Buffet heads the list of guides. She is the only woman included. Commenting on the final days of Parisian Dada in *Aires abstraites,* she pointed out the inevitable and rapid disintegration of the group because of rivalries among talents and opinions. She avoided going into much detail on the point, but it is obvious that she was referring to the power struggles among the three most vocal animators: Tzara, Breton, and Picabia.

The daring and rebellious spirit that Buffet exhibited during the Dada years persisted through World War II, when she and her daughter Jeannine Picabia became deeply involved in the Resistance movement and specifically in a cell known as "Gloria SMH," which Samuel Beckett joined in September 1941. Besides generously sheltering Allied parachutists and escaped prisoners of war, the sixty-year-old Buffet delivered hidden documents for the Belgian secret service, sometimes concealing them in a shopping bag or in her underwear. According to her debriefing files, "she used to get up at five o'clock in the morning, fetch a bag from a café near the Gare du Nord, and take an early train to Chalon-sur-Saône; often she did not get back until early the following day, going without food or sleep." She was once stopped and questioned by a young Gestapo officer while she was waiting for the train back to Paris.[39] Thankfully her early years of musical study in Berlin came in handy: Buffet spoke fluent German.

In 1976, at the age of ninety-six, Buffet was still offering commentary on Dada, its origins, and its future in her essay "Picabia Poète" for the Grand Palais's Picabia exposition catalog.[40] Again, just as she did in her 1950 article "Dada," Buffet classified modern art as Dadaist from the time Picabia and Duchamp joined forces in New York to the printing of the former's *Jésus-Christ Rastaquouère* and *Unique eunuque,* which, she said, were the last important poetic manifestations of 1920. She even noted a common thread that links the spirit of Dada from the 1917 issues of *391* to the student protests of May 1968 in Paris. Her distinctive vantage point and lucid analysis over many years placed Buffet in a rare position to provide piercing insight and a reliable interpretation of the Dada period.

Germaine Everling: A Ring around Picabia

While Buffet's poetry and manifestos demonstrate Dadaist affinities and her essays provide cultural analyses of important figures and movements in the arts, Everling's records of the period clearly constitute a personal narrative of her life among the artists of the time, most notably with her lover, Picabia. She admitted in her introduction to *L'Anneau de Saturne* that at first she resisted recalling "those past days" because the memory was painful. The bitterness of devoting twenty-two years to a difficult partner, who, after divorcing his wife, married his son's Swiss tutor, must have been hard to overcome. However, the act of writing the book delivered her: "I was able to envision Picabia again; in telling his story I had accepted him. I had understood that genius throws the one who carries the weight off balance. . . ."[41]

Everling's chronicle of her involvement with Picabia and Dada was first published as "C'était hier: DADA" in the June 1955 issue of *Les Oeuvres libres*. The text was later expanded to become *L'Anneau de Saturne,* published by Fayard in 1970. Everling's writing is remarkably intimate. She did not presume to offer historical analyses or a cultural study. Instead of poetry or essays, her genre is the personal memoir. It encircles herself, her lover, and their close associates. Nevertheless, perhaps even without intending to provide a contemplative record of her times, Everling could not avoid doing so; in her recollections of her life with Picabia, she had necessarily to reflect on the interactions she and her partner had with members of the Parisian Dada.

L'Anneau de Saturne is divided into three parts: "Intimité" (Intimacy), "Dada and Co," and "Le Commencement de la Fin" (The Beginning of the End). Each section is further divided into chapters (thirty-five in total) with descriptive titles such as "Comment je rencontrais Picabia" (How I Met Picabia) and "Le mouvement dada s'organise . . . dans un appartement meublé en Louis XV" (The Dada Movement is Organized . . . in an Apartment Decorated in Louis XV Style").

The first part of the memoir is a lyrical, joyous, and enthusiastic tale of the author's first encounter with Picabia, the hardships they faced trying to be together, and the birth of their son. Its nostalgic or sentimental tone is tempered by commentary. The author savored her past and treated her story with great care, as if it were her child. The second and third parts of the text record Dada events that involved Picabia while they document the relationships between various members of the Parisian Dada group. The text flows from chapter to chapter with vividly described scenes and recurring characters who are fleshed out with insightful detail.

Not only does Everling serve as a formidable witness to her and Picabia's engagement with members of the avant-garde, but she also recorded her partner's public and private dealings with his friends and his enemies. According to Everling, Picabia was an essential animator of Parisian Dada: "In 1921 the bomb known as 'Dada' exploded in Paris. Tzara had brought it with him from Zurich, but Picabia was its detonator."[42] History shows that introducing Tzara to the Parisian Dadaists was Picabia's greatest contribution to the French group. Everling pointed out that Picabia served as a trigger, a vital spark. As such, he inspired important artistic links connecting New York, Barcelona, Paris, and Zurich, producing and sustaining a network of correspondence among artists and writers he met.

To Picabia's famous 1921 Dada canvas *L'Oeil cacodylate,* Everling contributed the puzzling, or what she called "esoteric," message "J'espère toujours me réveiller!" (I hope always to awaken!). This enigmatic note on the left margin of the painting, to the left of the single, bewitching eye, poses questions about Everling's meaning. From what does she hope to awaken? Is it simply from a night's sleep to greet a new day? Is it waking from an unreal world to experience a truer state of being? Or, is it something more problematic, as awakening from Picabia's seductive hold over her? The inscription's sense remains indecipherable, and Everling offered no clues in her other writings. One is left to view the entire canvas simply as a sort of ambiguous autograph board that redefines what constitutes a work of art, as well as how it is constructed and by whom.

According to Jean Cocteau, this work was exhibited for quite some time at the Boeuf sur le Toit, in the rue du Colisée, Paris. In 1953 he said that he had been referring to Everling when he wrote: "Nothing believed itself less noticed than us, but the cacodylic eye wasn't the only one to observe us. A woman's eye undertook it with implacable care."[43] Cocteau was right to notice that there was an omnipresent, observing eye, which he described, not as poisonous, but as benevolent and sympathetic. Everling was an ever-present witness to Parisian Dada, whose meetings often took place in her apartment. Members of the group saw her as a nonthreatening onlooker more than as a participant at the time, and it was only many years later that she was urged by a friend to reveal the story of her life among the Dadaists.

Everling was not the only observing eye, however. Picabia's wife remained a constant in his life until their divorce in 1930. She participated in many avant-garde events and worked alongside her husband as they published their writings in the same periodicals. Buffet's inscription on *L'Oeil cacodylate* reads: "A Francis Picabia qui raconte des histoires de Nègre" (To Francis Picabia who tells tales). It is written in large green letters, in the same ink as the signature of Arnauld, on a découpé of a slyly smiling woman (Buffet's photograph) placed just above the sketch of the famous arsenic eye. The message and signature generate a curious question: Why did Gabrielle Buffet spell her name "Gabrièle"? It may seem a misspelling, but Buffet often used the alternate form to sign her artistic creations of the period. The accompanying message, however, remains mystifyingly accusatory and may reveal the ruse behind the entire painting. *L'Oeil cacodylate* is merely Picabia's practical joke.

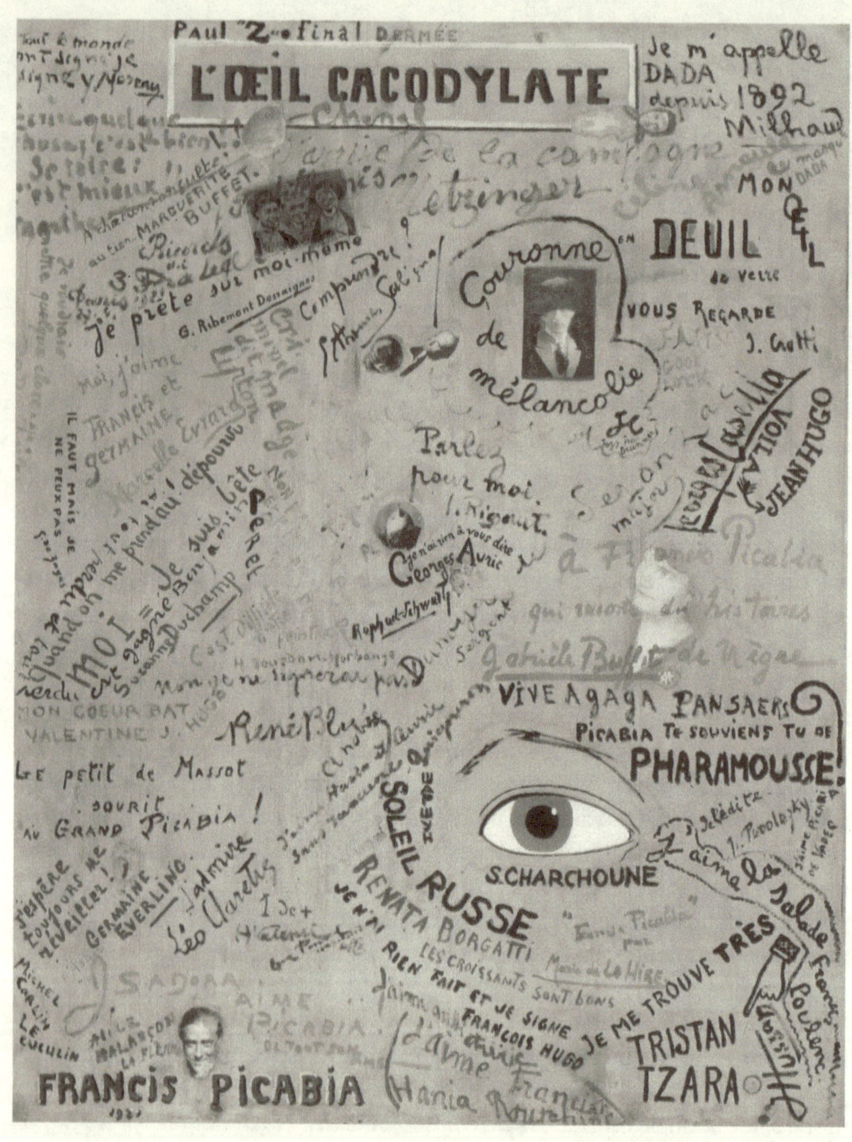

L'Oeil cacodylate, by Picabia, 1921, oil on cloth and collage with photographs. 148.6 × 117.4 cm. AM4408P © 2012 Artists Rights Society (ARS), New York/ADAGP, Paris. Location: Musee National d'Art Moderne, Centre Georges Pompidou, Paris. Photograph by Georges Meguerdtchian. CNAC/MNAM/Dist. RMN-Grand Palais/Art Resource, New York. Image Reference: ART153156. Image size: 6208 × 7678 px.

Mistress and wife found it necessary to share space in the tableau (or at least their signatures did), as they shared their lover's life. How did these two women negotiate their relationship with Picabia, and how did they perceive their relationship with one another? Although Buffet never mentioned Everling in her published writings, Everling certainly gave her reader a glimpse of her lover's wife and even an occasional evaluation of Buffet's work.

Picabia met Everling in November 1917, through the Mexican painter de Zayas, and he immediately began to court her. When she met Picabia, Everling, at age thirty, was separated from her husband and living with her twelve-year-old son, Michel, in what she described as a typical bourgeois apartment on the Boulevard Emile-Augier. Although she had been to other artists' studios, she related that Picabia's truly shocked her at her first visit because of its disorder of papers and cigarette butts that formed a carpet.

It is important to note that Everling's episodic narrative is replete with direct dialogue between Picabia and herself. The dialogue, like the chronicle of days, was recalled or recreated in light of later developments, feelings, and insights. Essentially she was composing and reinventing, not delivering reliable information based on painstakingly recorded notes. As with all memoirs that recollect events of the past, one must recognize the creative embroidery that accompanies the narration.

According to the memoir, when Picabia asked her if she was attached, Everling straightforwardly stated that she lived separately from her husband. She then turned the question on him, saying "but yourself, aren't you married and the father of three children?"[44] In a move to evoke her sympathy, he told her that his wife had left him under the housekeeper's care when he was sick in order to rejoin their children in Switzerland. He added that he did not think she would return. Not yet realizing the unusual relationship that Picabia had with his wife, Everling did not quite know what to think. She was intrigued by him, but wondered all the same why she would choose to be mixed up with a man such as Picabia, an artist "who painted cubes about which no one understood a thing!"[45]

Soon after Picabia and Everling's "honeymoon" trip to Martigues, the former announced his wife's imminent return but reassured his lover that his wife "will understand the situation perfectly. She's not attached to me at all; she is absolutely loyal; she'll accept to give me my freedom."[46] Surprisingly enough, the following day, Buffet invited Everling to the Picabia family home for dinner. Picabia had often praised his wife's abilities, so Everling was naturally expecting an intelligent, lively, and superior woman. She was undoubtedly intimidated by the idea of meeting her lover's accomplished wife, but she accepted the invitation nonetheless. Everling's first impressions of Buffet confirmed that Madame Picabia was indeed "une femme supérieure," who proved to be the perfect hostess to her guest.

Everling's memoir provides an uncommon look at her rival: "I had before me a small, slightly curved woman, very brunette, with a mobile face in which the character resided in an extraordinarily long and squared chin, a sign of will and obstinacy; a mouth with thin, slightly drawn in lips, black eyes whose look had such extraordinary acuity that they seemed to undress those they observed. But her voice, which I had already heard on the phone, was so marvelous and pleasing that it deflected the reservations that one could have felt based on the facial expression. . . . Here was, in any case, a being well above the ordinary—an unquestionable personality."[47] In this description Everling managed to issue compliments but in such a way that the overall portrait is not flattering. Further descriptions of Buffet mention her "malicious smile" and suggest that she perhaps lacked a bit of humanity. While reading the memoir, one must remember that one sees Buffet through the eyes of Picabia's mistress. Some jealousy or resentment naturally shapes every portrait of Everling's lover's wife.

Another episode reveals Everling's disapproving view of Buffet. According to her memoir, when Picabia eventually fell ill again, Everling spent most days at his bedside with his wife's consent, but eventually Buffet tired of the intrusion. Her temper exploded, and she intimidated Everling with threats that she would personally throw her out of the house. In an attempt to console his mistress, Picabia vowed to leave Buffet, but he insisted that he was too ill at the time. Ultimately he admitted to Everling, "It's horrible. . . . I think that I'll never have the courage to leave my wife and my children."[48]

Noticeable in the text is Everling's stitching together of anecdotes in an episodic manner. She did not provide her reader with the reassuring guideposts of dates. Although this may be annoying to the historian, it is an appropriate style for the memoir. One becomes privy to the intermittent and subjective workings of the author's memory. In this way Everling's tone remains familiar and her perspective appears direct, personal, and honest, at least as far as her biases allow.

To lend credibility to her narrative, Everling also included copies of notes and poems that Picabia sent to her whenever they were separated. One letter-poem of January 1918, which he had delivered to her by messenger, reveals Picabia's subtle method of control over his mistress:

FOR GERMAINE
Your eyes are blue, and your character is like mine.
You are the sweetest that one can imagine.
You astonish the serenade singers in Spain.
You are my treasure;
My little girl is dedicated to me.
And so, I'm feeling much better,
And I think that tomorrow we'll continue on our dewy path.[49]

POUR GERMAINE
Tes yeux sont bleus, et ton caractère ressemble au mien.
Tu es la plus douce qu'on puisse imaginer.
Tu étonnes les chanteurs de sérénades en Espagne.
Je t'ai comme une relique;
Ma petite fille m'est dédiée.
Aussi, je vais beaucoup mieux,
Et je pense que demain nous poursuivons notre chemin dans la rosée.

Picabia's manipulation of the submissive Germaine, his "petite fille," is significant. The letter-poem dictates her unquestioned devotion, drawing a direct correlation between the intensity of her dedication and his improving health. Her reward will be their "chemin dans la rosée."

Also in 1918, according to her narrative, Everling went to great lengths and endured personal sacrifices to secure the necessary papers to cross the wartime border and join Picabia in Switzerland. But during her second visit, Everling reported, "Gabrielle did not stop alerting me to the 'despotic' character of Picabia, 'his dreadful egoism, the true mortal canker that eats away at him.'"[50] In her retelling, Everling appeared to be quoting Buffet's words, but one can hardly accept them as such. They could well be her own nascent misgivings about the deceptive and despotic nature of the man they both loved, as she hinted in the introduction to *L'Anneau de Saturne.*

While they were in Switzerland, Buffet supposedly approached Everling and tried to discourage her from continuing to see Picabia, pointing out a recent affair as an example that he was unable to be true to either woman. According to Everling, Buffet even suggested that they leave her husband behind and return to Paris together to open an art gallery. But Everling confessed to her readers that she was in love with the artist and forgave him everything.

Always ready for adventure when his health was not an impediment, Picabia claimed to be tired of Switzerland, which he described to Everling as "that nonexistent country where love and art resemble albums of intellectual engravings."[51] Eventually the two lovers returned to Paris to live together, though Picabia continued to spend some time in the Parisian family home with his wife and children. Much to the surprise of his mistress, he announced at one point that his wife was pregnant. According to Everling, he explained away his behavior with: "It was for Christmas" and "it made her so happy!"[52]

Meanwhile Picabia was becoming involved in avant-garde movements in Paris. Everling recorded in *L'Anneau de Saturne* that the day after the Armistice, Picabia, Gleizes, Ferdinand Léger, and a few others took steps to reform the Cubist Section d'or that had formed in 1911. Picabia wanted to invite Arp and Janco, whom he had met while in Switzerland, to join the group in Paris, but Gleizes and his friends were against the idea. Everling reported Picabia's prediction: "I give you my word that shortly the word 'cubism' will expire and be replaced by another that will make more noise in the world than cubism has ever made."[53] Picabia was accurately predicting Dada's dominating and explosive arrival in 1920.

Everling qualified Picabia's statement by explaining that his reaction was not against Cubism per se, but against the attitude of certain members of the movement. According to Everling, it was at this point that Picabia committed to Dada and adopted a combative stance toward certain other groups of artists. She recalls that he sent the Cubists a canvas with "M . . . pour celui qui le regarde" (Monsieur . . . to whom it may concern) in black letters on a gray vacant background. The press got word of the insult and a scandal began.

Everling is undoubtedly referring to the 1921 canvas *Chapeau de paille?* (Straw Hat?), which features a collage advertisement mentioning the singer Marthe Chenal (who also autographed *L'Oeil cacodylate,* appeared in photographs with the group, and attended the Salle Gaveau Dada Festival with Picabia) with the question "CHAPEAU DE PAILLE?" in the opposite corner. The "to whom it may concern" inflammatory greeting crosses the canvas diagonally, leading to an exclamation mark in the upper right-hand corner. The piece is boldly signed below. The picture is an intertextual ruse in which Picabia invoked *Le Chapeau de paille* (circa 1625), attributed to Rubens, a portrait thought to be of Susanne Lunden, who is wearing, not a straw hat but one of black felt, a "chapeau de poil" (felt hat). Like *L'Oeil cacodylate,* the canvas is yet another mocking provocation, this time to Picabia's Cubist opponents.

While Picabia was setting fuses to ignite Parisian Dada, Everling was about to give birth to their son. The sixteenth chapter of Everling's *L'Anneau de Saturne* is appropriately titled "Un enfant naît . . . et Tristan Tzara arrive" (A Child Is Born . . . and Tristan Tzara Arrives). Soon after the birth of Picabia and Buffet's fourth, "Christmas-conception," child, Everling gave birth to Francis-Lorenzo in 1919. Everling reported that, when she went into labor, Breton and Picabia were sitting in her bedroom, deeply engaged in a discussion about Nietzsche. They had to be interrupted and chased out by friends so that she could use the bed for the delivery.

This chapter offers a front-row view as an important event takes place in the development of Parisian Dada—another birth of sorts. In January 1920 Picabia was out touring in one his favorite automobiles when a young foreign man arrived at Everling's apartment on the Boulevard Emile-Augier. She agreed to let him wait for Picabia's return. To his hostess's surprise he proceeded to install all his belongings, mostly piles of papers and journals, in her home. According to Everling, Tzara stayed a year, lodged in her living room. His arrival was greatly anticipated by the Parisian Dadaists, especially Breton, Dermée, and Picabia, with whom he had carried on a frequent correspondence. As early as 1917, Apollinaire had given Breton a copy of the first *Dada* review, which Tzara had sent from Zurich. Before August

1918 Tzara had already named Dermée (husband of Arnauld) the "chef rédacteur" and representative in France of *Dada*. Then, a year before Tzara's arrival, Picabia and Buffet had traveled to Switzerland to meet the Cabaret Voltaire group, which proved to be the final stage in uniting the Zurich and Parisian Dadaists.

Although she did not mention it in her memoir, Everling's home was also used as a sort of clearinghouse for Dada materials during this period. In 1921, for example, Tzara suggested an exposition of the works of Cologne Dadaist Max Ernst. Since Ernst could not acquire the papers necessary to travel to France so soon after the war, it was left to Breton and Aragon to organize everything. Packages of Ernst's controversial collages arrived at Everling's apartment to be opened, sorted, framed, and hung at the bookstore Au Sens Pareil by the two poets.

Chapter 17 of Everling's memoir, "Dada à la loupe" (Dada under the Magnifying Glass), provides her frank analysis of Parisian Dada and its players. It is reflective, allowing more evaluation and providing fewer anecdotes than previous chapters. First it describes the group that directed the journal *Littérature* (1919–24): Breton, Aragon, and Soupault. Everling remarked that Aragon and Breton were inseparable, that they shadowed each other. Furthermore she agreed with Picabia's assessment that the prolific Aragon was Dada's true friend or "amant de coeur." Soupault, on the other hand, was not really a Dadaist, because he had nothing to revolt against. He was "mediocre by upbringing and by undetermined tastes. He made himself out to be a graceful butterfly who refuses no flower but who has its preferences—and he soon showed which gave him his best booty."[54] Everling viewed Soupault as an opportunist without commitment to Dada. He supposedly resented having to participate in Tzara's theatrical pieces, while he criticized Picabia for being largely absent.

According to Everling, Breton was a natural leader who influenced the journal's collaborators, as well as an entire band of young intellectuals who came into contact with the *Littérature* group: "Just as all sailors, despite their different nationalities, have a similar walk, the review's collaborators had borrowed from Breton his slow and detached way of pronouncing each syllable and seemed to speak with the front of their mouths. Afterward, all the young intellectuals who had had contact with the group affected the same tone."[55] In 1920 Breton and Soupault collaborated to publish *Les Champs magnétiques* (*The Magnetic Fields*), which, they swore, was written according to the dictates of the subconscious. Everling described the product as a sort of poem of disenchantment, heavily influenced by the aesthetic of poet Anna de Noailles and by the speech of Lautréamont.

Everling's memoir includes frank evaluations of other Dadaists with whom she came into contact through Picabia. Speaking of Ribemont-Dessaignes, Everling concluded that his attraction to Dada allowed him to express his rancor, perhaps for being disowned by his father when he chose the life of an artist. She judged him "the most sincerely revolutionary of the Dadaists!"[56]

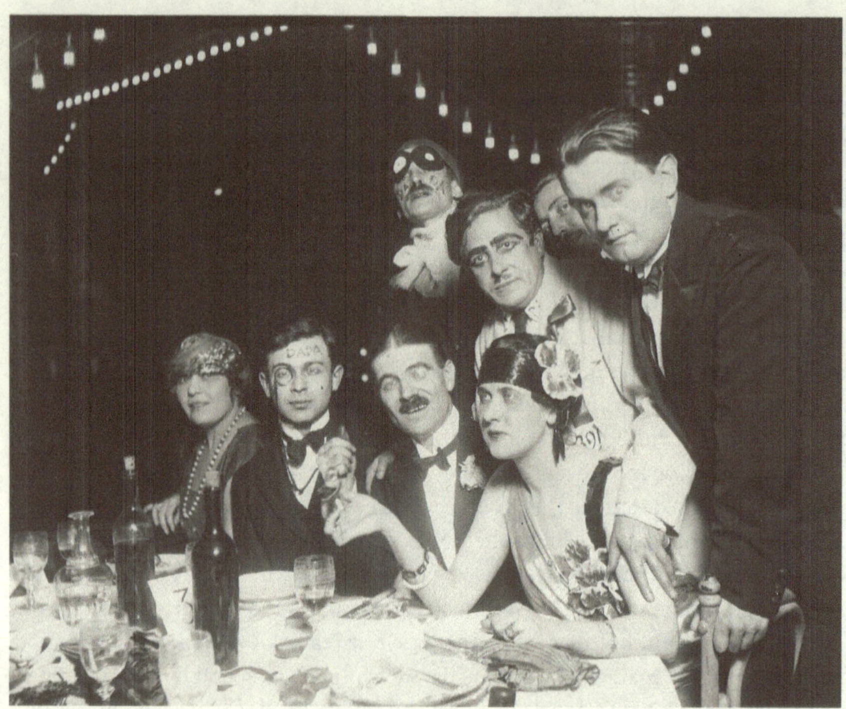

Guests at a Dada dinner, circa 1920–22: *(standing)* Georges Ribemont-Dessaignes, Francis Picabia, unidentified person, and Georges Auric; *(seated)*: Marthe Chenal, Tristan Tzara, Georges Casella, and Germaine Everling. Anonymous photograph, gelatin silver print. 12.5 × 15.9 cm. AM 2008-23. Location: Musee National d'Art Moderne, Centre Georges Pompidou, Paris. Photograph credit: CNAC/MNAM/Dist. RMN-Grand Palais/Art Resource, New York. Image Reference: ART438507. Image size: 3984 × 3192 px.

According to Everling, Paul Eluard did not have the temperament for Dada. Instead "there was in him the finesse of Verlaine, mixed with very personal complexes."[57] He believed too strongly in poetry and could not embrace the nihilism of Dada. Nevertheless Paul and Gala Eluard welcomed the spirit of Dada, but its revolt against accepted values and its promise of liberty seemed to offer them a mere distraction from their bourgeois lifestyle.

For Paul Dermée, Everling had high praise, but she reported that, although he was a first-rate friend to Dada, as was his wife, the Dadaists never completely appreciated his contributions. During the Section d'or debates between Cubists and Dadaists, Dermée unsuccessfully tried to reconcile the two groups. Overall he was less vocal and less controversial than the leaders of the *Littérature* or *391* groups.

Not only did Everling offer her impressions of Dada members, but she also gave glimpses of their outlandish behavior. Everling's description of a disruptive episode at the second Festival de Dada, May 22, 1920, demonstrates contemporary reactions to Dada events while also illustrating her dialogue-rich writing style, which turns the reader into an eyewitness:

> On the main floor, in an orchestra box, in the company of Marthe Chenal who was having a wonderful time, Picabia applauded with all his heart, crying out: "Long live Dada!"
>
> At that moment, a member of the audience in an orchestra seat, pushed to the paroxysm of anger and recognizing Picabia as one of the promoters of the movement, left his seat and, approaching the box, set about climbing into it. He brandished a menacing cane and cried, in the name of the Legion of Honor with which he was decorated. . . :
>
> "You are all bastards! . . . You are not French! . . . Down with all foreigners! . . . , etc."
>
> Picabia waited for him, impassable, his arms crossed. But Marthe Chenal, worried probably about her elegant attire, interposed between the two:
>
> "—You are not going to fight here, in front of a woman? It's crazy and . . . improper! . . . Just wait until you go outside!"
>
> "—All right, I agree, said the champion of the Order of the Brave to Picabia. I'll wait for you at the exit."[58]

Whether Everling witnessed the incident or not, her account makes her reader feel as if she had been there, beside Picabia. Her satiric tone is discernable in her description of the defender of the Legion of Honor and in her addition to her first version (in "C'était hier: DADA" of 1955) of the amusing detail about Marthe Chenal worrying about the men upsetting her smart attire.

In *L'Anneau de Saturne* Everling upheld the generally shared opinion that Duchamp, provocative creator of the *Nu descendant un escalier,* was certainly one of the most intelligent men of the epoch. She called him a "mathémagicien" who posed problems that had no solutions. His strong sense of independence, she maintained, would not allow him to join any group that obligated him in any way. It seems that his refusal to commit to "–isms" and his adoption of "antiart" make him the purist Dadaist of all.

There is evidence that Everling, in a rare contribution to Dada artistic creations, played a direct role in Duchamp's most famous version of the 1921 *Rrose Sélavy* (*Eros, It's the Life*) photographs. Arturo Schwarz reports that Duchamp inscribed on a copy of the second Man Ray portrait of "Rrose," the one in which his hands appear to embrace an oversized fur collar: "Hat and hands [belong to], Germaine Everling."[59] This seems to be the only image of Rrose Sélavy or La Belle

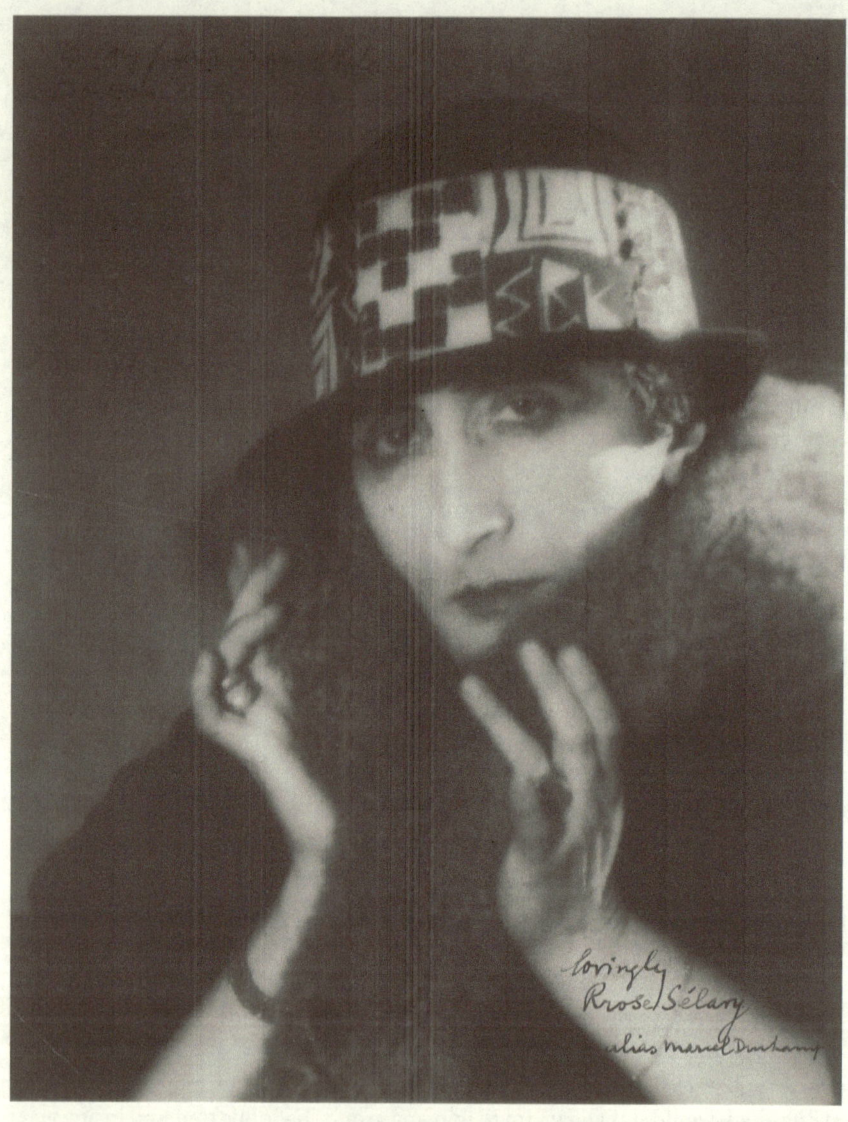

Marcel Duchamp as Rrose Sélavy, by Man Ray. Hands and clothing of Germaine Everling. © 2012 Man Ray Trust/ARS, New York/ADACP, Paris. Gelatin silver print, $8\frac{1}{2} \times 6\frac{13}{16}$ in. (21.6×17.3 cm). Signed in black ink at lower right: "lovingly / Rrose Sélavy / alias Marcel Duchamp" [cursive]. The Samuel S. White III and Vera White Collection, 1957. Location: Philadelphia Museum of Art, Philadelphia, U.S.A. Photograph credit: The Philadelphia Museum of Art/Art Resource, New York. Image Reference: ART180545. Image size: 4807×6144 px.

Haleine that includes hands, and clearly female hands richly augment the illusion of Duchamp's alter ego, a parody of the feminine consumer, richly clothed in Everling's garments and scented with eau de violette.

Moving on in her memoir from Duchamp to Parisian periodicals, Everling asserted the importance of journals to the growth of French Dada, noting that the true Dada publications of the time were ephemeral. In "C'était hier: DADA" she named five examples: $D^d\ O^4\ H^2$ (Ribemont-Dessaignes), *Littérature* (which later became *La Révolution Surréaliste*), *M'amenez-y* (which she attributed to "Cécile," instead of "Céline," Arnauld), *Proverbes* (Eluard), and *Z* (Dermée). In *L'Anneau de Saturne* she updated her list, omitting Ribemont-Dessaignes's and Arnauld's publications, probably because their journals were so short-lived, though that feature seemed to be essential to the definition of a true Dadaist periodical in her list of 1955. She noticeably did not mention Picabia's *391* or Tzara's *Dada* in her list, either because their origins were non-Parisian or they were too solidly established to be considered "ephemeral."

As Dada became better known, it changed in character. In Everling's opinion, Picabia finally separated himself from the Dadaists not because of differences in personalities but because of a difference in the definition of the essence of Dada. Picabia believed that in its spirit, Dada must be a storm, but some of its followers wanted to make it a permanent climate. For him the emphasis was always on the departure, the beginning. In this attitude he respected the original goals of Zurich Dadaists such as Ball and Arp, who likewise stressed the spontaneity of the Dada event.

Everling's take on the demise of Dada was that its manifestations attained a summit too quickly, and nothing, she said, was as dangerous as a paroxysm. In her opinion Dada was out of breath. She perceptively explained that a scandal that lasts is no longer a scandal because the ear, like the eye, gets used to the stimulation. Dada, she claimed, could not go any further in its absurdity, so something else became necessary. For some Dadaists, such as Breton, Soupault, and Aragon, this became a move toward Surrealism.

In a 1936 article printed in Sophie Täuber's review *Plastique,* Buffet concurred in her distinctive style that "the spirit that had blown so forcefully and ardently degenerated in the Parisian postwar climate into a polemic of the clique, or even of the individual."[60] Buffet, a more metaphorical writer than Everling, illustrated her point by likening manifestations of Dada to fireworks or a glass of champagne: "Dada acted on the spirit like a sparkling and stimulating drink, and could not become established without irredeemably losing its evanescent and imponderable virtues, its *raison d'*être."[61] However, some Parisian Dadaists longed for a more permanent arrangement: a school, manifestos, central leadership, and a hierarchy of artists.

According to Everling, Breton, Soupault, and their friends thought they had found just the answer in Surrealism. She claimed that "in reality, Surrealism was nothing more than a small way to continue Dada."[62] An object can be displaced so that it loses its initial identity. It can be moved from left to right or from right to left to make it look like a new object. Thus, she said, the spirit of Dada, presented at a new angle and given a new title, was put before the public. In this explanation, Everling accused Surrealism of being a recycled version of Dada.

The main difference between Dada and the new Surrealism was clear to Everling: "Dada had been a game; Surrealism would be a school."[63] Surrealism took the esoteric Dada and molded it into something that became accessible and graspable by the public, so much so that the new movement eventually grew to be acceptable to the status quo. The legacy of Dada became, in the form of Surrealism, popularized and recognizable through artists such as Salvador Dalí, but the playful and rebellious spirit of Dada was more often than not lost in the transformation to Parisian Surrealism, a school of art and literature that took itself so seriously that many of its practitioners dismissed the humorous and mocking jokes of Dada and, instead, formulated rules that, if broken, led to excommunication proceedings.

As an examination of their lives and writings show, Buffet and Everling were fundamentally different kinds of women who interacted with the avant-garde community according to their talents and personalities. When it came to their support or mothering of Dada, there was much divergence: Buffet contributed to the growth of the movement as a poet while she documented her observations and reactions as a critic. Throughout her life, Buffet proved to be brilliant, well connected, and assertive. It is safe to say that she would have had a successful career as a writer or musician without any connection to Picabia. In fact her responsibilities to her problematic husband and their children probably hindered her artistic production. Her level of interaction with the Dadaists was intense at times, as she helped to promote their ideas in New York, Barcelona, Zurich, and Paris. Everling on the other hand appears to have been caught up by Dada exclusively because of her relationship with Picabia. Fortunately she used her emotional bond to her advantage, and in publishing her memoir, she shared with readers her life amid the Dadaists. Those early years seem to have had a lifelong effect on Everling, ultimately compelling her to record her perceptions and memories. In *L'Anneau de Saturne* she showed no signs of attempting to advance her career as a writer. She merely confirmed her status as mistress and witness. It seems that the only goal of her chronicle is to validate her relationship with Picabia, for herself and for history.

Despite their differences, the literary contributions of these two female participants in the propagation and survival of Dada closely complement one another to create a more fully articulated picture of Dada, both as it traveled and as it settled in Paris. Buffet and Everling took advantage of their close proximity to the ever-duplicitous and egotistical Picabia to oversee and comment on Dada events and personalities. Their surviving texts focus as two eyes on the same subject, yielding a woman's intimate perspective on Dada that is unavailable from male memoirs of the period. To include the writings of Buffet and Everling in the study of Dada—both during and after the movement—adds another piece to the puzzle of this movement's definition, growth, and survival.

3. Céline Arnauld

Parisian Dada's Best-Kept Secret

Who remembers Céline Arnauld (1885/1895–1952) and the role she played in Parisian Dada? In their rush to the more popularized and thus more accessible Surrealism, the literary and art history communities treat Dada—a multinational, multimedia, antibourgeois manifestation of the 1910s and 1920s—as the neglected stepchild of the avant-garde. How then is one expected to notice a lone female poet whose works are difficult to locate and whose name appears infrequently in the male-authored histories of Dada? Surrounded by the more verbose members of the Parisian movement—Tzara, Breton, Ribemont-Dessaignes, and Picabia—and their competing and proliferating manifestos, who could get a word in edgewise? Arnauld did, but her works have become shrouded in obscurity. Although once lauded by Antonin Artaud, who referred to her poetry as "an explosion of blazing vigor,"[1] who now is publishing and reading her work?

Little is known of Arnauld's early life. In fact the dates of her birth and death have both been disputed. At least one source states she was born in Nice in 1898 while another maintains that Arnauld was born in Călăraşi, Romania, on September 20, 1885,[2] but her most recent biographer gives 1895 as the year of her birth.[3] There is evidence that Arnauld traveled with her father in India, Greece, Turkey, and Italy after the death of her mother. At an early age she reportedly read Johann Wolfgang von Goethe, Alphonse Lamartine, William Shakespeare, and

François-René de Chateaubriand, and she completed her *baccalauréat* in Romania. On her arrival in Paris in 1914, she changed her name from Carolina Goldstein to Céline Arnauld, studied Friedrich Nietzsche and Henri Bergson at the Sorbonne, and obtained her *diplôme de licence ès lettres.* She spent the rest of her life in Paris at several addresses: rue Descartes, rue du Cardinal-Lemoine, rue du Mont-Cénis, and rue Cassini.[4]

In Paris she met and married the Belgian-born poet Paul Dermée, with whom she formed an artistic modernist couple, much like the pairs Emmy Hennings and Hugo Ball, Sophie Täuber and Hans Arp, Sonia Terk and Robert Delauney, Hannah Höch and Raoul Hausmann, and Juliette Roche and Albert Gleizes. In her entry for Gérard Lacaze-Duthiers's *Anthologie des écrivains du V*^e (1953), Arnauld wrote: "I came to poetry through my companion Paul Dermée. He met me, at the Collège de France, in Pierre Janet's course, and eventually introduced me to the new Surrealist poetry."[5]

An interview in the 1930s popular press provides a quick view of Arnauld and her relationship with Dada. The "A Paris et ailleurs" section of the December 11, 1937, *Les Nouvelles littéraires* contains a humorous caricature of a starstruck Dermée gazing at Arnauld, who has an Eiffel Tower fancifully sketched over one shoulder. The drawing by G. Augsbourg shows the intimate linking of the two poets, their hands and legs interlaced. In the accompanying article, Fernand Lot described the working collaboration between Arnauld and Dermée as "à belle union, belle différence" (in beautiful union, beautiful difference), leading the reader to believe that they formed, at least in their working union, a complementary, though differently talented couple. In the interview Dermée revealed that Arnauld had a much deeper and richer interior life, while he acted exteriorly. When he mentioned that they both nevertheless belonged to the Surrealist movement, she interjected that "it used to be Dada." He corrected himself. Arnauld's interruption underlines the controversial intersection of the two avant-garde movements. She insisted on historical accuracy and in crediting Dada with its role in the genesis of Surrealism.

When the interviewer asked if they shared the same influences, both quickly answered no. Arnauld listed her "gods" as Arthur Rimbaud, Stéphane Mallarmé, the Comte de Lautréamont (Isidore-Lucien Ducasse), Charles Baudelaire, the British Romantic poets, Henrik Ibsen, and Pablo Picasso, thereby demonstrating the influences on the Surrealist period of her work and the sources of her longlasting poetic inspirations. Dermée attempted to speak for the couple: "We are aware of belonging to a magnificent era of lyric renaissance." Then he noted, "But poetry must return to being a little more human."[6] This is exactly what Arnauld became known for doing: rendering poetry more human.

There is evidence of frequent mutual artistic respect and support in this poetic pair: Arnauld's and Dermée's poems appear in the same Dada journals of the period, and Dermée sent his wife's novel and at least one of her poems to

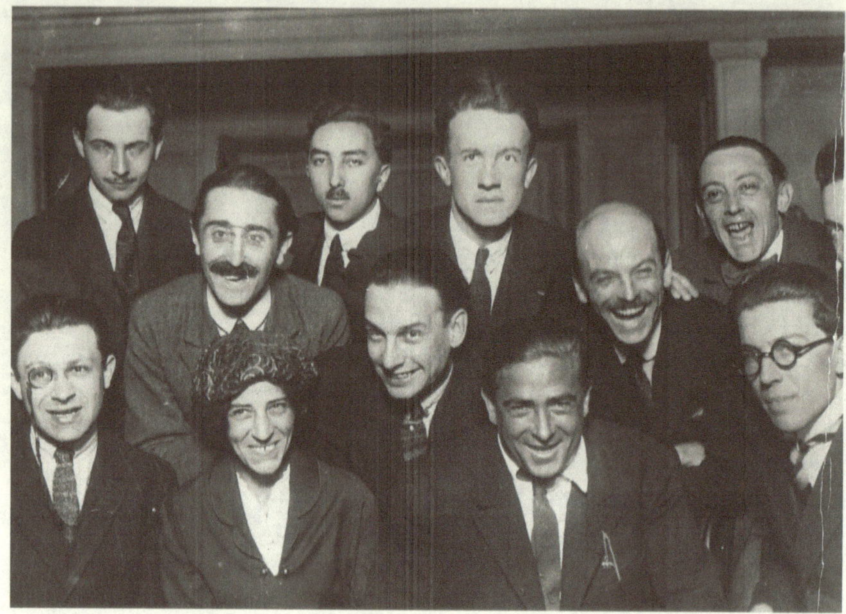

Céline Arnauld seated between Tristan Tzara and Francis Picabia in group of Parisian Dadaists, 1920. Unknown photographer. Reproduction from a black-and-white photograph, gelatin silver print. Museum of New Zealand Te Papa Tongarewa.

Tzara before his 1920 arrival in Paris. Dermée's admiration for his partner's work continued throughout his lifetime: in a 1936 publication he appreciatively pointed out the "primitive pantheism" of her work and referred to her poetry as "deeply humanized."[7]

Although largely unrecognized today, Arnauld was active enough in the Parisian avant-garde for her name to appear in some of the most significant histories of Dada, such as Sanouillet's *Dada à Paris* (1965) and Hugnet's *L'Aventure dada* (1975). Three of her poems are included in Bohn's 1993 anthology, *The Dada Market.* Until 1993 there were no known translations of her work into English. More recently Dawn Ades included three of Arnauld's poems in *A Dada Reader: A Critical Anthology* (2006), and Ruth Hemus devoted a well-illustrated chapter of her *Dada's Women* (2009) to Arnauld and her poetry. In French one can find several of Arnauld's poems included in Jeanine Moulin's *Poésie féminine: Epoque moderne* (1963) and her three editions of *Huit Siècles de Poésie féminine* (1963, 1966, and 1975). Historic photographs capture Arnauld with the likes of Picabia, Eluard, Soupault, Breton, Tzara, Ribemont-Dessaignes, and the rest of the Parisian Dada circle, or in a more serious solo portrait by Dadaist Christian Schad, who photographed each contributor to the 1920 issue of Tzara's *Dadaphone.* She is usually the only woman in these photographic records, wearing a confident smile or an enigmatic stare.

Dada Is Poetry/Poetry Is Dada

To appreciate Arnauld's poetic contributions to the development of Parisian Dada, it is important to understand the nature of the manifestations of this French avant-garde group. Paris is not the birthplace of Dada, nor is it most immediately associated with the movement. This is partly because the view of Parisian Dada has been obscured by its better known descendent, Surrealism, a movement readily identified with the French capital.

The focus of Parisian Dada differed from that of the movement in other sites. Groups in New York, Switzerland, and Germany are readily known for the pictorial artifacts they left behind. Not relying on a viewer's knowledge of the artist's language, such visual art forms are globally understood. Recognizable Dadaist-flavored paintings survive from the time that Duchamp and Picabia exhibited in the 1913 Armory Show. Later international refugees in politically neutral Zurich nurtured performance-oriented Dada, much of it accessible to any language through dance, music, trilingual recitations, costumes, and puppets. After the war Berlin Dada became known for its satiric antigovernment treatises but also for its politically charged and visually shocking drawings, posters, or photomontages. Although Parisian Dada did stage raucous, aggressive, and antiauthority pranks, it focused its attention instead on theater spectacles that privileged the spoken and written word, even when the meaning of such words was indecipherable. The new poetic language of Dada, alternating between the playful and the abrasive, was most strongly promoted through its French-language journals. Consequently Paris may surely claim to be the home of literary Dada.

The motivating Parisian Dadaists were Breton, Eluard, Soupault, Aragon, Benjamin Péret, Ribemont-Dessaignes, Dermée, and Arnauld. They were not dancers, actors, puppet makers, painters, or sculptors. All were poets, artists of words. They produced tomes of poetry, many literary magazines, and quite a few irreverent manifestos. When one adds to this group of poets the varied talents of Picabia, who brought elements from New York, Barcelona, and Zurich, and Tzara, a main animator of Swiss Dada, conditions became perfect for an explosion in avant-garde activities, but most especially in print. In 1920 alone this group produced a wealth of single-author volumes, poetic readings, and periodicals. In the early 1920s the three most significant international Dada publications were based in Paris: Picabia's *391* for ten of its nineteen issues, Breton's *Littérature* from 1919 to 1924, and Tzara's *Dada,* which moved from Zurich to Paris in 1920. These primary periodicals gave birth to at least four new and more modest publications: $D^d\ O^4\ H^2$ (directed by Ribemont-Dessaignes), *Proverbe* (directed by Eluard), *Z* (directed by Dermée), and *Projecteur* (launched by Arnauld on May 21, 1920).

This publishing frenzy was intense but short-lived. First Dada battled with the previously established Cubists for the French avant-garde label. Then, the Dadaist poets, after their quick and loud explosion in the early 1920s, began to drift into Surrealism, trading in their Dadaist antiestablishment antics for a more defined aesthetic. The historical fact of its members' changing allegiances also helps to explain why Parisian Dada is less conspicuous than its counterparts in Germany, where multiple cities hosted artists who remained for many years loyal to their Dadaist roots.

Amid the already transitory Parisian Dada, sandwiched by art historians between the widely known French versions of Cubism and Surrealism, one finds a single prolific female poet. Though one would not easily notice them today, Arnauld's publications and literary projects were copious, including at least fourteen volumes of poetry, a novel, and the literary magazine she created. Her early works: a volume of poetry, *La Lanterne Magique* (The Magic Lantern), in 1914; a novel, *Tournevire* (an archaic name for a nautical cable), in 1919; *Poèmes à claires-voies* (Openwork Poems) in 1920; a poetry collection, *Point de mire* (Focal Point) in 1921; and a novel of lyric dialogue, *Jeu d'*échecs (Chess Game), also in 1921—have been for many years out of print and unavailable except for the rare copy in a Parisian archive. Fortunately the 1936 publication *Anthologie Céline Arnauld: morceaux choisis de 1919 à 1935* (Céline Arnauld Anthologie: Chosen Pieces from 1919 to 1935) may still be found in a few university libraries. This comprehensive collection comprises texts that predate Parisian Dada, works from the Dada period, and some Surrealist-flavored writings, giving a clear view of Arnauld's early and mature career as a poet, when her writing, like that of her compatriots, vacillated between Dada and Surrealism like "two waves which one after the other cover each other," as Breton described the gradual transition during which those who were formerly Dada in Paris tried automatic writing and other forms of rendering the unconscious on the page or canvas.[8]

The first selection in *Anthologie Céline Arnauld* is the fourth chapter ("Condamnation") of the "roman poétique" *Tournevire,* accompanied by "Poèmes du concours entre les personnages" (Competition Poems between Characters), including "Farandole" and "Cinéma." "Farandole" is written in a typical Dadaist style with its disjunctive dancing images and its flirtation with an unresolved and ambiguous narrative:

> Wooden horses revolve around the Eiffel Tower
>   and the sun at its summit awaits the pilot . . .
>
> I saw your destiny
>   and I drank with delight
>   a glass once filled
>   with fever and gin . . .

I bought a book on the riverbank
    And between two pages
    I noticed your name
        my name
            a letter from the past

On the church square at Mareille
There was a funeral[9]

Les chevaux de bois tournent autour de la
Tour Eiffel
et le soleil au sommet attend l'aviateur . . .

J'ai vu ton destin
et j'ai bu avec délice
un verre rempli jadis
de fièvre et de gin . . .

J'ai acheté un livre sur le quai
Et entre deux feuillets
J'ai aperçu ton nom
    mon nom
        une lettre d'antan

Sur la place de l'église à Mareille
il y avait un enterrement

The unpunctuated poem at first appears sentimentally nostalgic, but it has a modernist edge that denies the reader the comfort of easy access. From the opening lines, the provocatively confusing image of wooden carousel horses (one widely recognized meaning of "dada" is "cheval de bois") encircling the modernist/iconic Eiffel Tower in the alliterative "tournent autour de la Tour" under the noon sun, estranges the reader but does not seem to disconcert the speaker, who projects contentment, knowing the future of the one she familiarly addresses ("J'ai vu ton destin"). She finds a sensual delight in her present drink, which she prefers over the "glass once filled with fever and gin." The poem then flirts with sentimentality when a book, bought at a riverside stall, reveals the unlikely discovery of the couple's names inscribed on a letter preserved from a time past. To avoid a detour into what could become a romanticized memory, the speaker abruptly shifts the focus and tone of the poem in the final lines to a church square at Mareille, where she matter-of-factly reports an anonymous interment. The final funereal image, though one may be inclined to force it into a narrative relationship with the letter in the book, remains mysteriously disconnected from the ambiguous found letter. Arnauld's "Farandole," with its iconic imagery and frustrated storyline, illustrates her first steps in the rupture between art and logic that Tzara called for in his 1918 manifesto.

More obviously in the Dada vein is "Cinéma" with its jolting and loosely related images: bulls leaping toward the sun, flaming horizons, and a dying giraffe:

> Carthaginian bulls with their heads bowed
> Were leaping toward the sun
>
> And on the roads of white-washed villages
> The flaming horizons hit like the surf
> I leaned toward the dying giraffe
> And drunk with dizziness I cursed your gaze
>
> The scimitar planted in the depths of my chest
> I vomited my life inclined on the screen
>
> And when the capstan raised the hide
> I surprised you grinding your teeth[10]
>
> Les boeufs carthaginois la tête embrasée
> Bondissaient vers le soleil
>
> Et sur les routes des villages blanchâtres
> Frappaient comme un ressac les horizons incendiés
> Je me suis penchée vers la girafe mourante
> Et ivre de vertige j'ai maudit ton regard
>
> Le cimeterre plongé au creux de ma poitrine
> J'ai vomi ma vie déclive sur l'écran
>
> Et quand le cabestan souleva la dépouille
> Je t'ai surprise à crisser des dents

In "Cinéma" the lyrical enchantment Arnauld had expressed in *Tournevire* suddenly gives way to a new form of expression, one that shocks by the violence of its images and its refusal to allow a coherent and logical narrative. The reader's reception of the poem is complicated by the speaker's unconventional and sometimes hallucinatory reactions to a modernist pictorial text: film. The speaker's unpunctuated and disjointed style of relating the cinematic experience results in the reader's encounter with the avant-garde's characteristic denial of stability and comfort. "Cinéma" displays an undeniably nightmarish scene (a blade in the chest, an animal hide), while its overriding aggressive tone (cursing the addressee's gaze, vomiting, and grating teeth) creates a Dada poem designed to offend. The poem will not reveal its secrets; consequently one remains uncomfortably bewildered by the evocation of nonsequential scenes of butchery projected in flashes on the movie screen. The reader thereby relives the poet's interaction with and reaction to the tangle of magnified images.

Tzara also focuses on the magic of film in the poem "Chant 20," which he published in June 1920 in his *Cinéma calendrier du coeur abstrait* (Calendar Cinema of the Abstract Heart). His poem echoes Arnauld's 1919 "Cinéma," as shown in the following excerpt:

> Hypnotized lamps of the salt mine
> make spittle pale in the vigilant mouth
> the train cars stopped dead in the zodiac
> a monster shows his brain of calcified glass
> here is the truth that escapes the cordial greeting
> and resembles the turtledove of ragtime[11]
>
> Les lampes hypnotisées de la mine de sel
> font pâlir le crachat dans la bouche vigilante
> les wagons figés dans le zodiaque
> un monstre montre son cerveau de verre calciné
> voilà la vérité qui s'échappe au salut cordial
> et ressemble à la tourterelle du rag-time

Again, disjointed images shift without a definable, logical narrative progression as the writer records the visual stimulus as it might appear enlarged on a cinema screen. The narrator's reaction to a technologically new truth (Tzara's "vérité") projected before the viewer reflects the realization reached earlier by Arnauld's speaker. In each case there is a striving to reconcile the larger-than-life images of the cinema with what the narrator traditionally accepts as reliable reality. In Arnauld's poem, however, the human element is foregrounded as the speaker ("je") interacts with violent empathy to the startling scenes, thereby causing them to be all the more horrendous to the reader.

One is left to wonder if it could have been Arnauld's "Cinéma" that Dermée mailed to Tzara with his December 1919 letter. It is possible. Dermée clearly referred to a poem by "Mme Céline Arnauld," which could have been "Cinéma,"[12] but because Dermée did not mention the title, one cannot determine whether this is a case of direct literary influence or if Arnauld and Tzara were merely reacting to a common stimulus. In any case both poets bore witness to the rise of the cinema through their Dadaist imagery and styling. Zurich Dada had already successfully experimented with the disjunction of sound on stage in recitations of simultaneous poems and *Lautgedichte* (sound poems). The flashing of the projected image of a film subsequently appealed to the Dada aesthetic in its ability to display disjointed visual images in a way that stage performance could not.[13]

Paris Explodes in 1920

As vividly described in Everling's *L'Anneau de Saturne,* Tzara arrived in Paris from Zurich in January 1920, having been urged to come by Breton and Picabia. Picabia had carried on a correspondence with the Romanian animator of Zurich Dada since 1918.

Dada as a purposeful group activity in Paris was born with Tzara's arrival. The events of that explosive year were set in motion when the already well-known Tzara appeared in public at the only Vendredi de Littérature, held on January 23 at the Palais des Fêtes, rue Saint-Martin. Sanouillet has provided a thorough examination of the evening's entertainments in *Dada à Paris.* Although one knows Arnauld's husband, Dermée, was peripherally involved, there is no mention of Arnauld's participation in the Vendredi de Littérature. While there is evidence that she took part in performance-oriented Dada, her primary focus was on writing, editing, and publishing.

In February and March 1920 two issues of *Dada* appeared in Paris: number 6 as *Bulletin Dada,* which served as a program for the Dada entries in the February 5 Salon des Indépendants, and number 7 as *Dadaphone,* which includes pieces by what Sanouillet has called all the well-known Dadaists. Arnauld was the only female Dadaist to contribute a poem, "Enigme-personnages," which was published alongside works by Tzara, Ribemont-Dessaignes, Breton, Cocteau, Eluard, Dermée, Serner, Ezra Pound, and others. She also contributed to Dermée's periodical *Z* that year. In the March issue of *Z,* one finds her poem "Avertisseur" (Alarm), which issues a warning within a disjointed narrative:

Sentiments
getting out of bed in the antiquary's
house
Morning
The airplane's wings
balance the reawakening of loves
on the train
The rails in tears
intelligence derails
and the mechanics vie dispassionately for
the songs of the Pullman coaches
My friends my friends
don't trust in sparks

fire erupts everywhere
even in your brains
Stop first station
the crazy station-master
—is it the display of sunlight
on the coach windows
or the anti-alcohol inspiration
of the morning in paper curls—
rambles on while juggling the packages
full to the brim with alarm-clock coffee
The catapults' power
breaks the too fragile wings of the airplane
                    see-saw of ancient tenderness
Hello my very dear friends
time passes
over feelings of getting out of bed
the rain falls suspicious and petty
Your words are shrapnel
on the sunflower wheels
The cemeteries extend to the dead grass . . .
Watch out for the open graves[14]

Les sentiments
descentes de lit dans la maison
de l'antiquaire
Matin
Les ailes de l'aéroplane
balancent le réveil des amours
en chemin de fer
Les rails en pleurs
l'intelligence déraille
et sans souci les mécaniciens se disputent
les chansons des wagons-lits
Mes amis mes amis
ne vous fiez pas à l'étincelle
le feu prend partout
même dans vos cervelles
Arrêt première station
le chef de gare sans raison
—est-ce l'étalage du soleil
sur les fenêtres du wagon
ou l'inspiration anti-alcool

du matin en papillotes—
divague en jonglant avec les colis
sévèrement remplis de café réveil-matin
La puissance des catapultes
brise les ailes trop fragiles de l'aéroplane
                balançoire de vieilles tendresses
Ohé mes très chers amis
sur les sentiments en descente de lit
le temps passe
la pluie tombe méfiante et mesquine
vos paroles sont des schrapnells
sur les roues tournesol
Les cimetières s'allongent jusqu'à l'herbe morte . . .
Prenez garde aux tombes ouvertes

In this poem post–World War I industrialized images of delicate plane's wings, train coaches, and weeping railroad tracks seem to be in an endangered state of disarray, disorder, or deterioration. The sharpness of coffee clangs like an alarm clock, while words emit sounds that bite like shrapnel and tear the round faces of flowers. Breakage, spilling, and derailing characterize the alcohol-deprived morning of the speaker, who warns unseen friends to be careful of sparks for fear of an overtaking fire, and of a walk across the cemetery, whose grass leads to open graves. The morning becomes something to avoid if not fear. Like Arnauld's earlier poem "Farandole," "Avertisseur" features modernist aviation imagery and the suggestion of a funeral; however, the nostalgic "Farandole" retains a detached, observational tone in its look at the past, while the more urgent "Avertisseur" introduces a skeptical and at the same time personal tone in the warning to "mes très chers amis."

In typical Dadaist fashion, the poem features the characteristic juxtaposition of seemingly random imagery and a rambling, ill-defined story out of unpunctuated phrases that purposefully obscure any construable narrative meaning. Just as Pierre Reverdy advocated in the March 1918 edition of *Nord-Sud*, the best poetic images are not born of comparisons but from the juxtapositions of distant but true realities. The more distant and accurate the correspondences between ideas are, the stronger the image. Arnauld's proliferating visual imagery of loose associations results in a multilayered escalation of movement in much the same way as a Futurist painting or Duchamp's *Nu descendant un escalier* explores space and movement in real time.

As Arnauld was readying "Avertisseur" for publication, she participated in the highly controversial February 25, 1920, assembly called by Roche's husband, the Cubist Gleizes, in the banquet rooms of the Boulevard de Montparnasse restaurant La Closerie des Lilas, a beloved Dada gathering place. According to Dermée's description in the "First and Final Report of the Secretary of the Golden Section: The Excommunicated," Gleizes invited Arnauld's Dadaist husband to the meeting, saying he had had enough of the battle between the two groups. It was to be determined whether or not there would be "a session on Dada" at the March 2, 1920, exposition.[15] For the Dadaists the purpose of the get-together was to rally forces to defend their cause, which was under attack by the more orthodox Cubists, who objected to what they perceived as a scandalous and dangerous Dada group threatening to overwhelm their upcoming combined Section d'or.

Dermée included dialogue in his satirical account of the evening, including pianist Germaine Albert-Birot's confession that she was, after all, a Dadaist and Juliette Roche's distancing herself from the affair as it became increasingly disagreeable. He also inserted an overheard conversation between Cubist-inspired Marthe Tour-Donas and Dadaist Arnauld. When Tour-Donas confided that she favored the "hermetic quality of Cubism" and that she was told that Dada was not serious, Arnauld supposedly corrected her, saying that the opposite was true: Cubism had "lots of leaks," and the Dadaists were a serious bunch, whereas she found the Cubists a group of "practical jokers."[16] Dermée's account is delightfully playful in its portrayal of the women who were currently involved in Dadaist activity in Paris. The speech he attributed to his wife illustrates Arnauld's sense of humor and biting sarcasm as well as her support for the Dadaists in their losing crusade against the established Cubists.

As the argument continued, the Dadaist point of view was represented by Tzara, Breton, Dermée, Arnauld, Picabia, Soupault, and Ribemont-Dessignes, who, according to Dermée, "demolished every one of [the Cubists'] pretexts for getting rid of us."[17] Nevertheless, when the vote was taken, Dada was expelled from the exposition. As Sanouillet has cleverly interpreted the results, "Dada was no longer part of the great family of avant-garde artists where everything goes, as long as one plays the game."[18] Certainly the Dadaists had no intention of adhering to the Cubists' restrictive rules; meanwhile the Cubists could not allow irreverent and provocative Dada art such as Picabia's ink-blot *La Sainte-Vierge* (Holy Virgin) or his mechanical *Tamis du vent* (Wind Sieve) to clutter up their exposition walls.

Taking their revenge through words, the Dadaists fired off a round of scathing manifestos and public displays of defiance. At the March 27 Maison de l'Oeuvre Soirée at the Salle Berlioz in the rue de Clichy, Arnauld played a pregnant woman in Tzara's *La Première aventure céleste de M. Antipyrine* and added vocalizations: "toudi-a-voua/soco bgaï affahou."[19] Meanwhile Picabia read his "Manifeste cannibale" in a grand gesture of Dada insubordination and soon thereafter launched his aggressive periodical *Cannibale,* with the first issue appearing on April 25, 1920. Eluard contributed a poetic/ironic piece titled "Présentations de circonstance," in which he introduced Tzara, Aragon, Soupault, Picabia, Breton, Dermée, Arnauld, Ribemont-Dessaignes, and himself. Eluard described the only female in the group: "Céline Arnauld, coiffed as ship and parrot, her eyelashes in gleaming verses,"[20] providing an abstract and exotic description of Arnauld's hair and makeup. First, he jokingly played with contradictory shapes (the angular ship and the rounded, smooth parrot's head) before mentioning her magical mascara shining with the language of her poetry. Eluard did not mention physical attributes of the other Dadaists, not even fanciful ones. Each of the men listed is defined by his actions instead of his appearance. Even Dermée is described as "our handsomest sportsman, a glory,"[21] putting emphasis on his performance, not on adornment.

Ironically Arnauld contributed the proactive and mocking "Dangereux" to the first issue of *Cannibale:* "To put an end to the stupid comedy of those who believe themselves the defenders of a nation that they poison with their art of gossip, I've invented a filmed song, a song that kills, a song that strangles and that disinfects the onion-peeling looks; it's the last film-rocket insecticide, showing at the Cinéma Céline Arnauld, at Montmartre."[22] The obvious invective tone and counterattack are clearly in the spirit of Picabia's *Cannibale.* Arnauld's bold writing formed part of the assault on the commonly accepted stuffy poetry of the era, poetry that the Dadaists refused aesthetically and ideologically. In "Dangereux" Arnauld's rebellion against the status quo goes beyond registering a complaint, beyond calling out the offenders; the poem threatens that she has taken action and created an alternative form of art. Curiously enough, this art takes the form of a song, but a song that is experienced through the sense of sight. Though it be violent, this filmed song's destruction of the poison that passes for art is to be viewed by the masses through the modern medium of her imaginary (and explosive) film, now being shown at her invented theater. Such a declaration of tearing down the old forms and substituting a risky alternative is typical of Dada behavior. In "Dangereux" Arnauld clearly transcended Eluard's limited description of the merely decorative poet of "eyelashes in gleaming verses."

In the second number of *Cannibale,* released on May 25 (the day before the Festival Dada took place), one finds Arnauld's poem "Mes Trois Péchés Dada" (My Three Dada Sins) on page 12. It is the precursor to her upcoming Dada manifesto. Her poem appears in the company of works by other prominent Dadaists: Aragon, Breton, Soupault, Ribemont-Dessaignes, Tzara, Cocteau, Dermée, Eluard, Duchamp, and Marguerite Buffet.

Going back up the hill
the wheel broken, bitter eyelid
was whistling the hymn of altar boys' cloaks
Parrots' eyes are nonsense marbles
You are neither God nor mantilla
nor parasol, nor alarm clock
You are the amphityron of Amphion without lyre
Lord gazing at your reflection without lyre

Hopscotch gives birth to a sunflower
the sunflower to the prayer
and my eyes to a broken wheel
that I was sending to Lord Abbot Merlin
For punishment I'll go sacrifice myself in the cellar
It's the fault of the lamp that's going out

*
* *

The awful luck
To drink whiskey in a lily
spiritual discussion of my treason against myself
then to sleep, to sleep until an offering
fallen from my eyes slides into my veins
But what I gave to the parrot
is not for you
Friendship is not written in shorthand

*
* *

And it was still that broken wheel
that was bothering me
To repair it
I took Lord Abbot Merlin as witness
the ladder like an image
the glass like a microscope
and my eyes like beautiful language
Finally, since everything is finished
we will go demolish the structure built on a wheel and a nail
in the cellar of spiritual discussions
of my Calvary in whiskey[23]

En remontant la colline
la roue cassée, prunelle amère
sifflait l'hymne des mantes enfants de choeur
Les yeux des perroquets sont des billes billevesées
Vous n'êtes ni Dieu, ni mantille
ni ombrelle, ni mécanisme de réveil
Vous êtes l'amphitryon d'Amphion sans lyre
Sire se mirant sans lyre
La marelle accouche d'un tournesol
le tournesol de la prière
et mes yeux d'une roue cassée

que j'envoyais au Sire Abbé Merlin
Pour me punir j'irai m'immoler dans le cellier
C'est la faute du fanal qui se mourrait

*
* *

L'affreuse chance
Boire du whisky dans un lys
discussion spirituelle de ma trahison envers moi-même
puis dormir, dormir jusqu'à ce qu'une aumône
tombée des yeux glisse dans mes veines
Mais ce que j'ai donné au perroquet
n'est pas pour vous
L'amitié ne s'écrit pas en sténographie

*
* *

Et c'était toujours cette roue cassée
qui me tourmentait
Pour la racommoder
je pris Sire Abbé Merlin comme témoin
l'échelle comme image
le verre comme microscope
et mes yeux comme beau langage
Enfin, puisque tout est fini
nous irons démolir l'édifice bâti sur une roue et un clou
dans le cellier aux discussions spirituelles
de mon calvaire en whiskey

Though the title of the poem causes the reader to anticipate a confessional tone and a list of the three Dada sins, neither is given. The speaker is annoyed by, but not contrite about, a broken wheel. A Dadaist nonsensical series—hopscotch gives birth to the flower, the sunflower to the prayer, and her eyes to a broken wheel, followed by the ladder like an image, the glass like a microscope, and her eyes like beautiful language—adds to the ambiguity of chronologies and correspondences as images pile one upon another and then melt away from view. The poem offers no key to its interpretation in the traditional sense. Instead, it defies the rules of poetic art by taunting the reader with recurring, layered images that do not fulfill clear symbolic functions, thus inviting a search for meaning.

One possible clue to its sense may be the recurring wheel, one of the best-known mechanical Dadaist icons, established by the 1913 ready-made *Roue de bicyclette sur un tabouret* (Bicycle Wheel on a Stool) by Marcel Duchamp. One wonders if Duchamp, recognized as a mentor and leader by the French Dadaists, could be the "Sire Abbé Merlin" of "Mes Trois Péchés Dada." If this is the case, then it seems that Arnauld assumed responsibility for the broken wheel (born from her eyes in the first stanza). She also announced her part in the future demolition of "l'édifice bâti sur une roue et un clou," because she seems to have discovered new language (also born from her eyes) to replace the outmoded image. Nevertheless she confessed that the broken wheel troubled her, and her participation in its destruction seems reluctant. It is only conjecture that in "Mes Trois Péchés Dada" Arnauld was referring to her refusal to follow the mechanical or ready-made aesthetic promoted by Picabia's ventilators and Duchamp's *Porte-bouteilles (Bottle Holder)* of 1914, *Fountain* of 1917, and *L.H.O.O.Q.* of 1919. One of her Dada sins seems to be her preference for beautiful language over objects. Arnauld called for a return, not to convention (because her poetry is not conformist), but to beauty born from a meditative state and reinforced by "discussions spirituelles," that is art that is neither technomechanical nor ready-made, but rather carefully and poetically wrought. In response to Eluard's poetic depiction of her eyes, the second stanza of "Mes Trois Péchés Dada" explains that hers are not the nonsense glass eyes of parrots but eyes that, despite the fading light, pour forth the gift of poetry.

In some ways, one is called to read this Dadaist poem as if it were a Dadaist painting. The movement of the mind, when it is forced to switch from one image to another in the poem, resembles the focus of the eye as it is led from one object to another across a Dadaist canvas. For example the viewer's gaze must often move between various images and words in an avant-garde painting such as *ARieTte d'oubli de la chapelle étourdie* (ARieTta about the Forgetfulness of the Absent-Minded Chapel) by Suzanne Duchamp, the only committed female visual artist in Parisian Dada, even if her involvement was short-lived and soon evolved into the Dada offshoot she and her husband named TABU.

Just as the text of Arnauld's poem foregrounds the shifting and evaporation of images, Duchamp's painting flirts with disconnected and connotatively inaccessible text, in both cases creating a merging of incongruent figurative and textual messages under the dominion of a ruling eye. The painting was created in 1920 and features a prominent glass eye in a male profile, while Arnauld's 1920 poem includes in each stanza a set of recurring narrative eyes that filter the series of images. In each case—painting and poem—the artist reminds the viewer of the implications of perception by placing her in a precarious subject position that is threatened by other witnessing eyes.

While "Mes Trois Péchés Dada" challenges the goals of art and suggests a new direction in Dadaist poetry—that is, verse born of beautiful language instead of mechanical structures—Arnauld's poem "Ombrelle Dada" (Dada Sunshade) sets out to define the art of poetry. Her sarcastic ars poetica appears in number 13 of *Littérature* (May 1920), alongside twenty-two other Dada manifestos by Picabia, Aragon, Breton, Tzara, Arp, Eluard, Soupault, Sernier, Dermée, Ribemont-Dessaignes, and Arensberg.

The issue, subtitled *Vingt-trois manifestes du Mouvement Dada* (Twenty-three Manifestos of the Dada Movement), was under the direction of Aragon, Breton, and Soupault. The so-called *manifestes* do not profess aesthetic beliefs but rather strike out at the status quo with provocative, irreverent jabs. For example Ribemont-Dessaignes declared that nothing is sacred, not religion, not art: "Dada likes to ring doorbells, strike matches to ignite hair and beards. It puts mustard in the ciboriums, urine in the holy-water basin, and margarine in painters' tubes of color."[24] Dermée, Arnauld, Arp, and Arensberg add their manifestos on page 19. In a similar nihilist and irreligious vein, Dermée's declaration claims: "Dada God-killer. The oldest and most formidable enemy of Dada is called GOD!"[25]

Unlike the male contributors' declarations, Arnauld's manifesto poem "Ombrelle Dada" offers a playful but intellectual definition of her art that relies on a combination of poetic imagery ("a parasol, a taxi, an encyclopedia, or a toothpick") and a scientific understanding of movement and depth of field perception (the telegraph pole):

> You don't like my manifesto?
> You've come here full of hostility and you're going to boo
> even before hearing me?
> That's perfect!! So just go on, the wheel turns, turns since
> Adam, nothing's changed, except that we have only
> two feet instead of four.
> But you really make me laugh and I want to pay you back for
> your nice welcome by speaking to you about Aaart, about Poetry etc.
> etc. ipecacuanha.
> Have you ever seen on the sides of the road between the nettles and
> the flat tires, a telegraph pole painfully growing?
> But as soon as it has outgrown its neighbors, it climbs so fast that
> you can no longer stop it . . . never!
> It opens itself in the open sky, lights up, inflates, it's a
> parasol, a taxi, an encyclopedia, or a toothpick.
> Are you happy now? Oh well, that's all that
> I had to say to you. That's what Poetry is, believe me.
> —Poetry = toothpick, encyclopedia, taxi, or sunshade,
> and if you're not pleased . . .
> TO THE NESLE TOWER[26]

> Vous n'aimez pas mon manifeste?
> Vous êtes venus ici pleins d'hostilité et vous allez me siffler
> avant même de m'entendre?
> C'est parfait!! Continuez donc, la roue tourne, tourne depuis

> feu Adam, rien n'est changé, sauf que nous n'avons plus que deux pattes au lieu de quatre.
>
> Mais vous me faites trop rire et je veux vous récompenser de votre bon accueil, en vous parlant d'Aaart, de Poésie et d'etc. d'etc. ipécacuanha.
>
> Avez-vous déjà vu au bord des routes entre les orties et les pneus crevés, un poteau télégraphique pousser péniblement?
>
> Mais dès qu'il a dépassé ses voisins, il monte si vite que vous ne pourriez plus l'arrêter . . . jamais!
>
> Il s'ouvre alors en plein ciel, s'illumine, se gonfle, c'est une ombrelle, un taxi, une encyclopédie ou un cure-dent.
>
> Êtes-vous contents maintenant? Eh bien, c'est tout ce que j'avais à vous dire. C'est ça la Poéésie, croyez-moi.
>
> —Poésie = cure-dent, encyclopédie, taxi ou abri-ombrelle, et si vous n'êtes pas contents . . .
>
> A LA TOUR DE NESLE

The image of the wheel reappears in the manifesto, beginning the suggestion of movement in the poem that is continued in the speaker's evocation of speeding in an automobile down back roads and observing a post that seems to grow larger as the viewer approaches. At its closest and tallest point the telegraph pole unexpectedly mutates into a series of objects, underlying the multifaceted and transitory nature of art. Instead of delivering a prescriptive definition of poetry, the poem opens the genre to all possibilities of the imagination. Just as Dada itself was a shape-shifting version of the avant-garde, forming and re-forming from one genre to the next as it displaced itself across the map, the appearance of poetry, according to Arnauld, continually changes.

Though accusatory, Arnauld's manifesto does not resort to scatology or blasphemy. Instead it plays with sound and typography: "Aaart," "Poéésie," and "ipécacuanha," her version of what she elsewhere abbreviated into increments of sound as I.P.K., echoing Duchamp's L.H.O.O.Q joke. The "Ombrelle Dada" manifesto is distinctly Arnauld's in its literary allusion. The poet's teasing threat to those who refuse her definition of poetry (toothpick, encyclopedia, taxi, or sunshade) relies on the reader's understanding of her mock menacing reference to *La Tour de Nesle,* the title of Alexandre Dumas' 1832 novel and the tower built by Philippe Auguste as part of the city wall, destroyed in 1663. According to legend, this is the tower in which Marguerite de Bourgogne (1290–1315) entertained her lovers and then perhaps had them executed. Queen of Navarre, then of France by her marriage (1305) to the future Louis X, she was ultimately arrested for adultery and smothered. The scholarly reference to a bloody historical site does not detract from Arnauld's overall message about poetry, suggesting that everything depends

21 Mai 1920

PROJECTEUR

Directrice : **Céline Arnauld**
29, Rue du Mont-Cenis
PARIS

Dépositaire
AU SANS PAREIL
37, Avenue Kléber, Paris

Le N° : 1 fr. — Sur Chine 5 ex. : 10 fr.
ABONNEMENT
12 Numéros : 10 fr.

PROSPECTUS PROJECTEUR

Projecteur est une lanterne pour aveugles. Il ne marchande pas ses lumières, elles sont gratuites. *Projecteur* se moque de tout : argent, gloire et réclame — il inonde de soleil ceux qui vivent dans le froid, dans l'obscurité et dans l'ennui. D'ailleurs, la lumière est aussi produite par une pullulation madréporique dans les espaces célestes.

CÉLINE ARNAULD
Céline Arnauld

Front page of Céline Arnauld's 1920 Dada journal. Courtesy of the University of Iowa International Dada Archive.

on the physical act of seeing. Opening one's eyes to the countless possibilities of perception augmented by one's fancy is a recurring message of the avant-garde. Despite Arnauld's clever and apt contribution to issue 13 of *Littérature,* her surname is unfortunately misspelled as "Arnault" in the list of contributors.[27]

Meanwhile, also in May 1920, Arnauld launched *Projecteur,* her first periodical. Henri Béhar, editor of Tzara's poetry, mistakenly gave credit for the journal to Dermée.[28] *Projecteur* might very well have been the same journal as the anticipated but never published "M'Amenez-y," which itself might have had previous titles, such as "Ipéca" or "I.P.K.," alluding to the vomit-inducing medication mentioned in "Ombrelle Dada." Arnauld announced her intentions for *Projecteur* in the following prospectus, printed on the front of the journal: "*Projecteur* is a lantern for the blind. It doesn't sell its lights, they're free. *Projecteur* makes fun of everything: money, glory, advertising—it floods with sun those who live in the cold, in the darkness and in ennui. Moreover, light is also produced by a profusion of madreporian (warm-water corals) in celestial spaces."[29] With its professed goal of mocking "money, glory, advertising," Arnauld's journal clearly sets out to serve the Dada agenda. Yet, there is her distinct preoccupation with the visual, with light, projection, clarity, and the proliferation of esoteric objects that is characteristic of Arnauld's work of the early Dada years. Reminiscent of "Dangereux" with its "filmed song," the audible is highlighted again in a text about sight, as evidenced by her alliterative and layered final sentence of "p" and "s" sounds: "aussi produite par une pullulation madréporique dans les espaces célestes."

Despite the call for a new poetry, the May 21, 1920, issue of *Projecteur* contains the now customary Dada works by predictable poets. There are poems and short prose pieces by Breton, Picabia, Eluard, Soupault, Dermée, Tzara, and Aragon, with two poems by Arnauld: "Luna Park" and "Les Ronge-bois" (The Wood Gnawers).[30] "Luna Park," appearing on page six of *Projecteur,* reveals the tone and mission that she chose for her journal.

Sinister display of this optic mirror
stuck to my shoulder
a miner's lamp horoscope of the bad days
tattoo of my enemies
submerged at the bottom of sad reservoirs
crystallized by elusive flashes of lightning

My hands extend beyond their reach
to take hold of the flower
barge in the din of the ocean
bagpipes of dreamers

In their fort the snails
turn the wheel of the Universe
But the spontaneity of emotions
in life . . .
It's the sunken hydra
on the only chit-chat of the racing turfs
incredible bargain of ices in the Palaces

At Luna Park they juggle
hearts of crystal
The horoscope in tumblers
listens to the mimes speak . . .

Don't be afraid of me
I'm only the ephemeral reflection
of the projector
morning serenade by megaphone[31]

Sinistre étalage de cette glace optique
plaquée sur mon épaule
photophore horoscope des mauvais jours
tatouage de mes ennemis
submergés au fond des tristes réservoirs
cristallisés par des éclairs fuyants

Mes mains s'allongent démesurément
pour saisir la fleur
péniche en rumeurs sur l'océan
cornemuse de rêveurs

Dans leur fort les escargots
tournent la roue de l'Univers
Mais la spontanéité des sentiments
dans la vie . . .
C'est l'hydre sombrée
sur l'unique sornette des turfs
aubaine des glaces dans les Palaces

Au Luna Park on jongle
avec les coeurs en cristal
L'horoscope en gobelets
écoute parler les mimes . . .

Ne vous méfiez pas de moi
je ne suis que le reflet éphémère
du projecteur
aubade à porte-voix

The title "Luna Park" evokes the inviting image of moonlight and the promise of amusement park entertainment. The argentine glow pervades the first stanza and increases the reflective nature of the poem, as seen in the mirror that is plated, like silver, to the speaker's shoulder. This reflecting optic device reveals, under the beam of a miner's lamp, a horoscope of bad days, tattooed into permanence by the narrator's enemies. Although sunken in a reservoir of water, the unpleasant forecast reappears by elusive flashes of lightning.

In the second stanza the poet moves from moonlight and mirror to a third reflective surface, water. The reader views a dream that allows an unnatural extension of the hand to reach a flower, while in the background an ocean din lulls a barge with the sound of dreamers' bagpipes. The vastness of the ocean links easily with the multitude of celestial bodies in the heavens in the following stanza. The snails, which from the safe fortress of their shells turn the wheel of the universe, seem to multiply like the heads of the hydra, like emotions. This profusion of celestial, marine, and human characteristics echoes the "pullulation madréporique," mentioned on *Projecteur*'s cover page. And, as Arnauld stated in her prospectus, the result is light, clarifying light, which serves as "une lanterne pour aveugles," a lantern for the blind, inundating with sunlight those who live in cold and darkness.

Luna Park offers otherworldly delights. One sees crystal hearts juggled and hears mimes speak. The narrator addresses the listener, confiding that she is not to be feared. She is merely the ephemeral reflection of the projector, the megaphone for the message. To underscore the feeling of an escaping moment, the poem abounds in terms that defy solidity or permanence in favor of fragility: "glace optique," "fuyants," "péniche en rumeurs sur l'océan," "aubaine des glaces dans les Palaces," "cristal," "gobelets," "reflet," et "éphémère." Even the sound of "des glaces dans les Palaces" glides away from one's grasp.

In "Luna Park" the speaker, her poem, and the journal in which it is printed share the same task, to serve as a fleeting transmitter of the era. Permanence is unsought and undesirable. "Luna Park" is yet another poetic manifesto that expresses the purpose of Dada art. Arnauld's understanding of the aesthetic and ideological goals of Dada, if one can use the word *goals,* is clearly expressed in her refusal of the "tatouage de mes ennemis" in favor of the ever-multiplying and ephemeral creations that are nevertheless nothing more than mirrored images under a temporary but clarifying light.

Projecteur announces on its back cover the Festival Dada to be held May 26, 1920, at the Salle Gaveau on rue la Boétie, with entertaining presentations on "le Sexe de Dada" (Dada's Sex) and "le Nombril interlope" (The Shady Navel). The choice of the Salle Gaveau, a location whose prestige was supposedly tainted by the event, naturally alarmed Parisians. It would not have been hard for Paris to expect something outrageous after reading a teasing preview of the coming attractions: "All Dadaists will have their heads shaved on stage," and the following accusation printed in the program distributed in the street: "Each of you has a bookkeeper in your heart, a watch, and a little packet of shit."[32] On the official program of the festival, Arnauld is ambiguously listed as the author of the dialogue *Jeu d'*échecs (Chess Game), a title that she gave to her lyric novel of 1921.

The festival included Tzara's performance piece "Vaseline symphonique," which required twenty actors and caused Breton to run in agony from the room "gnashing his teeth."[33] Contributions by Picabia, Dermée, Arnauld, and Eluard completed an evening that was punctuated by the sound of the popular foxtrot "Pelican" on the organ, which was usually used for playing Bach. The audience included André Gide, Jules Romains, Paul Valéry, Jacques Rivière, and Jacques Copeau representing the *Nouvelle Revue Française,* while Rachilde, Paul Léautard, and André Fontainas appeared for the *Mercure.* Other spectators included Natalie Barney, Jean Metzinger, Gleizes, and Léger. An attorney general of the Supreme Court of Appeal, Léon Brulot, was unable to make his way into the crowded room and reportedly sent his card to Picabia later, saying that he had left full of respect for a disorder that was so well organized. He wondered if the obstruction that prevented his entry was an intentional Dada ploy.[34]

Clearly Dada made an impression on the Parisian public and thus found a literary home in 1920, despite the efforts of Cubists such as Gleizes whose "L'Affaire

Dada" accused Dadaists of creating a rotting "cadaver," from which he called on others to make something beautiful grow. Ribemont-Dessaignes and Picabia promptly attacked Gleizes in the second issue of *Cannibale*. This feuding was typical among the male members of competing avant-garde movements. The relationship between groups was clearly inflammatory, but in the case of Dada, it was probably also unifying and beneficial because Dada did not have a central leader or manifesto around which to rally.

Amid all the controversial activity of 1920, Arnauld's volume of verse *Poèmes à claires-voies* appeared. These poems testify to an influence that drew Arnauld even further from her previous lyrical and narrative style to experiment with a typography that emphasizes the visual juxtapositions of her images. Critic Elie Moroy, who published *La Littérature définie par les femmes écrivains* in 1931, gave the following assessment of Arnauld's 1920 collection: "It's supple, it's gay, it causes a shudder. It escapes well away from the grey cages of tradition."[35] Arnauld's *Poèmes à claires-voies* seeks original structures for her vivid imagery.

In addition Arnauld contributed to Eluard's periodical *Proverbe,* which ran from February 1920 through July 1921. Her work appears as well in *Le Pilhaou-Thibaou,* a sixteen-page "illustrated" supplement to Picabia's *391,* published in Paris on June 10, 1921. During *391*'s ten years in the French capital, Arnauld was a contributor alongside Apollinaire, Aragon, Arensberg, Arp, Breton, Buffet, Cocteau, Crotti, Robert Desnos, Dermée, Eluard, Gleizes, Max Jacob, Laurencin, René Magritte, Ray, Ribemont-Dessaignes, Erik Satie, Soupault, Tzara, and Varèse. She was part of the group that surrounded Picabia and contributed to his projects, such as *L'Oeil cacodylate,* the painting he exhibited at the Salon d'Automne. To this work, featuring approximately fifty signatures and messages from friends who visited Picabia in his studio, Céline Arnauld signed her name in the upper right corner in green paint.

From Poetry to Suicide

The audacity of *L'Oeil cadodylate* clearly illustrates how Picabia's brash, outlandish, and aggressive style might be viewed in contrast to Arnauld's more refined Dada expression in a poem such as "Luna Park." In his 1976 *Expressionnisme, Dada, Surréalisme et autres ismes,* Serge Faucherau offered the following commentary on the style exhibited in Arnauld's 1921 collection of poetry: "*Point de mire* is a return to the fantasy of Max Jacob, exempt from the verbal excesses which Tzara, Picabia, or Pansaers excel at." Faucherau described Arnauld's more restrained poetry as elegant, "but perhaps a bit too pleasant."[36] The pleasant, or "amiable," qualities of her poetry challenge Dada's reputation as a purposely offensive antiart rebellion represented primarily by a male-dominated group of avant-garde artists who were meanwhile being labeled by Antonin Artaud as "several artificial assemblers of mechanical images."[37] However, Arnauld's "Cinéma," "Dangereux," "Trois Péchés Dada," and "Ombrelle Dada" do indeed set out to provoke and scandalize.

They do not handle the reader gently. Even when the content is humorous, as in the case of "Ombrelle Dada," the speaker's voice is not pleasant in tone, but instead ridiculing.

Nevertheless Faucherau's description of Arnauld's poetic language draws on the contrasts he saw with Ribemont-Dessaignes's or Picabia's writings. Hers is elegant, rich, musical, and textured with images. It remains almost detached in its critique of bourgeois life and art and devoid of any name-calling or direct personal attack on her contemporaries. In fact Arnauld's poetry remains so aesthetically and intellectually grounded that for some readers it might seem to lack the conviction and raw power of the more aggressive verse of her compatriots. Her poetry has charm. It first relies on the sharp juxtaposition of carefully crafted images to startle, after which its pleasing language seeps into the senses.

Critics label much of her work as Surrealist; however, Arnauld revealed in her "Comment je suis venue à la poésie" that, although she discovered Rimbaud in 1921, she participated in the avant-garde, "all the while remaining independent."[38] In a self-evaluation of her work, written just months before her death, she explained her perspective: "In love with music and philosophy, the Surrealist excesses did not mix well with my lyricism. I preferred to hold myself in the silent domain of the interior life where everything is love and knowledge. In my writing there is an agonizing desire to embrace the Universe, to live life fully. Of bitterness too, that bitterness of whatever is not the dupe of recantations. I've made my way like an intoxication, my nomadic life has given me but one religion, that of the marvelous. I am proud of my independence within the modern poetic movement. I've followed no one, not lowered myself with compromises, and scorned publicity. I've stayed a Poet."[39]

Arnauld's uncompromising, independent attitude that does not encourage self-promotion is closer to the original goals of Dada as set forth by the earliest Zurich Dadaists. It was, however, one of the reasons why she went unnoticed for so many years by historians of the Parisian avant-garde. They chronicled instead poets who participated more heatedly in the habitual Dada manifestations of overt rebellion. The more scandalous the act, the more attention it drew.

In comparison with the writings of her male colleagues, Arnauld's poetry is certainly more lyrical, more personal, and thematically less risk taking. Whether this was simply her taste or the result of her writing from the outside edge of the tougher "boys' club" of Dada is hard to tell. This much is clear: while Picabia, Breton, Tzara, and Soupault often wrote in response to each other, Arnauld's poetry responds primarily to itself. In this way Arnauld's poetry follows no rules as it registers its revolt against the ruling aesthetic.

By 1923 a new poetic trend was beginning to be strongly felt in Paris. Published just before Parisian Dada began its decline, *Guêpier de diamants* (Diamond Trap) documents Arnauld's gradual movement away from her former antiart rebellion and toward the aesthetic of the surreal. The sixty-seven-page volume, published in Auvers by Ça Ira in 1923, contains an eight-page prose work dated July 17, 1922, also titled "Guêpier de diamants." While the seductive lyric dialogue between two alternating voices, ELLE and LUI, exhibits Dadaist traits in its disjunctive narrative voices, its tone nevertheless suggests Arnauld's new visionary style as evidenced in this example:

> HIM
>
> ———I know a country where the gravediggers bury the living, the dead bury themselves, and that's why there are so many famous dead there.
>
> HER
>
> ———The evil spell was crushed against the tombs impervious to storms; the release was effected through a shower of diamonds and the bronzed salutations of the sun, always more superb and more ingenuously suspended in its Eldorado engraving. Capricious and interlaced with sighs, the door of the cooper opened itself to the vines and antelopes, pure of all treason and ennobled with charm and childlike grace. . . .[40]

In this excerpt, the rich imagery and flowing rhythm of layered prose simulate the hypnotic vertigo of a dream sequence with echo. Each descriptive phrase, heavy with visually evocative adjectives, ties to it a succeeding phrase through syntactical transpositions or a series of alternate expressions, giving hallucinatory approximations of scenes instead of realistic representations of them. The text exhibits an unrestrained movement of the mind from one image to another, suggesting a kind of automatic writing (an essential element of Surrealism) that is nevertheless carefully calculated in its pattern of images.

In 1924 Arnauld's work appeared in the now-obscure *Interventions: Gazette internationale des Lettres et des Arts modernes* and in its continuation, *Le Mouvement accéléré: Organe accélérateur de la Révolution artistique et littéraire,* which voiced its condemnation of Breton. Other collaborators on these two periodicals edited by Dermée include Picabia, Ribemont-Dessaignes, Yvan Goll, René Crevel, and Frantisek Kupka. *Interventions* also included an article about Arnauld, written by what Sanouillet has described as "an affectionate friend."[41]

A valuable 1936 publication, "La Critique et Céline Arnauld," provides a collection of critical perspectives of Arnauld's work by her contemporaries. Tristan Rémy underlined her "surreal atmosphere" in the two-act passion play *L'Apaisement de l'Eclipse* (The Calming of the Eclipse) and noted that "even though she searches in the deepest part of herself, she remains under the sign of surrealism."[42] Like many poets and artists who began their careers in Dada (such as Breton, Ernst, Man Ray, and Soupault), Arnauld was influenced by and eventually showed signs of the new Surrealist aesthetic in her post-Dadaist poetry.

Appended to her 1936 *Heures intactes,* one finds Pierre-Louis Flouquet's "Opinions sur 'La Nuit rêve tout haut' suivie de 'Le Clavier secret'—1934." In this document Flouquet, director of *Les Cahiers du Journal des Poètes,* claimed that Arnauld was the first woman who embraced the literature of pure creation, that is, the avant-garde. He further lauded her fresh and strong imagination and her rare technical resources. Of her *L'Apaisement de L'Eclipse,* he wrote that such an astonishing poetic passion in two acts must be classified among France's greatest lyrics, forging a unique syntax, style, and vocabulary by its amplitude. This is high praise from the director of a series that had as its stated mission to present and defend authentic poetry, without regard to forms or doctrines. Furthermore Flouquet was not alone in his commendation of *L'Apaisement de L'Eclipse.* An anonymous review of Arnauld's work in the August 15, 1925, issue of *La Vie* points to the poet's ability to humanize poetry. Her contemporaries often remarked that Arnauld's writing seemed sensitive and human oriented when compared to the mechanical and experimental poetry of her male colleagues. *L'Apaisement de L'Eclipse* was well received by critics and won respect for Arnauld as a poet of her generation. In addition to Flouquet's appreciation, Arnauld also received favorable reviews in *Le Mercure de France, La Revue des Poètes, Paris-Nice,* and *L'Express du Midi.*

During her prolific poetic career Arnauld contributed to many publications, among them *Dada, 391, Littérature, Cannibale, Z, L'Esprit Nouveau, Action, Zénit, Proverbe, Création, Les Images de Paris, Ça Ira, Le Journal des Poètes, La Revue Monsane, La Flandre Littéraire, Muba, L'Art Contemporain, Le 7*[e] *Art, Documents Internationaux de L'Esprit Nouveau,* and *Le Phare de Neuilly,* indicating her high level of involvement in Dada and the Parisian avant-garde.

Arnauld was a consistent presence in Dada activities in Paris. Although she contributed to the propagation of Dada through proclamations and manifestos, she was nevertheless not an ideologue. She participated but did not take a leading part in the more performance-oriented side of Dada, unlike Tzara and others who continued the methods of the Swiss Dadaists. Her artistic production was not noticeably political, like the work of many of the German Dadaists such as George Grosz and Hannah Höch with their provocative posters or anti-Wilhelmian photomontages. Instead she concentrated on creating disquieting but beautiful poems according to her own aesthetic. She chose poetry as her art, words as her medium, and the literary magazine as her vehicle. She deserves to be remembered as the Dadaist poet whose imagination dared to invent its own brand of avant-garde poetic imagery.

Although she worked within a circle of Dadaists, Arnauld's art remains noticeably personal and distinguishable. One thing that sets her apart from her peers is that she did not write about her fellow Dadaists. Other women involved in Parisian Dada (such as Everling, Buffet, and Roche) left behind written records about the group, but Arnauld produced no memoir or essays of literary criticism.

Furthermore Arnauld distanced herself from the competitive one-upmanship of practical joking that is commonly found in the poetry of Picabia, Tzara, or the future male Surrealists. She also refrained from the attacks and counterattacks launched by Ribemont-Dessaignes and Picabia against the likes of Gleizes. Her poems may be either aggressive or playful, but they never attack an individual and are never frivolous.

In the July 1921 issue of *391*, Arnauld gave cleverly worded advice to the warring male members of the group. The final lines of her "Extrait de Saturne" scold and counsel: "What an accumulation of hate, of rancour, of bad behavior behind this calm! Believe me, vomit all that out in bad words, write it, shout it before the world and you will be relieved. It is necessary to purge the spirit as well as the body. Everything can be said in anger and still keep a pure heart. 'Know oneself'; in other words: 'Soap yourself before soaping others.'"[43] As the playful disciplinarian of the Parisian group, Arnauld tempered her admonitions with humor.

Arnauld's publishing career continued as her poetry appeared in journals and in her collections, such as *La Nuit rêve tout haut* (The Night Dreams Aloud), published in 1934; *Le Clavier secret* (The Secret Keyboard), poems from 1925–34, also published in 1934; *Heures intactes* (Intact Hours), published in Brussels in 1936 and listed in at least one source as *Hermès intactes;*[44] *Anthologie Céline Arnauld,* also published in 1936; *Les Réseaux du Réveil* (The Networks of Awakening), poems published in 1937; *La Nuit pleure tout haut* (The Night Cries Aloud), published in 1939, but listed as "edition destroyed by the occupant"; *Rien qu'une Étoile* (Nothing But a Star), followed by *Plains-Chants sauvages* (Wild Plainsongs), written between 1940 and August 1944 but not published until 1948. It is difficult to determine the path of her career between 1948 and 1952. Her publishing seems to have abruptly stopped.

Just as her date and place of birth have been disputed, sources also disagree on the date of Arnauld's death. According to the editors of Huelsenbeck's *Dada Almanac,* she committed suicide the day after the death of her husband.[45] Although Dermée's death is recorded as December 27, 1951, most sources list the year of Arnauld's death as 1952. The *Dictionnaire littéraire des femmes de la langue française* (1996) avoids listing a date of death altogether.

It is known that the couple was living across from the Paris Observatoire, rue Cassini at the time of their deaths, and that Dermée suffered for several months with the illness that eventually claimed his life. The *Dada Almanac* perhaps exaggerates the proximity of the dates of death for dramatic effect, though most sources do emphasize that Arnauld's suicide followed shortly after Dermée's death because she was unable to endure her grief. Rousselot stated that "she committed suicide, in 1952, so as not to survive the death of her husband."[46] The University of Iowa Dada Archive lists her date of death as December 23, 1952, nearly a full year after her husband's.[47] However, Hemus, after consulting Arnauld's heirs, holds that the poet took her life one month after Dermée's death.[48]

This confusion surrounding the date of her suicide (whether intentional for effect or the accidental symptom of a general disregard for accurate information about female poets) is but yet another illustration of the lack of serious attention given to this noteworthy Dadaist. As the only fully committed female Parisian Dada poet, Arnauld deserves finally to receive some of the respect she has been denied since the 1940s. In her *Poésie féminine: Epoque moderne* Moulin has pointed out that Arnauld's little-known texts give an idea of what women were achieving intellectually and psychologically in the domain of pure invention during a period in which tastes, morals, and society were undergoing unprecedented changes.[49] For this reason alone, Arnauld's poetry merits rediscovery, reprinting, and reinstatement in the annals of literary history, and her contribution to the explosion of Dada in Paris should be further recognized and appreciated.

4. Juliette Roche

Dada Scandals and Scoundrels

Although Juliette Roche (1884–1980[1]) was an astute observer and recorder of the twentieth-century avant-garde through her paintings and poetry, it has been difficult to catch a glimpse of this important eyewitness herself. The story of her life, as she chose to tell it in her "Mémoires," remains unpublished. Her collection of poems (*Demi Cercle*) and a novella (*La Minéralisation de Dudley Craving Mac Adam*) were last published in the 1920s. Many of her paintings are lost. To date, there has been only one retrospective of her art. A formidable poet, critic, and painter in her own right, who contributed to the avant-garde through articles and interviews until her death, Roche is often remembered merely as the wife of the controversial Cubist Albert Gleizes, whose hostility toward the Dadaists in the April 1920 issue of *Action* invited scathing attacks by Picabia and Ribemont-Dessaignes. However, prior to this falling out, both Roche and Gleizes were active participants in at least three international sites of Dadaist activity: New York, Barcelona, and Paris.

When viewing the battleground of fervent male egos that characterizes New York and Parisian Dada, how could one expect historians to notice the contributions of Roche, a gifted and insightful writer and painter who happened to be married to one of the most vocal and enduring theorists in the debate between conflicting manifestations of the avant-garde? Who hears her words over the continual din emanating from Picabia, Ribemont-Dessaignes, Tzara, and Breton? Although she appears to be yet another hushed female Dadaist, it is not a voice that she lacked but an audience. One must make the effort to listen. Roche's writings are not timid; she is opinionated, straightforward, and can speak for herself. Nevertheless her words are largely unheard, unknown, and unavailable outside a few European archives.

Thanks to Carolyn Burke's extensive research presented in "Recollecting Dada: Juliette Roche" (1998), Roche's role as artist, agent, and eyewitness to Dadaist activities in New York, Barcelona, and Paris has been brought to light.[2] Through her paintings, but especially through her writing, Roche refused the role of Dada nurturer or supporter adopted by Hennings, Buffet, Everling, and Arnauld. Instead she served as an avid eyewitness, reluctant participant, and demanding critic of Dada events and personalities. Her testimony helps to clarify the definition and history of Dada. While she scrutinized and evaluated her contemporaries, she also took into account her role as an observing figure. Each painting and written text that she left behind, each interview and photograph of her, serves as a consciously produced self-portrait. By inspecting the artifacts of Roche's long career, one can determine the contribution of the woman who dared to satirize the arrogant New York Dada celebrities in her novella à clef, *La Minéralisation de Dudley Craving Mac Adam* (The Mineralization of Dudley Craving Mac Adam). Who was this chronicler of Dada, this woman chosen by the charmed Picabia as the measuring *manomètre* of the avant-garde?

Daughter of Politics

Raised as the only child of the wealthy and politically connected Jules Roche, Marie Juliette Lucy was born in Paris, August 29, 1884. After losing her mother at a young age, she became close to her father, who regularly discussed his political career with her and revealed in confidence his conversations with Kaiser Wilhelm of Prussia. According to her unpublished memoir, the adolescent Juliette often accompanied her father to the regatta at Kiel in northern Germany, where he entered into business deals with the kaiser and Crown Prince Albert of Monaco in hopes of uniting Europe through a common economic union or *Zollverein*. Juliette's father saw France as part of this European union, and through personal acts of diplomacy, he actively sought to diminish the mounting hostilities between Germany and England. The daughter of Jules Roche was also expected to do her part to preserve peace. At age sixteen Juliette was called on to use her fluency in English by acting as the interpreter at a private meeting arranged by her father between future prime ministers Aristide Briand and Winston Churchill. Later Roche remembered little about the content of the meeting, blaming her lack of interest in political matters on her youth, but she did record in her memoir that she was favorably impressed with Briand's quick comprehension and eloquence.[3]

Not long afterward, Juliette and her best friend, Nanie, came into contact with members of the nationalist, monarchist movement L'Action française. Naïve to political distinctions, the girls were inspired by the personality of the future mayor of Lyon, the young Edouard Herriot, who recited to them from their favorite poets (Paul Verlaine and Charles Baudelaire) and recommended others to read. Nanie eventually married one of her young socialist friends at age nineteen, but Juliette did not appreciate politics, professed to be uninterested in marriage of any kind, and continued to pursue instead literature, music, and painting.[4] She began her formal study of art at the rigorous Académie Ranson under the direction of Maurice Denis, Paul Sérusier, and Félix Valloton, whom she later joined in the Nabis, a post-Impressionist, pre-Fauve group that included Pierre Bonnard, Aristide Maillol, and Eduard Vuillard. Although she was the youngest of the group and female, she was elected to join, reportedly because of her uncommon talent.

The story of Roche's early life seems to be composed of pleasant anecdotes and social events. Hers was a life of privilege and ease; her concerns were personal and not yet pressing. According to Lea Vergine, one day Roche questioned Denis about what she should paint: what she saw or what she imagined. He purportedly replied: "Drawing is something that you think and you put a line around."[5] But Roche, who traveled in many circles under diverse influences, thought of many things. Art was merely one of them. Poetry was another. Her first collection of poems *Des Mots* . . . was published in 1907 under the pseudonym "Herco."[6]

Unhurriedly searching for her artistic niche, Roche indulged her curiosity about Futurism, the mostly Italian multimedia avant-garde movement that had broken into France when Filippo Marinetti's manifesto was published in *Le Figaro* in 1909. Roche was escorted by Marinetti himself through the 1910 Futurist exhibition in Paris. In her memoir she characterized the tour as tranquil until, after the Futurist leader gave his talk, Ukrainian Cubist-Constructivist sculptor Alexander Archipenko approached Marinetti's table and pointedly asked him whether he thought his Futurism was the only worthwhile art. Something in Archipenko's tone provoked the Futurist to answer him with a punch in the face. The table was overturned; a fistfight broke out in the gallery; police arrived; and arrests were made. Amazingly Roche had posed a similar question during her private tour, to which Marinetti reportedly replied that, although he preferred Impressionism, Futurism, with its emphasis on technology and speed, was what was presently needed. While Roche saw no need for such modernity in her painting, her poetry shows her preoccupation with avant-garde forms.

Roche incorporated many influences from the visual arts into her poetry. By 1913, the same year in which she exhibited in the Salon des Indépendants, she was creating poems that featured modified printed "ready-mades" by inserting already printed advertising slogans and texts into her writing. In some ways this poetry inhabits the border between traditional verse and the kind of canvases that Berlin Dadaist Hannah Höch later produced as photomontages or as her 1922 *Haussprüche* (Household Sayings). Roche merged two of her great passions (poetry and the visual arts) in her early writings. In her 1913 poem "Toulon-Cannes," for example, alternating narrative text and fantasized dialogue or song are punctuated with bold-type advertisements such as "Hotel Astoria entirely renovated" and "Rome Elysée Palace / 400 Rooms open all year long."[7] The graphic effect is visually jarring, even disturbing in its interrupted linear narrative, but at the same time the result is thematically synthesizing because the boldface insertions are integrated into the aristocratic tone of the text's travel narrative. Later poems, such as "BREVOORT" and "N'Existe Pas / Pôle Tempéré," take this effect to a more extreme and abstract form.

Between 1910 and 1914 Roche frequented rival Parisian salons, each with its own political or aesthetic orientation. Because of family connections, most notably the comptesse de Greffulhe (the model for Proust's Madame de Guermantes), all doors were open to her. The young poetic painter moved freely between "the rue d'Athènes" (the Goldsteins' apartment where one might find Maurice Ravel, Odilon Redon, Gide, Valéry, and Jules Roche's godson Jean Cocteau) and Ricciotto Canudo's home (where she came into contact with avant-garde trends). By 1913 she was included in the Tuesday meetings of poets at the Closerie des Lilas, frequented by Apollinaire. All in all, Roche led a privileged life of travel, literature, music, and brilliant conversation. As Pierre Alibert has pointed out: "To study painting at the Académie Ranson and to go dancing on Sunday with Sérusier, Valloton, Denis when Ravel is at the piano is a fate not reserved for the common people. Likewise, it's not the good fortune of everyone to be beautiful. And Juliette Roche was beautiful, in face and bearing. Dresses by Poiret certainly augmented nature, but the photo of her around 1911—she was thus 27 years old—shows that then too she was at the top of the class. And even though everything converged to make the daughter of Jules Roche the most perfect of snobs, she was saved by painting."[8]

By 1912 Roche had discovered the latest avant-garde rebellion in Cubism, and she began to spend time with its practitioners. Through her introduction to Cubism, she arranged to meet Albert Gleizes, whom she married on September 8, 1915, with Cocteau as her witness. According to Gleizes's biographer Peter Brooke, it was an unusual marriage "between two people who, one might have thought, were temperamentally unsuited to each other. There was little in common between the down-to-earth, morally earnest son of a prosperous artisan, Albert Gleizes, and the witty, sophisticated, high-society woman, Juliette Roche, more than able to hold her own in the world described in the novels of Marcel Proust."[9] For this reason some might have thought it a mere marriage of convenience, releasing

Gleizes from military duty and allowing him financial independence from commercial restraints on his art; however, the couple remained committed, loyal, and inseparable until Gleizes's death in June 1953.

Despite her evolving personal relationship with Gleizes, a Cubist painter and theorist, Roche remained professionally a devoted disciple of the Nabis, who emphasized color and personal symbolism. Alibert has noted her tenacity: "She would traverse the fifty most agitated years in the history of Western painting without changing what she had adhered to before the war of 1914, consciously and with complete lucidly, with a rare intelligence of her resources, of her limits. This is what caused her to have one of the liveliest spirits of the time because nothing could fool her."[10] Nevertheless Roche had to sacrifice her long-time friends Denis and Valloton before her marriage, because they considered her Cubist husband the enemy. Vergine points out the difficulty of the artist's situation: what she painted was still "Nabis," but she was not accepted by the group of former friends who now ostracized her.[11] On the other hand, her figurative, metaphorical style of painting was certainly not appreciated by the Cubists. Consequently, when it came to the support of fellow artists, Roche was alone in a virtual no-man's land.

However, such problems could not deter Roche. Instead she prepared her first important exhibition, which took place March 2–7, 1914, at the Galerie Bernheim-Jeune, a premiere Parisian site. Her paintings were a success, with the minister of fine arts figuring among the many buyers. Meanwhile she was still writing actively. "Jardin Public" of 1914 warns of the upcoming event that would interrupt her art and Parisian life. In the poem she warns "—The city already contained its noises of war."[12]

In the spring of 1914 Roche introduced Gleizes to her long-time friend Cocteau, who, prior to the encounter, opposed the current avant-garde trends in painting. In her unpublished memoir, Roche recorded the potentially disastrous meeting:

> I had been imprudent enough to start a portrait of Cocteau. During the Easter holidays in my studio I did the portrait, or rather tried to do it. His continual agitation and too amusing comments prevented me from working. . . . An unexpected ring at the doorbell alarmed me. It was Albert Gleizes, whom I hadn't been expecting. It was a catastrophe. . . . For a year Cocteau had been pleasantly making fun of "my" Cubists, and also of those of Roger de la Fresnaye, and we politely replied that he was ripe for the academy. Terrible things were about to happen. I pronounced the two names as badly as possible in a strangled voice in the feeble hope that they would not understand them, and, so as not to be present at the probable outcome, I disappeared backstage to make some tea. When I reappeared with my teapot, they were sitting close to each other with a delighted air, exchanging cards, telephone numbers and

> arranging a further meeting. Eight days later, Cocteau could no longer talk about anything other than Jacques Villon, Duchamp-Villon, Albert Gleizes. Missia [*sic*] Godebska reproached me severely: "Why did you put Jean in touch with the Cubists? He is a man of the right, he isn't a man of the left. . . . He will be lost in that crowd."[13]

Later the rise and fall of the couple's relationship with Cocteau became a barometer measuring their interactions with various and competing avant-garde factions. In 1914 Cocteau enlisted Gleizes to do illustrations for his patriotic periodical, *Le Mot,* and to collaborate on his adaptation of *A Midsummer Night's Dream.* However, Gleizes was not invited to contribute to Cocteau's 1917 *Parade.* By that time there had been a shift of loyalties.

Because of their divergent social backgrounds and aesthetic goals, Roche and Gleizes experienced occasional difficulties in agreeing on friendships with other artists. They had each been independent in their tastes when they met, and they continued to be so. Instead of a shared social circle, it was more likely their antiwar politics that brought them together.

About her marriage Roche admitted many years later that "without the war I never would have married."[14] According to Brooke, Gleizes sent a postcard to Roche from the front at Toul to indicate that he was alive, contradicting rumors of his death that had been circulating in the Salon des Indépendants. She surprised him with a long, impassioned antiwar letter, and their political and personal commitment to each other began. According to Alibert, because of her father's political influence, Roche managed to acquire the paperwork to visit Gleizes several times. At Toul, where Gleizes was in charge of organizing cultural events for the troops, he sketched his future bride and also painted the portrait *La Parisienne.* When the love affair became a question of marriage, Monsieur Roche reportedly sent a cousin to interview the young man. She returned with this conclusion: "He is as crazy as she is, it will work out fine."[15] Gleizes received a discharge from military service in August 1915 owing to behind-the-scenes efforts by Roche, who, as described in her memoir, had appealed directly to Briand, then minister of justice, in a one-hour meeting. A month later the couple was married and, proclaiming a pacifist stance, they left Europe for America on September 11, 1915.

Dada in New York, Barcelona, and Paris

The newlyweds settled in New York at the English-style Albermarle Hotel and were escorted around the city by the "full of whiskey" Duchamp, whom Gleizes had met at the studio of Duchamp's brother Jacques Villon. There they found themselves connected to the expatriate circle of artists and writers of the Arensberg salon. They frequented the Museum of Natural History and wandered through the city, often emerging from the subway to find overwhelming and undesirable industrial

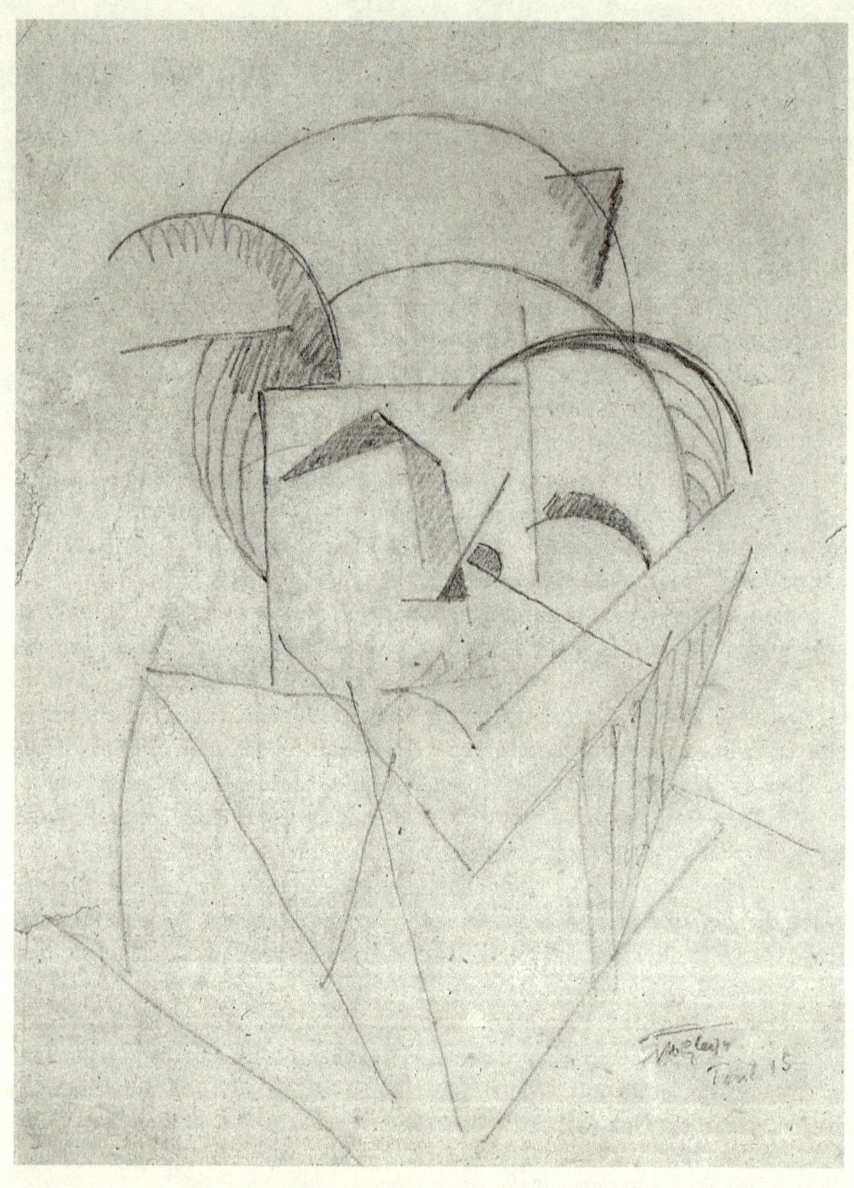

Study for the Portrait of Juliette Roche-Gleizes, by Albert Gleizes. Ink on paper, 27 × 21 cm. © 2012 Artists Rights Society (ARS), New York/ADAGP, Paris. Location: Fondation Albert Gleizes, Paris, France. Photograph credit: Banque d'Images, ADAGP/Art Resource, New York Image reference: ART313405. Image size: 227 × 300 px.

neighborhoods of concrete and metal. During this time, they served (in name, at least) as journalists and foreign correspondents, Roche for *Le Gaulois* and Gleizes for his father-in-law's *La République Française.*[16]

In New York the French honeymooners attracted attention. The *New York Tribune* of October 9, 1915, ran an article by Sarah Addington on page 9, which featured the headlines: "New York Is More Alive and Stimulating than France Ever Was, Say Two French Painters" and "Albert Gleizes, Noted Cubist Painter, and His Artist-Journalist Bride Also Assert That War Was an Inevitable Climax to a Life in Europe That Was Too Charming a Circus to Endure." The four-column article includes a posed photograph of the couple with Roche seated in the foreground. Her body is turned to reveal her hands comfortably clasping her knees, but her gaze is unflinchingly directed into the lens of the camera. Behind her stands her husband of one month, leaning on one elbow toward his wife, with his face turned slightly at an angle from the camera. The caption reads: "Albert Gleizes, Cubist Painter, and His Wife Juliette Roche Gleizes; Daughter of a French Newspaper Owner, She Would Nevertheless Limit News in War Time to Government Bulletins." Juliette, described as a "lean, dark beauty" and "a slight figure, purple clad," was noted as the daughter of a member of the *Chambres des Deputés,* newspaper editor, and former French cabinet minister. The press in New York considered her a distinguished foreign celebrity.

Addington's article goes well beyond a society feature story about visiting artists, as its politically nuanced headings suggest. The interview for the article was conducted with and through Roche, who had learned to speak English from her childhood governess. Addington barely interacted with Gleizes during the interview, "since [Roche's] husband could only sit by and guess at what [Roche] was saying." As Brooke has noted, "on certain matters, mainly politically and pacifist, it was [Roche] who took the lead."[17] As the spokesperson for the couple, Roche first conveyed her enthusiasm for, and her husband's appreciation of, New York's beauty: "The lights, electric signs, most nourishing to artists. See!"[18] She gracefully indicated her husband's Cubist canvases depicting the bright lights of Broadway in their hotel-room-turned-studio.

Instead of discussing art or the artists' impressions of New York, most of Addington's article concerns politics and the war in Europe. The article allows readers to see Roche and hear her voice: "Mme. Gleizes does not talk excitedly or mournfully about the great world tragedy; hers is rather an attitude of poise and resignation . . . ." Roche described the causes of war as "a fateful, inevitable force, working just like gravity, pulling us down, down, whenever we soared too high." She continued: "You know, we knew two or three years ago that something was going to happen. The French people felt that the climax had been reached, that the breaking point had come. Life had become too easy, too charming. It could not go on, this refined, delightful circus. Tragedy was in the air; it tingled from one person to another; we were afraid of what we did not know. Then, like a prophecy fulfilled, came the awful fact."[19]

Roche, like many skeptical artists of the period—especially those, like Ball, who formed the Zurich Dada group—viewed the war as an unnecessary waste of human resources. According to Addington's article, Roche described it as a war of imperialistic greed: "A few men grabbing at each other's pockets for possession. Mere robbery. No larger, no more thrilling motive. I can see how an internal revolution might be good, how an uprising of people for a cause, for a conviction, might be the most salutary of movements, even if lives are lost. But this, ah! Stupid!"[20] According to Addington, Roche likewise pointed out the powerful and potentially corruptive influence of the press in inciting war, pointing to misrepresentations, false interpretations, and harmful editorials as the most dangerous obstacles to peace. Roche is quoted as saying that "perhaps even the war could have been averted if the newspapers had been more helpful."[21]

Other political topics covered in the interview include suffrage and women's rights. Roche explained that her husband never voted and that she (who did not have the right to vote) agreed with his decision. They were both, she said, feminists, "for we believe in equal artistic, industrial and economic opportunity for men and women . . . ."[22]

In her article, Addington remarked that "Madame Gleizes" showed a "startling intellectual independence from her husband," notably in her artistic expressions. Roche straightforwardly announced that she was not a Cubist even though "Cubist art is a definite reflection of the life we lead these days. Cubist art tries to see all the aspects of an object and get the essence of it, concentrated; we in our living are trying to get all viewpoints and all visions, and perhaps our lives are as unintelligible as a Cubist picture is to some people." Roche described her own art as "Japanesey" and said that she would never be a Cubist. "No, even my husband cannot influence me there," she declared.[23]

The view of Roche created by Addington's interview is of a self-confident, articulate, cosmopolitan, and charming individual who successfully presented herself to the American reader. As anyone who has been interviewed by the press can attest, managing to appear in a positive light is, in itself, not an easy task, but combined with the responsibilities of representing multiple viewpoints and doing so in one's second language, the task becomes even more daunting. In her position vis à vis the interviewer and her potential readers, Roche was made to speak for her husband, the French nation, Europeans at war, painters, members of the avant-garde, modern women, members of her social class, and so forth. That is because, in every way that she differed from the reader of the *New York Tribune* of 1915, she was necessarily made to represent that point of view. Reading this subtext of the interview demonstrates how bold, but also how skillfully diplomatic, Roche could be, especially since she later felt dreadfully betrayed when she was informed that the *Tribune* was a pro-German publication owned by William Randolph Hearst. She immediately resolved to give no more interviews for American newspapers because the political leanings of the press were so unclear to her.[24]

Mixing in politics had other dangers, as Roche recounted in her memoir. When Madame Seidlitz—resident of a luxury apartment in the Plaza Hotel where she welcomed many famous visitors—explained to Roche that she was selling forested lands in the Balkans to the Canadians, she requested that her French acquaintance oversee the paperwork in Russia. Although her husband insisted it was an absurd idea, Roche proceeded to arrange the necessary travel documents. When all was ready, Madame Seidlitz also asked Roche to deliver two important letters that she dared not trust to the post. This caused Roche to panic, especially when she discovered that one of the letters was addressed to the Russian czarina. Perhaps overwhelmed by the stress of her "mission," she soon became ill and was ordered by her doctor not to travel.[25]

Besides catching a glimpse of Roche through her memoir and through a newspaper interview, another possible view of the artist comes from a colorful Cubist canvas begun in France but finished in New York around 1915. The portrait, done by her husband, was exhibited at the Musée des Beaux-Arts de Lyon in a 2001 exposition titled Le Cubisme en majesté. The painting—an oil on canvas with a background of bold, geometric blocks of green, yellow, pink, red, orange, and white—evokes a fragmented fashion-designer sketch of a stately woman, made wistful by the sweeping vertical and diagonal dark lines in the foreground. Angles and curves are highlighted by patches of cobalt blue, white, shades of gray, and black. The effect is abstract and disjointed, but the woman's head rises unmistakably from a high stiff collar and is topped by the approximation of a stylish hat. The portrait bears the title *La Parisienne (Juliette Roche).*[26] To some extent, the posture of the woman echoes that of Roche in a 1911 photograph in which she wears a turban and poses, hand on hip, with one elbow angled across the frame. In both portraits, as well as in the newspaper photograph, Roche appears at ease, superior, and self-possessed. Her gaze affirms that if she were to step out of the frame of her portrait, she would move forward with complete confidence and grace.

In a more relaxed pose, Roche appears in a self-portrait on a balcony that overlooks a park. Her palette is of greens and golds. She wears a loose turban, skirt, jacket, and violet necktie. With her hands on her hips, she is leaning back comfortably on a railing. Her eyes meet those of her viewers in a calm and dreamy gaze.

In quite a different kind of portrait, this time by Picabia, Roche becomes objectified as a mechanized measure of gas pressure. According to Burke, the (now lost) *Juliette Gleizes au manomètre* probably hints that such a device indicates a woman's sexual temperature and "may have dated about the same time of the 1915 *Tribune* interview." Burke has suggested that perhaps Picabia's strong male ego was "struck by the journalist's taking [Roche] as seriously as, or more seriously than, her husband."[27] Evidence in Roche's memoir shows, however, that this mechanoportrait—part of Picabia's series of pseudomechanical contraptions of wheels, pulleys, and pistons—was probably executed in Spain, because Roche mentioned that, although her husband had already met Picabia, it was not until Picabia arrived in Barcelona in August 1916 that *she* was introduced to him and his wife, Gabrielle. She also recounts that she interrogated Picabia as to the meaning of his *manomètre,* and he, "with his Mona Lisa smile," had merely replied that it was up to her to explain the meaning to him, that God does not explain his creation. "We," he insisted, "name things for God—this is a dog, this is a tree." Puzzled and annoyed by his response, Roche turned to fellow Catalonian resident Marie Laurencin (whom Picabia had portrayed as a *ventilateur,* or fan), but Roche found her to be no help in solving the mystery. Laurencin counseled her friend not to listen to the stories of painters. Marie confided that if, in the days of Montmartre's Bateau Lavoir, she had listened to Apollinaire, Picasso, and Gris about what painting is or what it is not, she would never have been able to pick up a paintbrush again.[28]

On the other hand, if the *manomètre* painting was executed in 1915, Roche's own mixed media piece *Nature morte au hachoir* of the same year might have been her "mechanical" response to Picabia. The uncharacteristically dark-hued painting, which includes tiny press clippings from French and American newspapers, as well as an Austrian ration coupon, features a prominent meat grinder with whirling blades, surrounded by figurative allusions to chessboards, wheels, and several capital letters, among which the combination W-A-R is distinguishable. The more likely inspiration for her unusual creation—distinct from her other pictorial works in both subject matter and palate—is her pacifist reaction to the beginning of World War I combined with the influence of the Dada artists around her, especially Duchamp and Picabia. This painting is considered the only canvas that manifests Roche's Dadaist aesthetic in the plastic arts, and as such it was included in the most recent Dada retrospective at the Musée Georges Pompidou in 2005.[29]

New York offered endless opportunities and exposed Roche to new personalities. She found the Arensbergs generous and friendly, opening their home to many expatriate artists and writers. Among those artists in New York was Man Ray. Roche recounted in her memoir that she and Gleizes encountered the photographer one day in Washington Square where he proceeded to show a great deal of excitement over what he termed "the most prodigious thing ever discovered." He was, however, so completely incapable of describing it that the couple could not guess what he was referring to. Finally he took them home with him to read the article in question. It was, Roche revealed, on perpetual motion.[30] This discovery could hardly have been a novel concept to Ray, who in 1908 had designed and drawn his own *Perpetual Motion* of rotating wheels and twisting belts.

Roche's poetry of the period is heavily influenced by the people and places she encountered in New York. Two poems from her first New York visit appear in her 1920 collection *Demi Cercle,* a volume that is strong in visual poetry augmented by sound. Roche dates "Chanteurs nègres" ("Negro Singers") and "Down-Town" to 1915, thus identifying them as her first impressions of the metropolis. As such, they record what surprised her most in the city and the stylistic influences under which she wrote at that time. In "Chanteurs nègres" she wrote:

> Their feet draw ellipses
> (exoticism and geometry)
>
> by this movement communicates
> with all of Africa
> with its herds of elephants
> with its black swamps sputtering with mosquitoes
> and its howling sorcerers, their dances, their music,
> and their potions and their tam-tams and their snakes.[31]
>
> Leurs pieds dessinent des ellipses . . .
> (exotisme et géométrie)
>
> par ce mouvement communique
> avec toute l'Afrique,
> avec ses troupeaux d'éléphants,
> avec ses marais noirs crépitants de moustiques
> et ses sorciers hurleurs, leurs danses, leurs musiques,
> et leurs grigris et leurs tam-tams et leurs serpents.

The jazz of black musicians leads the speaker's imagination from the performers before her to a Eurostereotyped fantasy of exotic African culture. The poem begins not with singers, as one would expect from the title, but with the dancing movement of feet tracing geometric shapes. The style of Roche's free verse is made appropriately rhythmic in the poem through end rhymes (communique/Afrique/moustiques/musiques, elephants/serpents) and the alliterative repetition of words and sound combinations: "grisgris," "tam-tams," "avec toute/avec ses/avec ses/et ses/et leurs," and the five "leurs" following "hurleurs," which prolong the echo of the howl. Each emphasized sound element evokes the rhythm of drumming. The singers in the title prove to be wailing sorcerers who evoke for the speaker the dark world of conjurers and charms. Sound and movement converge in this poem, which relays information about the era, class, and race of the speaker through her description of people who for her represent the exotic "other."

With its focus on an entirely different setting, "Down-Town" captures urban movement and sound in a Futurist style. The narrator's perspective shifts almost immediately from a view of the elevated train passing outside the window to an actual or imaged trip through the city, weaving between skyscrapers, then through Little Italy, Chinatown, and Wall Street, where telephones ring all night in empty offices. The effect of the poem is a dizzy ride offering fleeting views of a modern cityscape seen from the south-traveling train. This short, stark poem features flashes of disjointed, shifting images in the form of an El rider's list of neighborhoods. Missing are the layered adjectives of more narrative poems such as "Jardin Public" from one year earlier. Instead, "Down-Town" is direct, unembellished, and one can even say audio- and videographic as it winds its way from the out-of-reach heights of midtown to the audible music of accordions and ringing phones. The abrupt observation of the final line ties the vaults of the banking industry to weapons of war with satirical Dadaist effect.

Outside there is
the elevated,
the dizziness against the grain of the sky-scrapers that turns
above the passers-by,
the Italian quarter with its dark trattorias and its accordions,
the crimes committed in Chinatown
and the opium dens.
Wall Street
offices closed for the night where the telephone
rings uselessly

banks,

The new safes are shaped like naval cannons.[32]

Au dehors il y a
l'elevated,
le vertige à rebours des sky-scrapers qui tourne
au-dessus des passants,
le quartier italien avec ses trattorias sombres et ses accordéons,
les crimes qu'on commet dans la ville chinoise
et les fumeries d'opium.
Wall-Street
les offices fermés pour la nuit où le téléphone

sonne inutilement

les banques,

Les nouveaux coffre-forts sont en forme de canons de marine.

As seen in "Chanteurs nègres" and "Down-Town," Roche's new "American" poetry is devoid of ornament, relying on the essentials of language—nouns and verbs—to capture the sights and sounds of New York. Both these poems find their visual complements in her paintings. The colorful, swirling *Brooklyn* includes evocative and illuminated language, "WILL O' THE WISP" and "CHOP SUEY," superimposed over skyscrapers, while a glowing stage with three performers attracts a male figure to take the journey around and through the city.

Meanwhile, Roche's caricature of *Danseurs de Night-club* poses two tight-waist, pink-clad women between a couple of dancing men in top hats, one in blackface, in front of a pair of four-story apartment buildings. Her husband's canvases of the same period, *Jazz* and *Down Town,* also enhance her already highly pictorial poems and attest to the common influences on the two artists.

At this time Roche was also experimenting with printing techniques and the placement of words in her poetry. "Déjà-Vu" dates from this period. Its text spreads erratically in irregular stanzas across two pages in her *Demi Cercle* collection, forcing the readers' eyes to move from top to bottom to top to right to middle to bottom as they might while viewing dissected figures on a Cubist canvas. This is poetry to be seen, not heard or read for its meaning. It adopts the tricks of commercial advertising, drawing in the eye by its attention to font and print size. At the same time and in contrast to earlier poems commenting on the stimulating excitement of New York, "Déjà-Vu" shows the beginnings of cynicism and disillusionment with the city's commercialism. Poems written by her husband during this period also disparage the omnipresent advertising slogans of New York.

At the same time that Roche and Gleizes were beginning to feel disenchanted by the city at the beginning of 1916, Roche's father was asking her to return to Europe because of the war. She too believed that it would be easier to stay in contact with him and get news of what was happening in France if she were in Spain. At the end of May, she and her husband arrived in Barcelona, where they found a home available to them because Jules Roche was head of the board of directors of a Franco-Hispanic society that owned a spacious apartment, complete with a cook ready to prepare them Catalan feasts. Laurencin and her German husband had already taken refuge in Barcelona, and, although Roche and Gleizes were cautioned not to associate with the so-called traitors, the two couples dined together frequently. By August 1916, Picabia and Buffet had also arrived in the Catalan capital.

In her memoir Roche recounted how the three couples met most days at six under the palms and spent the evenings together. Although she found Picabia and Buffet charming at first, especially appreciating their melodic voices, she nevertheless soon came to see another side of them. Roche claimed she never met a less "sympathique" person than Picabia, that he manifested a certain "aggressivité" that was abhorrent to her. As for "Gaby," Roche found it curious that the sophisticated Gabrielle Buffet dreamed of a house with nothing in it, no furniture, because that way it could be flushed out with a "grand jet d'eau."[33]

This unlikely group of six expatriates was joined by various younger Spanish painters whose names Roche later did not recall, but who eventually formed the basis of the *391* group. War made improbable friends of otherwise quite different personalities when they found themselves refugees linked linguistically or by political allegiance to the same nation. The couples reportedly spent much of their time in casinos and on the beach. Roche appears in a well-known 1916 photograph of celebrities in swimsuits taken at the resort of Tossa de Mar. She is seated on the edge of a beached boat, beside a scantily clad Picabia. She is fully dressed in a long dark skirt, white blouse, jacket, hat, and white ankle boots. She holds a parasol and grins broadly at Picabia's antics. Picabia had reasons for encouraging Roche's participation in his group: it was through her that his first four issues of *391* made the trip to France to reach a new Parisian audience. Her father's contacts made wartime travel possible for her and Gleizes.[34]

Roche also continued to paint and exhibit. She produced her *Ramblas,* depicting Catalan women in colorful and fashionable attire fluttering carefully detailed fans while strolling the boulevard under widely stretched palms. In the autumn of 1916, she and her husband organized an exposition of their works at a known center of avant-garde art, Barcelona's Galerie Dalmau, where Picabia later exhibited a mixture of his new pared-down mechanical style alongside his portraits of *Espagnoles* (Spanish Women). According to Burke, the Roche/Gleizes November 29 to December 12 exposition at Dalmau, denigrated by Picabia, was not successful.[35] Some critics pointed to the hermetic and cerebral aspect of Gleizes's paintings as defects.

Although Roche's poetry remained in the Dada vein, her painting only once wavered from its original "Japanesey" style, in *Nature morte au hachoir.* Dating from Roche's Barcelona period is her more typical *Auto-portrait à l'estampe japonaise* (Self-Portrait with Japanese Print). As in earlier views of herself, she offers the artist's body in profile with her gaze directed over her left shoulder, straight at her viewers. She is dressed in a vivid blue and white diamond-patterned dress with a striking navy bonnet that appears slightly "République française" in styling, with chin strap and floret of red and white. A thin white dog sits alert on her lap. In the upper left corner of the painting hangs a colorful Japanese print of a woman in a domestic setting. She in turn is seated before a painting, this one featuring an oversized potted plant. The layering of the painting within a canvas within a painting produces a *mise-en-abîme* effect that invites the viewer's eye to enter into and through the canvas, but it also serves a pragmatic purpose: it creates the opportunity to portray diverse subjects and styles that demonstrate the versatility of the artist. The self-portrait thus depicts a figure who boldly relays information about herself as a woman and as a painter through saturated color, patriotic costume, self-assured posture, and a variety of pictorial subjects.[36]

In February 1917, the couple returned to New York, where Roche collaborated with Marcel Duchamp and Katherine Dreier on the first exposition of the Society of Independent Artists, which opened on April 10. The event featured more than two thousand exhibits from twelve hundred artists, both American and European, and was modeled on the French Salon des Indépendants, awarding no prizes and open to anyone paying a modest fee. While it is well known that Duchamp entered his now-famous *Fountain* (or urinal), art historians do not record which works Roche exhibited or what became of them. Perhaps they met with the same fate as her mystical *American Picnic* (circa 1915–19), which has been lost. Curiously Roche did not speculate in her memoir on what became of her paintings, nor did she reveal which ones were shown.

Several visually striking poems in *Demi Cercle* date from this second New York period. The best examples of how Roche integrated overheard dialogue, nonlinear typography, and graphic design are the pictorial poems "Brevoort" of 1917 and "N'Existe Pas / Pôle tempéré" ("Does Not Exist / Temperate Pole") of 1919.

"Brevoort," named after a hotel and its café in Washington Square, is composed of overheard conversations, recorded then chopped up and arranged to move the viewer's eye around the page. These typographical signposts, which vary as the conversations change are keys to navigating from one fragment to another, but they additionally slow the reader's movement. The letters *O, Z,* and the *V* of a drinking glass draw in the eye to search for logical correspondences between the phrases that encircle the darkened triangle in the center of the poem. All messages are set in motion around the line held by the triangle: "Voici venir le temps des grandes guerres" ("Here comes the time of the big wars"), attributed to Nietzsche. The startling placement of scattered verses distorts their social, political, and aesthetic contents but reveals more generalized and alarming themes of disorientation, disjunction, and war. The effect is unsettling. Viewers are forced to spy on the faceless, nameless speakers, but detective work frustratingly yields partial information, assertions without explanations, and voices without motivations. It seems as if Roche composed her poem from flashes of conversation on the frankly discussed topics she overheard.

Similar in style and resembling a sign or poster, the untitled poem referred to as "N'Existe Pas" announces its message in indecipherable code, creating a nonlinear, nonnarrative, but hyperrealistic, composite of conversational excerpts, complete with pauses and breaks that replicate the incomplete gathering of information through eavesdropping. The placement of each line slows the act of

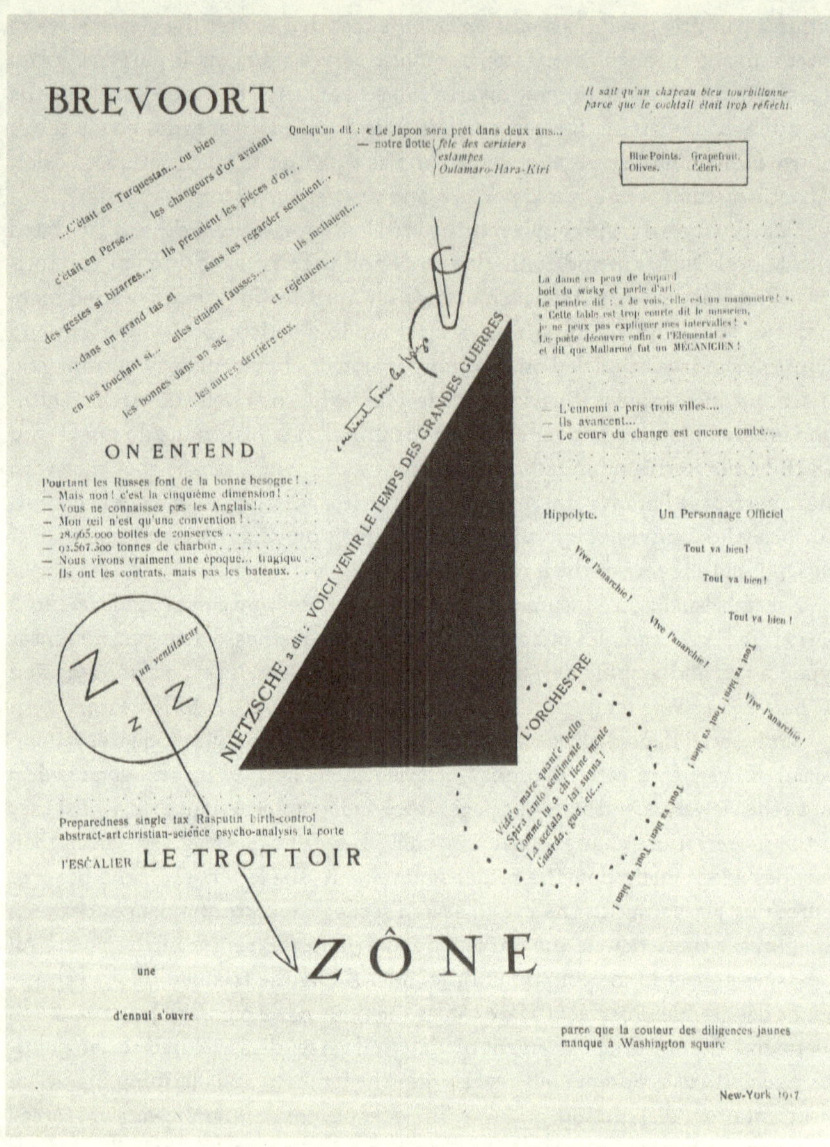

Two pictorial poems in Juliette Roche's 1920 collection *Demi Cercle.* Images courtesy of the Beinecke Rare Book and Manuscript Library © 2012 Artists Rights Society (ARS), New York/ADAGP, Paris.

pyjama toujours bleu

comme certaine difficulté à suivre la conversation

buste de Tolstoï football

l'inconfort des meubles esthétiques

annonce la réminiscence

confesseur athlète

Jiardino Guardi

N'EXISTE PAS

jusqu'à la ressemblance

idéoplastie

PÔLE TEMPÉRÉ

sous un parasol

je ne joue qu'en do

à Saint-Cucufa

J. C.

je ne joue qu'en fa

au Colorado

je ne joue qu'en sol

fa bémol faux

H. P.
R.

M. D.

l'œil slave sucrant la tasse à thé
déblaye les conceptions courage
araignée

matricule 10872-B.

KODAK

Fr. 2.50

la chaleur d'une pipe allumée
et le froid du verre sur la peau

étaient tout un climat

reading. For example, a small font is interspersed with a large one, and horizontal lines are interrupted by verse that runs on the diagonal, in curves, or in the design of a star. Despite the seeming confusion, visual clues urge interpretation: the chessboard with initials "M.D." and "H.P.R." appearing on opposite sides hints at Marcel Duchamp and Henri-Pierre Roché, close friends who collaborated with Beatrice Wood on the *Blindman*, a New York Dada periodical. Meanwhile "J.C.," Jean Crotti, sits across the room. The setting resembles one of the nightly gatherings at the Arensbergs' apartment at 33 West Sixty-seventh Street, where artists, writers, and intellectuals exchanged ideas and birthed movements. Roche had a knack for listening and recording what she heard. This poem also suggests a visual re-creation of the scene with the boldly vertical "KODAK" of her implied camera. Later she practiced similar listening and recording techniques in her fictionalized *Minéralisation of Dudley Craving Mac Adam*. Her writings from this New York period reveal her to be a witness, a chronicler, and a stylistically experimental poet who did not shy away from contemporary political topics such as controversial reactions to the war in Europe.

"N'Existe Pas" was republished in 1921 in *La Vie des Lettres et des Arts* alongside poetry by Aragon, Breton, Eluard, and Picabia—as well as Tzara's "Dada Manifeste sur l'amour faible et l'amour amer" (Dada Manifesto on Weak Love and Bitter Love) and Dermée's "Vernissage au Whiskey Picabia" (Exposition with Picabia Whiskey). Roche's experimental poetry is appropriately integrated into the largely Dadaist issue.

Beyond her somber mechanical painting of a meat grinder and her bold eavesdropping poems, there exists yet another view of Roche as a practicing Dadaist: Picabia supposedly memorialized her in his black, blue, and gold Dadaist *Vertu* (1915), one of his compositions of mechanized anthropomorphism that led to his recurring "theme of sexual mechanics and the parody of love and art," as described in the catalog to the 2003 Paris exposition of his works.[37] Just as his lost *Juliette Gleizes au manomètre* figures as one of his mechanosexual portraits of Dada members, so does *Vertu*. One certainly learns more about Picabia than about Roche from these nonhuman portraits. It is apparent that Picabia was fascinated by the socialite writer and painter. Whether he was admiring or mocking Roche in his portraits of her is immaterial. The fact is that he was preoccupied with her as a subject. Despite his later disagreements with her husband, Picabia made it clear that he regarded Roche as a continuing member of the Dada group, even including her name on a handwritten list of exclusive "Dadas" to be invited to his April 1920 private showing at the Galerie au Sans Pareil in Paris.

Picabia's fascination with Roche was not reciprocated. In New York, Picabia and Buffet lived downstairs from Roche and Gleizes in 1917. In her memoirs, Roche alludes to the loud parties and unhealthy bohemian lifestyle surrounding Picabia. Furthermore, she gives a convincing example of Picabia's annoying pranks when she reports that she generally avoided reading the daily newspapers in 1917 because they were full of bad news of the war, but that her intrusive neighbor would unfailingly arrive at her door, install himself in the living room next to her and read certain paragraphs aloud. Then he would return home to tell Gaby he had depressed Juliette, and so he felt much better![38]

Roche's answer to Picabia's arrogant tributes and the Dadaists' bothersome behavior was the novella à clef *La Minéralisation de Dudley Craving Mac Adam,* the story of an ineffectual poet who wanders a gasoline-stenched, 99°F Manhattan, where "underfoot, the asphalt is melting," and passersby must grab hold of their trapped legs and pull in order to make their way down the street.[39] Mac Adam is a lethargic creature of habit, a man who finds inertia more inviting than making the smallest effort to decide to take a taxi. The title character develops as an amalgam of Cravan, Duchamp, and Arensberg. Another character, Lloyd Willow, who also conjures up Cravan by alluding to his family name (Lloyd) and his uncommon height, identifies himself as a military deserter, swindler, forger, and polygamist.

During his downtown wanderings, Mac Adam's story is interrupted by the inner monologues of an array of characters who amusingly resemble members of the New York Dada group. An unnamed corpulent individual in the basement bar scene bears a striking resemblance to Picabia, "a fat philosopher, slightly Guatemalan, with fingers full of rings."[40] Roche becomes the fictionalized Juliette Granit, with a wordplay on her name "Roche," meaning "rock." Her character welcomes the change of air on the new continent, away from war. For the setting, the author drew on the Arensbergs' apartment and Duchamp's neighboring studio to create Mac Adam's residence, which appears in the third part of the narrative, while the labyrinthine wanderings of the main character echo Roche's description in her memoir of her first (and only) attempt to reach Duchamp's apartment across a fragile passerelle above the rooftops.

Burke has rightly asserted that the novella is Roche's own "manometer" rendering of New York Dada.[41] The author's reference to the mechanical is primarily seen in the means of Mac Adam's death: he is "mineralized," his body emitting the odor of ozone after sucking all night on a piece of copper (mixed with liquor), thus metamorphosing himself into something similar to Picabia's emotionless, automatic, and lifeless constructions. Roche's novella is satiric proof that in her tussle with Picabia and other New York based artists, she got the last word and let the egotistical colony of avant-garde artists know that all along she was watching and recording her observations. Supposedly, only Duchamp appreciated the humor of her satire.

Written in New York in 1918, the hallucinatory and dark narrative was first published in 1922 in number eight of *La Vie des letters et des arts* after Roche's return to France. The text was republished as a separate and ornate booklet in 1924 by Croutzet et Depost of Paris. This second edition features a hand painted cover and one illustration: a collage poem on page 19 that advertises tires, oil, limousines, and "TONIGHT! The greatest war drama ever filmed!" The typographical and collage elements add a rebellious and ironic Dadaist touch.

Perhaps because of its frank insider's critique of the celebrities of the Arensberg group, Roche's otherwise obscure satire enjoyed the attention of a larger audience through a 1964 French multimedia production that included three projectors, spotlights, a pianist, and paintings by Roche. André Benedetto, founder of the Théâtre des Carmes in Avignon, said that he decided to stage Roche's novella in his effort to include many different ideas that would defy the established order. In his presentation of *La Minéralisation de Dudley Craving Mac Adam,* he hoped to bring to the stage the rebellious French artists as they were in New York in 1917, but by choosing to show the avant-garde artists and literary figures through Roche's fictionalized chronicle, he necessarily staged a satire of them.[42]

Although the year 1918 was an artistically productive one for Roche with her work on *La Minéralisation,* her husband's creativity suffered during their quiet year in the suburb of Pelham, New York. Brooke suspects that a nervous breakdown led to Gleizes's religious conversion. According to Roche, it was in August 1918 that "she was tranquilly painting a picture of circus acrobats when Gleizes burst in in a state of great distress and declared: 'A terrible thing has happened to me. I have found God [je retrouve Dieu]. God exists. We cannot do without Him.' According to the story as she told it to Walter Firpo, she pragmatically replied: 'Well, Albert, don't worry. Take a cup of tea and you will soon feel better.'"[43]

Roche and Gleizes reacted differently to New York, the war, and "an intolerable summer with Picabia, who was destroying himself with drugs."[44] Roche struck back with her poetry and her scathing novella, while Gleizes saw his work as "relatively arbitrary, disorganized and melodramatic—indeed even histrionic."[45] Roche again showed herself to be resilient, motivated, and self-reliant.

After trips to Bermuda and Cuba, Roche and Gleizes returned in 1919 to Paris, where Gleizes began to form an artists' union. Jacques Villon gave Gleizes the use of Raymond Duchamp-Villon's studio. Meanwhile, Parisian Dada was beginning to heat up, thanks to the efforts of Picabia, Ribemont-Dessaignes, Breton, Soupault, and Dermée. The final spark needed to ignite the bonfire was Tzara's arrival from Zurich.

Breaking Up with the Dadaists

Although he made no secret of his disdain for Gleizes (whom he accused of impotency[46]), Picabia seems to have been intrigued enough by Roche to include her in his list of Dadaists and in a March 28, 1919 letter to Tzara at Zurich. In the letter Picabia tried to entice his new friend to Paris, while at the same time characteristically providing a caustic description of those who happened to be annoying him at the time. After harshly criticizing Cocteau, Picabia mentioned that Roche was also in Paris, but that she would soon be leaving again for New York where she found life easier.[47]

It is hard to tell if Picabia was using Roche as an enticement to Tzara or if he was criticizing her preference for life in the United States. Why would he even mention her to Tzara, who had certainly not met her before? Perhaps her participation in early Dada activities in New York or her role in bringing *391* to Paris had been revealed to Tzara in a previous communication. Perhaps she was known to Tzara as Picabia's symbolic *manomètre* or through her poetry published in Dada periodicals. In any case, in the fourth and fifth issues of *Dada,* Picabia mentioned that Roche, unlike her husband, was loyal to Dada, grouping her with supporters such as Stieglitz, Buffet, Duchamp, Tzara, Arp, Crotti, and De Zayas.

Although two of her paintings were displayed in the Whitney Museum of American Art's 1996–97 exposition *Making Mischief: Dada Invades New York* and yet another had its debut at the 2005–6 exposition *Dada* at the Centre Georges Pompidou, Roche did not eagerly label herself a Dadaist. Her 1915 still life from the Pompidou exhibit (which also represented Dada collage at Turin's *Galleria Civica d'Arte Moderna* exposition in 2007) includes a conspicuous collage detail and—because of its handle, blades, and wheel—is blatantly a tribute to or a parody of the mechanical-Dada portraits of Picabia or Duchamp. Nevertheless, with the exception of this one painting, Roche, who was surrounded by Cubist and Dada influences, developed her own fanciful style that is more reminiscent of Laurencin's paintings. On the other hand, Roche thoroughly explored Dadaist techniques through her avant-garde poetry as she incorporated variations in typographical layout or simulated collage techniques, along with her own addition: the recording of simulated, overheard dialogue.

Although her cynical portrayal of the New York Dadaists showed Roche's condemnation of their behavior as early as 1918, it was in 1920 that she and her husband officially broke from the Parisian Dada group. This time it was Gleizes's determination that caused the rupture. Roche set the scene by suggesting that "Paris was finding it difficult to recover from the war. In matters of art, all sense of reason and proportion had vanished, and the confusion seemed inextricable."[48] Soon, this perceived lack of "reason and proportion" among Dadaists led Gleizes to attack his former associates.

In his essay "L'Affaire Dada," Gleizes accused the "leaders-dadaistes" of propelling the group into spiritual anarchy. The essay states: "From the point of view of pathology, the case of the Dadaist-leaders is easily graspable. It is their absolute lack of a directing will that dooms them to the spiritual anarchy in which they look for a justification of their individuality."[49] Roche tried to prevent her husband from publicly venting his anger in the periodical *Action,* but to no avail. In true Dada form, Ribemont-Dessaignes and Picabia immediately took up the challenge through Picabia's publication of Ribemont-Dessaignes's Dadaist poem "L'Affaire Gleizes" in the second issue of *Cannibale* (25 May 1920).

It was not only with Dadaists that the couple broke relations. By the time of the 1917 ballet *Parade* (a collaborative performance effort by Cocteau, Satie, and Picasso), Cocteau had already replaced Gleizes with Picasso as his Cubist mentor. The relationship between the Gleizeses and their formerly close friend continued to deteriorate after the war. There are widely different versions of how the final 1920 break came about, whether it was Roche's idea or her husband's, but it seems likely that Gleizes resented Cocteau's frivolous lifestyle, which included bars, nightclubs, alcohol, and drugs. According to Roche's 1945 account: "I had forgiven Albert Gleizes for his brutal rupture with Cocteau after the war of 1914."[50] This statement confirms the interpretation offered by Brooke of the couple's complex relationship: "Juliette felt at home in the Paris café life, and still enjoyed the brilliance and wit of Cocteau's circle. Gleizes, however, insisted that if she did not break off the contact as well, he would leave her. Subsequent accounts by people who knew the Gleizes's well in the 1940s sometimes represent Gleizes as a rather henpecked husband, over-submissive to Mme Gleizes's whims. But it should be remembered that Juliette Roche made an enormous sacrifice when she accepted and agreed to cooperate with her husband's idealism which was to take them ever further away from the intellectual and cultural coteries of Paris in which she had been brought up. Intellectually she accepted and defended Gleizes's arguments but it is doubtful if she ever felt entirely at ease with them."[51]

In this respect, Roche's dilemma resembles that of Hennings, who was also pulled away from the culture she had always known to adopt a life of seclusion in the country where her husband could write his philosophical and religious books. Nonetheless, both women seemed to find ways to grow as artists and writers within the new constraints put upon them. In fact, when involved in less socially taxing activities, they both became more productive, though more conventional, writers.

The Country Life

By 1921 Roche was again exhibiting her paintings, first at the Bourgeois and Mantross galleries and later at the International Exposition of Geneva. Meanwhile, Gleizes was taking on pupils, not for economic reasons, but to promote collective artistic activity. The couple was already financially at ease because of Roche's family money when in 1923 her father died, leaving her a wealthy woman indeed. She owned her apartment in Paris on the Boulevard Lannes, but the couple resided primarily at Serrières, formerly Jules Roche's property in the Ardèche. Gleizes's biographers suggest that he had difficulty coming to terms with the responsibility of immense wealth, and that it weighed on his conscience.

Roche's money, however, made his dreams possible: financial independence from commercial art and the means to establish a community of artists. With the inheritance, the couple purchased the agricultural properties Les Méjades and Archaimbaud near St. Rémy de Provence. In 1927 they rented the Moly Sabata estate on the other side of the Rhône, where Gleizes founded the Ateliers agricoles et artisanaux de Moly-Sabata. There, pupils could gather, according to Roche, "to escape from the normal conditions of modern life and make their living by craftsmanship of one kind and another."[52] But maintaining the property was difficult, according to Anne Dangar, the Australian pottery artist who ran Moly Sabata for many years. Brooke has maintained that Dangar had "reason to complain at Mme Gleizes's aristocratic amusement and aesthetic appreciation of the poverty in which [Dangar] was often obliged to live."[53] A few years after the experiment had begun, Gleizes wrote to his friend and fellow painter, Robert Delaunay, revealing the ideals behind the trial community: "I no longer believe that this society can last, rotten to the marrow as it is with mercantilism, and I believe that we must, as far as one can, turn decisively to what will succeed it . . . ."[54] The artists' collective became the pathway to this spiritual revival.

While her husband painted, met with students, and tried his hand at farming, Roche devoted herself to creative writing and scholarship. Whereas her avant-garde poems frankly relay the topics she heard discussed in New York and her novella satirizes the mischievous and self-destructive group of European artists of which she had been a part, her later work moves in an entirely different direction. Around 1927 she began to produce a body of creative scholarly work that reveals yet another side of this enigmatic woman. Isolated from the raving Dadaists and a hectic social life with friends such as Cocteau, Roche found time to study poets of the past. It is in an erudite text that one finds the true irony of the situation of the female artist and writer in the modernist era: while her own poetry and novella à clef remain out of print and her memoir remains unpublished and inaccessible to the public, Roche was single-handedly responsible for bringing to light the previously obscure writings of an overlooked Huguenot poet, Christophle de Gamon (1575–1621). Gamon's works include *La Semaine, ou la Création du monde* (1609), an epic poem that refutes Du Bartas's 1578 overindulgent epic of the same title. Gamon also left behind a collection of poems on biblical themes.

Besides selecting and resurrecting pieces of Gamon's neglected oeuvre for publication, Roche wrote an insightful, scholarly study of his poetry, published in 1927 as "Christophle de Gamon, honnête homme," which serves as the introduction to *Excerpta* in the collection "Le Rayon du Mandarin" by René-Louis Doyon. The volume was published as number 6 of the first series by La Connaissance, Paris.

Roche's introductory remarks begin by pointing out the unjust neglect suffered by the early Protestant poet and the disservice done by those who had previously commented on his poetry, namely Charles-Augustin Sainte-Beuve and Jean Marc Bernard (whom she called the spiritual son of the mysticonationalist Maurice Barrès). Roche admitted that Gamon was not prolific, colorful, or particularly innovative. He was, on the other hand, an "honnête homme," according to Roche, and that quality influenced his poetry, which is more akin to that of the troubadours and the *chansons de gestes* of the medieval period than to the poetry of his contemporary François de Malherbe.

Roche appreciated Gamon's playful use of sound and his flights of fantasy—exactly what Bernard condemned—in alliteration, puns, and other forms of wordplay. Furthermore she ingeniously compared the architectural surprises of Gamon's poetry with those of the cathedral of Puy. Speaking of the cathedral's ornate décor, Roche poetically described a protruding hand: "In the crux of his heavy palm the sprays of vaulting come to an end. That hand is all that can be seen of a voracious and dangerous walled creature. The shelled paintings in the chapels at Chaise-Dieu, the figures in stained glass and tapestries also tell singular stories."[55] Her visually evocative prose reveals her appreciation of history and legend. She found this same quality of hidden surprises in Gamon's work: "Gamon carries in him this good humor, a little mocking, that good, robust, and jovial sense of the old image makers."[56]

Roche also praised Gamon's ability to capture the terrain of his homeland, les Cévennes, in his poetry: "One rediscovers in his poems the aroma of those large, harsh plateaus, covered with lean cultures and encircled by extinguished volcanoes, to the poor villages, reddened by brutal summers and entrenched all winter under the menace of the 'burles,' but from where one nevertheless feels Provence so near, with the sumptuous dust of its hot towns, with its sleepy sycamores and all its Mediterranean pleasure for living."[57] Her own poetic powers of description are evident in this commentary, while her literary criticism is informed by imagination and good judgment, as evidenced by the claim that the most sensible way to appreciate a writer is to do so in the context of his or her physical surroundings.

Appropriately Roche's poems written in both New York and Bermuda strongly reflect their geographical origins, recreating the sounds, colors, and movements of their diverse locations. The New York poems fittingly employ Dadaist techniques of fragmentation and typography to capture the sights and sounds of the city, while the Bermuda poems transmit the light and color of the island through word choices and emphases.

Her admiration for Gamon also rested upon his ability to create his art discretely and privately during a period of religious threats and butchery that underlined for him the absurdity of man. Comparisons with avant-garde artists' creations during World War I censorship come to mind. While Dadaists were known for encouraging political confrontation and provocation, Gamon chose a different path during his era of violence. Avoiding political and theological debates, Gamon turned to nature, learning the mysteries of the seasons and the virtues of herbs. Roche, in a moment that reveals the intimacy of her imagined kinship with Gamon, suspected him of having quite carefully hidden a few old manuscripts on alchemy. This affection and familiarity echoes in her direct address to her subject: "Christophle de Gamon, you would have been a charming countryside neighbor.[58]

At the end of her study, Roche pointed out a liaison between Gamon's poetry and the philosophy of the East that links to his ancestral lineage. Backed by anthropological studies affirming that Asian tribes settled les Cévennes, she imaginatively evoked facial features of the peasant that suggest a link to East Asia in cheekbones, skin tint, and contour of the eyes, concluding: "In the meditation of Gamon, in his tranquil and polite acceptance of existence, perhaps one can rediscover the sharp smile of some far distant grandfather with bridled eyes."[59] Roche's writing, which was so satirical and biting during the Dada era, had become, under the influence of her rural surroundings, contemplative, laudatory, and optimistic.

Also inspired by admiration for a noteworthy but seldom praised individual, her essay on Charles Henry, the French mathematician and mentor to Post-impressionist Georges Seurat, shows her concern for another overlooked genius after his death. This piece, published in *Cahier de l'étoile* in 1930, paints an intimate portrait of Henry by quoting his words of despair ("The world is a factory of stupidity") and of hope ("Death is nothing more than a physio-chemical phenomenon with no importance: it's only after my death that I will begin to amuse myself seriously").[60]

Roche invited readers into the interiors of Henry's private spaces: his office, his dining room, and finally his hospital room. The intimacy she recreated evokes a tone of respect as her essay relays how this man enriched the lives of those around him: "His spirit was a keyboard of a thousand octaves, containing the most imperceptible intervals and capable of rendering every sound."[61] The essay shows Roche's devotion and motivation to write a personal tribute in honor of her friend. Her appraisal of Henry's life and work is far from a dry biographical sketch; it is a poetic rendering, showing Roche's diversity as a writer.

Again returning to her painting, Roche exhibited with the Musicalist group in 1936 and then in 1938 with the Artistes contemporains at the Petit Palais in Paris. In 1939 her works appeared at the Musée Galliera in Paris with the Cercle Porza, an international group of artists that included Raoul Dufy and Le Corbusier.[62]

During the following years and throughout World War II, the Gleizeses spent most of their time at St. Rémy-de-Provence. They continued to take on projects to help other artists in their careers. Roche and her husband became a source of financial and emotional support for the artist Gaston Chaissac (1910–1964) who suffered from a lifetime of severe depression.

In 1956, the same year in which she was named Officier de la Ligue Internationale du Bien Public, Roche published yet another tribute, this time to her husband who had died three years earlier. The occasion of her writing was the fall

1956 exhibition of Gleizes's works at the Marlborough Gallery in London. She wrote the preface for the catalog in English. More academic and less emotional than her essay on Henry, the preface on Gleizes is succinct but fully informative. It achieves a perfect balance of providing a complete biography of the painter without extraneous detail. More specifically, Roche explained the evolution of Gleizes and his relationship to his art by marking the point at which the painting becomes an object in its own right.

The style of Roche's essay is impersonal. It never mentions Roche or her role in Gleizes's life. There are a few times, however, when one can infer her feelings about what she reported. At one point the essay seems to imply, by her choice of words, her dislike of his "four years of almost monastic seclusion" in the countryside and his success with students and followers when "his home was invaded every day by a horde of visitors, known and unknown."[63] Finally her report of what a friend said to Gleizes reveals, in a round-about way, her own relationship with him: "You are well known . . . and yet you are not known at all. We each of us know one side of you—the painter, the man of action, the writer, the Christian, the thinker. Very few of us know them all."[64] This intimate knowledge of Albert Gleizes was reserved for his life partner, Juliette Roche.

Her calm, respectful, and scholarly assessment of her husband's life and work less than three years after his death demonstrates Roche's quintessentially professional attitude. The preface highlights the importance of his work and refrains from sentimentality. Even though she became for a time a curator of her late husband's memory, as did Hennings after Ball's death and Sonia Delaunay after the death of Robert Delaunay, the focus Roche's writings of 1955 ("Belle journée est passée") and 1974 ("Albert Gleizes et son temps") gradually yields to her personal memoir. The unpublished story of her life and times is augmented by April–August 1977 interviews with Roche conducted by Burke at Les Méjades.[65]

In 1962 Lucien Blanc persuaded Roche to allow him to mount a retrospective of her paintings in Montpellier. For the catalog *Galerie Miroir: Juliette Roche exposition du 15 au 28 décembre 1962*, Henri Gineste presented a one-page text, "Juliette Roche crée une oeuvre remarquable" ("Juliette Roche Creates a Remarkable Work"), and Blanc offered a foreword of eleven pages that includes black and white reproductions of ten of her paintings, an extended biography of Gleizes, and three half-pages of text about Roche and her works. Blanc justified the rather lengthy treatment of her husband by explaining that it is important to put her work in context beside his. Blanc suggested that she gained much from her association with Gleizes, but what did Gleizes take from his relationship with Roche? In his biography of Gleizes, Alibert described the complementary pairing of the couple in their work, though not in their personalities. He further pointed out Gleizes's good fortune to have had a critic and sounding board such as Roche, a most vigilant and exacting censor, who never ceased to astonish.[66] The fact that Roche was herself a painter who provided unswerving emotional and financial support for her husband's work, certainly affected Gleizes and encouraged him to become the artist and thinker he was.

Roche should no longer be obscured by her husband's immense talent as a painter or by his controversial fame among the Dadaists. Taking into account her novella, interviews, poems, and scholarship, there is now a clearer vision of Roche and how she viewed herself as an artist amid the avant-garde circles she frequented. Her image comes forth from behind a curtain of obscurity to reveal the woman now known as an inspiration of Cubist, Dadaist and other portraits, a perceptive eyewitness of New York Dada, a courier of Dada's periodicals from Barcelona to Paris, and a creator and supporter of Dadaist poetry. In all her roles Roche emerges as an intelligent, socially advantaged, well educated, adventurous, devoted, articulate, capable, talented, experimental, and not easily intimidated woman who constructed a lasting self-portrait through her works. She used her writings, as much as her painted self-portraits, to construct images of herself for history's viewing and assessment. What she left behind identifies her as an innovative artist and astute critic: her poems, her novella, her literary criticism, her single Dadaist painting, and her memoir define her as no Picabian *manomètre* can.

Although she did not consider herself an adherent, Roche was nevertheless closely involved with Dadaist activities in New York, Barcelona, and Paris. Her reluctance to join the Dada club may be partly because of her upbringing and studies at the Académie Ranson, or because she was close family friends with Cocteau (who was shunned by the Dadaists), or because of her growing dislike of Picabia, or possibly because of her husband's loyalty to the Cubist adversaries of the Dadaists. But, what most likely kept her from enthusiastically and overtly declaring her allegiance to the Dadaist cause was primarily a question of her own taste, both in painting and in her choice of friends and colleagues. While her poetry and novella confirm her contributions to the Dadaist agenda, most of her paintings remained figurative and Postimpressionist. Her early experiences among key political figures, renowned or notorious artists, and the social elite in France, combined with her wartime interactions with the Dadaists in Paris and New York, exposed Roche to an uncommon mixture of influences that explains her simultaneous involvement with and independence from the avant-garde group.[67]

5. Hannah Höch

Expanding the Dada Network

If one mentions the name Hannah Höch (1889–1978) today, a look of proud recognition spreads across the face of many Berliners. They express a degree of proprietorship over the grande dame of Dada, who spent most of her eighty-nine years in their city. It is clear from the extensive archival holdings and scholarship on Höch that she has received more critical attention than any other woman treated in this study. Art historians have regarded the multitalented Höch as the only female member of Berlin Dada, and some have credited her with having initiated a technique called photomontage with her partner Raoul Hausmann. But she also helped to build key artistic networks beyond the Berlin group through her close relationships with Arp, Kurt Schwitters, Til Brugman, and the van Doesburgs. Furthermore she documented these interactions in her paintings, collages, and writings. These traceable interactions resulted in her remarkable diversity as an artist and established an important cross-pollination of art and literature that extended beyond national and linguistic boundaries.

By 1918 Berlin Dada was already politically militant. Its principle male participants included Richard Huelsenbeck, the *Weltdada* who had returned to Germany in February 1917; John Heartfield, called the *Monteurdada* because of his photomontages; Johannes Baader, the mentally unstable *Oberdada;* George Grosz, the highly political *Marschall Dada* or *Propagandada;* and Raoul Hausmann, the *Dadasoph* or philosopher of the group. Höch, introduced to the group as Hausmann's partner, became known as the *Dadasophin.*

According to Peter Krieger, Berlin Dada was officially baptized on April 12, 1918, in the Berlin Neue Sezession at Kurfurstendamm 238 with a speech from Richard Huelsenbeck, recently returned from the original Dada site in Zürich.[1] A few days later, he published the first German Dada manifesto, an angry rejection of Futurism and Expressionism in favor of three types of poetry: Bruitist, which embraces noise in the machine age; Simultaneist, which favors juxtapositions in pieces read simultaneously; and Static, which promotes the fragmentation and disintegration of the text. Other artists, writers, and publishers joined the group, including Wieland Herzfeld, Franz Jung, Otto Dix, Otto and Adya Van Rees (from Zurich), Serge Charchoune, Walter Mehring, and Carl Boesner.

Firmly established in Berlin, the Dadaists hosted the Ersten International DADA-Fair (First International Dada Fair) on June 5, 1920, in the gallery of Otto Burchard. The vast exhibition of 174 Dada works from Germany, France, the Netherlands, and Switzerland was condemned by the authorities for obscenity, antimilitarism, and subversion. Clearly the first DADA-Fair was a triumph: Dadaists had met their goals to provoke, to rebel, and to introduce new materials to art.

Despite Hausmann's preference for the destruction of all the exhibition pieces at the closing of the fair, most of the Dada artifacts survived. Höch, one of the few avant-garde artists to remain in Germany during World War II, is responsible for having preserved many Dada works during the Nazi years in Berlin, thereby jeopardizing her safety were she to be accused of being a decadent artist or harboring what Joseph Goebbels termed in 1937 "entartete Kunst" (decadent art). Later she reflected on her actions during this period: "I sometimes wonder today how I was courageous or foolish enough to keep so preciously all this incriminating material in my own home during those dreadful years. There was enough concealed . . . to condemn me and all the former Dadaists who were still in Germany. . . . [I could never] bring myself to destroy all these works of my friends—Hausmann and Schwitters—and all my precious souvenirs of the days when we worked together so enthusiastically as a group."[2] Little did Nazi party members realize that in her seemingly innocent flower garden, isolated on the northern fringes of the capital, Höch had reportedly buried her treasures in two teakwood naval chests inside sheet metal. The fact that she took risks to safeguard such a large quantity of Dada materials demonstrates the value that she put on them.

Hannah Höch (the second "h" in her given name was reportedly added by Hausmann to create a palindrome[3]) was born Johanne Höch in Gotha (Thüringen), November 1, 1889, the eldest of five daughters. She learned gardening from her father, a subdirector in an insurance company, and attended the Höhere Töchterschule (school for young ladies) until age fifteen. After a trial year as a bookkeeper in her father's office, she left her comfortable middle-class, small-town existence at age twenty-two to study painting at the Kunstgewerbeschule (School of Applied Arts) in Berlin-Charlottenburg with Harold Bengen in 1912. That same year Höch was exposed to her first dose of the latest avant-garde and antibourgeois art when she attended the Futurist exhibition in the gallery Der Sturm in the German capital. Stimulated by the new trends in art, she traveled to Cologne to see the first Werkbund-Ausstellung (Work Federation Exhibition) by a network of architects, artists, and artisans in 1914. Soon after, Höch's work in applied arts began to show the influence of this modernist commercial and industrial design.

The outbreak of World War I interrupted the young artist's studies. After all the art schools in Berlin closed, Höch served for a short time with the Red Cross in Gotha and then returned to Berlin in 1915 to study drawing under Emil Orlik, a member of the Berlin Secession and a proponent of crafts-oriented art. Shortly after her return to the capital, she entered the Lehranstalt des Berliner Kunstgewerbe-Museums (School of the Museum of Applied Arts), while she began her friendship with the Viennese-born Hausmann, who became her lover and companion for the next seven years.

While an art student in 1915, Höch found work as a pattern designer at the Ullstein Verlag, illustrating magazines such as the popular *Illustrierte* three days a week. She continued to work for Ullstein throughout the Dada years, until 1926. The violence of World War I inevitably affected the course of her studies in Berlin. The State School of the Museum of Applied Arts was transformed into a hospital, and classroom space made way for sickbeds.

Höch's short poem "Krieg" dates from May 1916 and reflects her growing awareness of the casualties of war. Though not recognized as a poet, Höch turned to verse from time to time to record her reactions to events or people. In "Krieg"[4] she movingly and candidly expressed her feelings of outrage toward a hopeless and seemingly endless war, which was inflicting communal grief and pain with the fall of each individual soldier. Höch was able to make the war personal and communal, labeling "our" way as "harrowing and hopeless." The poem shifts from intimate imagery—"our voices / choke with sorrow"; "our eyes whose tears have long since dried up"—to that of mythological dimensions, suggesting an insatiable monster devouring a godforsaken humanity that lies "bleeding to death in grief." The short, stark phrases and syntax, made abrupt by frequent line breaks, reflect the harshness of the message. The poem is brief, spare, and to the point. At the end it declares that there are no more words just as there are no more tears.

The war was not the only disruption to Höch's studies. Hausmann was also a significant distraction. As Heinz Ohff wrote in a 1967 manuscript, "Was fürs Erste nicht erscheinen kann" (What Presently Cannot Fail to Appear): "She worked at Ullstein, ten years, for her bread. In other words, she fed Hausmann, while she was also tyrannized by him. She could only paint in secret during those last years, behind his back, in an attic room in Büsingstraße. When he would reach the 108th step, she could hear him through the door left ajar, abandon her work, and receive him in the studio that she hardly ever used."[5] Ohff has offered a grim picture of Höch's working conditions: she was torn between her precious free time to paint and her appeasement of Hausmann. Although respected by his peers, the arrogant Hausmann was not beloved by them. Still Höch fell in love with him and devoted seven tumultuous years to their problem-ridden relationship, as witnessed by the frequent letters and poems the two exchanged, now available in Cornelia Thater-Schulz's edition of *Hannah Höch: Eine Lebenscollage 1889–1918* (Hannah Höch: A Life's Collage), published in 1989.

Despite the interruptions of the war, her job, and Hausmann's demands, Höch was able to begin producing a body of work during these personally difficult years. In a 1959 interview with Edouard Roditi, she revealed the underlying competition between the two artists when she claimed that until 1916 Hausmann remained a "figurative expressionist," "whereas I had already begun in 1915 to design and paint abstract compositions in the same general tradition as those Kandinsky had first exhibited a couple of years earlier in Munich."[6] It is worth pointing out that some of Höch's earliest collages and photomontages date from 1916, leading Eberhard Roters to insist that Höch expressed herself through collage long before she worked with Hausmann on Dada photomontages. According to Höch's memory (as recorded by Suzanne Pagé[7]), her photomontages sprang from early sources: what began with a childhood collection of comic postcards and collages became a lifelong hobby as evidenced in the *Hannah Höch Album*, published in 2004.

The 114 pages of photographs in the *Album* represent Höch's personal collection of more than 400 photographic images and clearly demonstrate the artist's established habit of assemblage, her eclectic selections, and the suggestive juxtapositions that she most likely employed as a preliminary step toward the creation of collage. The photographs fall into easily identifiable categories: cats, babies and children, African women, dancers, nature (flowers, animals, seascapes, and landscapes), feats of technology (such as bridges), the human body, aerial views of U.S. cities, and portraits of celebrities (such as Josephine Baker and Man Ray's photograph of Nelly van Doesburg).

Höch's preferred version of collage—photomontage—came about as a result of technical advances in the field of photography during World War I. The proliferation of German illustrated newspapers granted artists easy access to photographs for clipping and collecting. In the years after the war, Höch found an inexhaustible quantity of photographs in magazines and daily newspapers and coupled them with her own photographs, drawings, or lithographs, gradually developing elaborate and provocative social satires. In an April 1959 letter to Mehring, Höch maintained that, in her estimation, "collage was born with the Dada

Movement, and it never ceased to hold me. I always believed that one should not only use it for tendentious works or applied art, as the Malik group did, but that it was a form of expression complete in itself and could culminate in purely aesthetic work."[8] Höch must be recognized as instrumental in elevating the production of collage from a craft to a fine art. Earlier artists had incorporated collage elements into their paintings (notably Picasso and Gris), but none relied exclusively on collage or photomontage as the foundation of the work.

Höch's first abstract collage was the 1916 work *Weisse Wolke* (White Clouds), which she produced while working at Ullstein. Although black-and-white photographic reproductions of this work are available, the original is missing, so the texture and layering of the collage work cannot be determined. It is believed to have measured 12.5 × 12 cm and been made from stencils used in woodcut, which she had been studying at the Museum of Applied Arts under Oskar Bangemann. While the angular abstract figures on the left side of the piece suggest an urban scene in stark light with dark contrasts, the right half develops a more organic motif of leaflike prints with less contrast in its shading. Höch's handwritten note on the back of her personal photograph of the work explains that it was the model for an engraving she did for Orlik's class.[9] This simple study incorporates forms adopted from nature, a motif she soon would abandon as she moved either to more abstract or to recognizable but distorted human images under the influence of Dada.

Also dating from this year is her oil-on-linen piece *Der Anfang* (The Beginning). Formed of circles and half circles that emerge from an irregular black-outlined rectangular grid, the piece illustrates an entirely different approach from the *Weisse Wolke,* in which materials are applied to a smooth, inconspicuous surface. In *Der Anfang* the linen surface renders its distinctive texture visible. In addition the oil allows for layering and depth, creating visible brush stokes interspersed with the exposed linen fabric. An oil on canvas, also titled *Der Anfang,* from 1918–20 (30 × 26 cm), is noticeably darker and more angular, showing her progression away from rounded organic forms to sharp-edged shapes reminiscent of the mechanical objects much favored by Dadaists such as Picabia and Duchamp. This oil on canvas *Der Anfang* reflects the avant-garde influences she was beginning to incorporate into her creations. In 1917 she was still producing some watercolor and tempera pieces, mostly as organic abstract forms, and a portrait titled *Kind mit Glas* (Child with Glass); by 1918, however, she had abandoned all organic shapes for mechanical or distorted ones, with and without collage elements.

The Hausmann Years

Around this time Höch came into contact with the Dada group through her work with Hausmann, who moved into her studio at Büsingstrasse 16 despite the fact that he was married and had a ten-year-old daughter. During the early years of their relationship, Höch took part in the first manifestations of Berlin Dada, displaying her photomontages and puppets in 1918 in conjunction with the avant-garde artists of the Club Dada: Huelsenbeck, Hausmann, Grosz, Heartfield, and Baader.

In a November 1975 interview conducted by Pagé, Höch explained the mood of the Berlin artists, describing how before 1919 German artists were corseted in by the war and then with the armistice suddenly felt set free. It was not only the Dadaists who experienced this sense of liberty but also workers, members of the Spartakus movement, antiwar or religious movements, militarists, anarchists, and suffragettes.[10] Out of this turbulent period was born one of Höch's best-known works, her Dada "manifesto," *Schnitt mit dem Küchenmesser durch die letzte weimarer Bierbauchkulturepoche Deutschlands* (Cut with the Kitchen Knife through the Last Weimar Beer-Belly Cultural Epoch of Germany).

Höch took part in the 1919 exposition at the gallery of I. B. Neumann on the Kurfürstendamm, where Huelsenbeck opened with a public Dada manifesto. As far as her level of participation, Höch said she had written *Grotesken* (farcical tales) and read them with Hausmann and Mynona (Salomo Friedlaender), but she did not have any hand in the manifestos, the best-known being the political "Dadaisten gegen Weimar" (Dadaists against Weimar), signed by Baader, Hausmann, Tzara, Grosz, Janco, Huelsenbeck, Arp, Franz Jung, E. Ernst, and A. R. Meyer. Her abstract watercolors and drawings appeared alongside works by Hausmann, Grosz, Baader, and Mehring. Meanwhile Höch was also taking part in Novembergruppe events (1920–23, 1925–26, and 1930–31) with socialist-minded German Expressionists who sought a new unity in arts, crafts, and architecture while bringing artists into closer contact with workers.

Beginning in 1919, Dada periodicals began to appear with regularity in the capital. Höch and Baader collaborated with Hausmann to found his periodical *Der Dada.* Meanwhile Grosz and Jung established *Jederman sein eigner Fußball* (Everyone His Own Football), which was suppressed after the first issue. It featured an obscene poem by Mehring, for which the editor, Wieland Herzfeld, served a five-week jail sentence. *Die Pleite* (Bankruptcy) was forbidden to publish its January 1920 issue because of its antigovernment content. Berlin Dadaists were meeting their provocative objective "to be the disruptive faction in the great international movement in art," according to Huelsenbeck.[11]

Höch's work from 1919 includes carefully designed collages of camera-made images, such as *Bürgerliches Brautpaar (Streit)* (Bourgeois Couple [Quarrel]) and *Da-Dandy,* both illustrating her assembly of distorted shapes and illusionary figures cut from popular magazines and leading to the legendary pieces *Schnitt mit dem Küchenmesser* and *Dada-Rundschau* (Dada Panorama). In these later works Höch reached her full powers of collage construction, integrating reconstructed human figures and disjointed text into a quilt of movement and humorous or satiric commentary on politics, art, and the social status of women. What these works represent for the understanding of Berlin Dada cannot be underestimated.

Their content is at once aggressive and playful, while their engineering is a tour de force of assembled fantastic metamorphoses and jarring juxtapositions, which influenced Hausmann and other Berlin Dadaists at least as much as their experiments influenced Höch's works.

Schnitt mit dem Küchenmesser ranks as one of the strongest examples of Berlin Dada's disgust with German politics, especially its nationalist bent following World War I. While the Club Dada crafted its own satirical condemnations of the Weimar Republic, Höch was composing her critique of government with a new twist: her rebellion against personal oppression. In *Schnitt mit dem Küchenmesser* Höch included embarrassingly manipulated photographs of General Paul von Hindenburg, Kaiser Wilhelm II, President Friedrich Ebert, and Defense Minister Gustav Noske, mixed with images of Karl Marx, Lenin, Karl Liebknecht, and Albert Einstein, alongside Dadaists Heartfield, Grosz, Herzfelde, Baader, Hausmann, and even herself. Höch's title implies that she was using a kitchen knife to slice into the beer belly of modern industrial society and political figures (rather than using it to make dinner), adding another dimension to her photomontage manifesto. Not only does the work critique the usual political and social targets of the Dadaists—from a feminine perspective Höch also included commentary on traditionally female domestic duties, such as preparing food. If the title *Schnitt mit dem Küchenmesser* is to be read as a reference to how these pictures were cut out, there is no denying a suggestion of something sinister and brutal about the newspaper figures being attacked with a kitchen knife. In later works Höch further examined women's roles, questioning notions of domesticity, motherhood, and beauty.

Beside her collage work stands Höch's first *Dada-Montage,* a sculptural assemblage that was exhibited in the 1920 Ersten Internationalen DADA-Messe. This exhibition, organized by Heartfield, Grosz, and Hausmann, featured Dada products from Zurich, Cologne, Paris, Amsterdam, and Berlin. It included Höch's *Schnitt mit dem Küchenmesser, Ali Baba, Mechanisches Brautpaar* (Mechanical Couple, now lost), *Diktatur der Dadaisten* (Dictatorship of Dadaists, now lost), *Dada-Rundschau,* and two Dada Puppen (Dada dolls), as well as works by Ernst, Arp, and Picabia.

Like Hennings and Täuber, Höch created cloth dolls for various Dada events and exhibitions. In her 1975 interview with Pagé, Höch explained that she saw the puppets and dolls as symbols of mankind, lost on the terrestrial globe. Unlike the marionettes made by the Zurich Dada women, however, Höch's dolls were for exhibition rather than for use in theatrical performance. They are still regularly exhibited, most recently as part of the 2006 Dada exposition mounted by the Centre George Pompidou and in the 2007–8 Höch: Aller Anfang Ist DADA! retrospective in Berlin and Basel. Höch's Dada Puppen stand in stark contrast to typical German bisque dolls of the 1920s with their rosy cheeks and lifelike features. Instead of baby dolls with painted eyelashes, pink lips, and elaborate trousseaux, her adult female dolls have bodies made of strips of fabric and board and heads of stuffed cloth topped by untidy yarn hair. Their bulging eyes and high breasts with beaded nipples question the nature of feminine beauty and satirize society's preference for the soft, sweet-looking faces and appealing body shapes seen in commercially produced dolls of the time. Höch's rendering of the female body continues her commentary on the role of women as artists and as subjects of art within the avant-garde.

The state of Höch's relationship with the Club Dada was often influenced by the status of her relationship with Hausmann, especially in the early years of Berlin Dada. Hausmann's mistreatment of Höch, which Ohff referred to, illustrates the lack of respect by some male Dadaists who were initially disinclined to value and welcome women artists. Höch explained: "Most of our male colleagues continued for a long while to look upon us as charming and gifted amateurs, denying us implicitly any real professional status. Hans Arp and Kurt Schwitters, in my experience, were rare examples of the kind of artist who can really treat a woman as a colleague."[12]

Despite the fact that Höch already had a reputation as a successful artist, the Berlin Dadaists somewhat reluctantly admitted her into their "boys' club," so in the beginning she was forced to remain mostly on the margins of the group. Though her work had appeared in a May 1920 exhibition in Chicago called Das Beste der jungen Kunst Deutschlands (The Best of Young German Art), Grosz and Heartfield reportedly did not want her to take part in the June–July 1920 International DADA-Messe. They gave her the condescending pet name "Hannchen" (little Hanna), which annoyed her. The most irritating joke was their inclusion of "Hannchen Höch" in the catalog when her *Schnitt mit dem Küchenmesser* was exhibited. To compound the injury, they changed *Küchenmesser* to *Kuchenmesser* ("kitchen" knife to the less menacing "cake" knife). With her characteristic good humor, Höch tricked the tricksters by cutting out the misspelled label and adding it to her collage.[13] This was not the last time that Höch used her fellow Dadaists' words to critique them.

Beyond playing practical jokes with names, Berlin Dadaists were also known for assigning Dada nicknames to members. Instead of being seen as humiliating or degrading, these labels were worn as badges of membership that demonstrated one's acceptance into the group. Baader christened Höch with the name *Dadasophin,* since she was identified as the female companion of Hausmann, the *Dadasoph.* By this act, the Berlin Dadaists demonstrated their acceptance of Höch into their company, but only, it seems, in relation to Hausmann.

Höch blamed Hausmann when her name was misspelled on the tickets to the February 8, 1921, Vortragsabend held at Kurfürstendamm 232, where she read *Grotesken* with Mynona and Hausmann. Her name is printed as "Hanna Hösch,"[14] and in Hanne Bergius's *Das Lachen Dadas,* the incorrectly printed ticket shows the striking out of the "s," both lightly with a diagonal stroke, then darkly with a vertical stroke. An indecipherable note is scribbled next to the error.[15] One can only imagine Höch's frustration when her name was consistently misspelled or her titles were mockingly altered. The young Höch seems to have exercised incredible patience with the men who tormented her.

As far as her role as the only active female Dadaist in Berlin, Höch later told Pagé that she played a modest part; her works were accepted by the male members, and mere acceptance was sufficient for her. It was only later, she said, that she started to speak up, "in the days of their comradeship."[16] Her later correspondence with the early Dadaists shows the evolution of their relationships through letters exchanged between 1925 and 1958. In the early days of Dada, however, Höch did manage to find subversive ways of speaking up—and speaking about Dada—through her autobiographical pieces, among them her *Haussprüche* (Household Sayings).

Part of her silence and acquiescence around the Dada group was because of her volatile relationship with Hausmann. Karoline Hille's 2000 study, *Hannah Höch und Raoul Hausmann: Eine Berliner Dada-Geschichte* (Hannah Höch and Raoul Hausmann: A Berlin Dada Story), could also be subtitled *Eine Berliner Liebesgeschichte* (A Berlin Love Story). The eight chapters recount the meeting of the two figures, their courtship, their correspondence, their participation in avant-garde activities in Berlin, their disagreements, and their bitter separation. According to Höch, it was with Hausmann that she learned "to plumb the unfathomable depths of philosophical thought,"[17] owing in part to his intense interest in the works of Nietzsche. Höch also credited him with having led her to the Dada group, an action that changed the course of her art and her life. In a 1959 interview, Höch claimed: "Hausmann remains in my eyes the artist who, among the early Berlin Dadaists, was gifted with the greatest fantasy and inventiveness. Poor Raoul was always a restless spirit. He needed constant encouragement in order to carry out his ideas and achieve anything at all lasting. If I hadn't devoted much of my time to looking after him and encouraging him, I might have achieved more myself. Ever since we parted, Hausmann has found it difficult to create or to impose himself as an artist, though he still continued for many years to provide his friends and associates with an inexhaustible source of ideas."[18]

Despite Höch's sympathetic assessment of her former partner, some of her biographers (among them Ute Scheub and Hille) portray Hausmann as an abusive villain for the way he mistreated Höch. Bergius has implied that Hausmann could not part with his wife or Hannah, because he envisioned them as two different and essential kinds of women. His wife, Elfriede Hausmann-Schaeffer, embodied for him the maternal woman, while Höch was the sexually available artist. According to Bergius, "the double-portrait of Hannah Höch and Raoul Hausmann (1920) makes us realize the dominant role of Hausmann and reveals the contradiction between his notion of female emancipation, as he conceived of it . . . and his anarchistic stand that women were not an important subject of history."[19]

The portrait Bergius referred to is Hausmann's watercolor *Doppelporträt Hausmann und Höch,* in which he painted himself as a pensive, pessimistic philosopher, slouching at the breakfast table, his body facing Höch but clearly not engaging with her since his gaze wanders upward. Höch is depicted in a hyperfeminized pose: her body twisted, accenting her thighs, breasts, poised wrist, long neck, and exaggeratedly long eyelashes in coy profile. The colors are warm and applied in patches over a black ink drawing. Previous to this portrait is the couple in Hausmann's *Selbstbildnis mit Hannah Höch* from 1915. The piece, mostly in Cubist blocks of blues and browns with a yellow-faced Höch, has a haunting quality. The female face is alive, flooded with light, eyes open, while the male head floats, rising in the background with closed eyes of perfect detachment. Both paintings depict a disinterested and unreachable man alongside an animated woman. The two paintings define the limitations of his relationship with Höch. He was never completely available to his lover.

Evidently Höch yearned for respect and a more dependable situation that did not include Hausmann's wife, a relationship with "a full man for me—and not a part of a man."[20] Many disputes punctuated their seven-year relationship, some causing Höch to flee Berlin for her family home in Gotha. In the autumn of 1920, she set off with a sister and a girlfriend to walk from Berlin to Rome. The goal was to distance herself physically, mentally, and emotionally from Hausmann and the Dada group.

Adding to the turmoil of their relationship, Höch became pregnant twice and underwent two abortions, one on May 16, 1916, and another on January 18, 1918. A May 1916 letter from Höch to Hausmann reveals her self-doubt while reassuring him of her love. The letter refers ambiguously to his wish and what he wants from her but confesses that she does not feel herself woman enough for him, that she does not have enough passion to satisfy him. She asks for a few days alone. Hausmann's own reflections, dating from December 12, 1920, recount that he shared with Baader that he felt it was entirely his own fault that he did not make clear to Höch his desire for her to give birth to his child. He claimed his guilt, however, in a roundabout way, saying that he should have "bid her to stop" and should have shown her that it "would have been possible" to have the child. He confessed that it was his "lack of clarity and his self-deception about his true desires" that resulted in their children not being born.[21]

Two autobiographically inspired canvases from the 1920s suggest that Höch found a visual way to immortalize her hostile feelings toward Hausmann. The figures of quarreling parents and accusing infants recur in works such as *Frau und Saturn* (Woman and Saturn) of 1922 and *Zwei Köpfe* (Two Heads), created in 1923 and altered in 1926. The fact that Höch kept these two paintings hanging prominently in her art studio as late as 1976 (as evidenced in a photograph by Stefan Moses) suggests how personal and significant they were to her, even fifty years later.

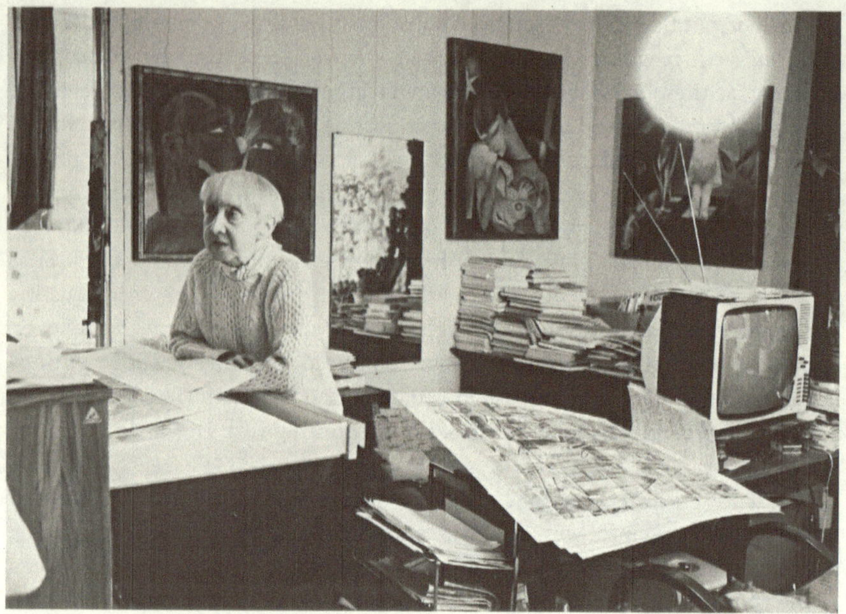

Hannah Höch in her studio, 1976. Photograph by Stefan Moses. Courtesy of the Berlinische Galerie Museum für Moderne Kunst.

Frau und Saturn, is an oil canvas of 86 × 66 cm in size and depicts a close and protective embrace of an infant by a mother who has one breast bared. Although abstract and angular, it is nevertheless clear in detail, especially in the emotion on the woman's face. Her large almond-shaped eyes are gently closed, her full lips rub against the baby's cheek, and her head is bowed over the child while her right arm cradles the naked figure closely to her upper body in a Madonna-and-child pose. There is an amazing likeness between the woman depicted in the painting and the photographs and self-portraits of Höch, above all in the characteristic *Bubikopf* haircut, or bob. Overshadowing the peaceful representation of mother and child is a forbidding, dark, and tense figure: a man with eyes tightly shut and a stubbornly down-turned mouth, a man who faces away from the embracing couple in seeming disapproval. A star near his right ear is labeled "Saturn," and on each side of a block boundary separating the adult figures are the stylized letters *h* and *h,* possibly for Hausmann and Höch. In the Berlinische Galerie Archives of the photographic prints from Höch's personal collection, there can be found two black-and-white reproductions of the painting with her notes. Surprisingly one copy is labeled *Frau und Saturn,* while the other prints of the same painting are labeled *2 Köpfe.* Her choice of an alternate title directly links the painting with another autobiographical piece, *Zwei Köpfe.*

Zwei Köpfe of 1923, previously titled *Imaginäre Brücke* (Imaginary Bridge), shows two futurist-styled heads that resemble the wooden *Dada Köpfe* sculptures produced by Höch and Täuber. These figures, however, are gendered and linked by a baby that rests across the lips of the female figure. In the early version, the infant appears soft and fleshed out as if in a Renaissance painting. In the later version the baby is angular and abstract, a caricature. Its angry gaze is directed accusingly toward the woman. She, in turn, looks levelly at the male figure, who responds with a furrowed brow and an upward, evasive gaze that ignores the infant and mother. Furthermore the male's mouth forms a tunnel that seems ready to aspirate the child from the woman's lips, thus providing a remedy to the threat of a potential family. The painting suggests that it is the male figure who terminates the pregnancy, although the woman stands accused.

Frau und Saturn and both versions of *Zwei Köpfe* can be read as autobiographical texts, revealing Höch's feelings about motherhood, rejection, and the termination of her pregnancies. What she could not resolve in a letter to Hausmann, she could work out through her art. Her message is clear: she resented Hausmann's inaction, while she documented the loss of the (unborn) children who resulted from their sexual relationship.

Later evidence of her loss is apparent in the abundance of photographs of children and infants in Höch's circa 1933 *Album*, suggesting a continued preoccupation with the mother and child theme. After her 1938 marriage and subsequent divorce from businessman and pianist Kurt Matthies (nineteen years her junior), Höch described their relationship with a revealing statement: "I needed a child; he needed a mother."[22] Höch's disappointments with Hausmann's lack of commitment seem to have influenced her life choices for many years.

But there were also positive and long-lasting effects of Höch's problematic relationship with her Dadaist lover. Through Hausmann, Höch gained access to, and developed important and lifelong friendships with, other artists. During their years together, Höch and Hausmann accompanied Kurt and Helma Schwitters to take Dada to Prague in September 1921. In the German press, only the men are announced as "exzentrische Gäste" (eccentric guests), whom Prague rejoices in greeting. But Höch and Kurt Schwitters were the true travel partners, hiking in the countryside together and climbing the Dubitzer Kirchl for a panoramic view of the Elbe. Hannah noted on a scenic postcard that "Helma and Hausmann did not want to go up with us."[23] Finally Höch had found in Schwitters a man with whom she could enjoy a relationship based on true friendship and mutual respect. Their companionship lasted a lifetime.

As Höch distanced herself more and more from the power struggles of the Berlin Dadaists, she was able to move toward her own aesthetic. At the same time she expanded her Dadaist contacts beyond Berlin to include Arp and Schwitters and created the 1922 collage that Ohff has called "das Schlüsselbild der Dada-Bewegung," the key picture of the Dada movement, otherwise known as *Meine*

Haussprüche (My Household Sayings, or Proverbs to Live By). By this time Berlin Dada had seen its zenith, and the Club Dada was winding down: Grosz, a main animator of the Berliners, left the group in 1922, and the remaining German Dadaists joined forces with De Stijl, the Moscow Constructivists, and the Zurich and Paris Dadaists at Weimar in September 1922. In *Meine Haussprüche,* Höch would rescue pieces of the disintegrating movement, preserve them, and interpret them.

The title of the work, *Meine Haussprüche,* appears entirely ironic: the statements are not hers, nor are they household sayings. Instead Höch cited many Dada personalities as well as Nietzsche and Goethe. Armin Schulz has identified four types of "sayings," which Höch recorded in cursive script: 1) Huelsenbeck's proclamations that mention Dada directly; 2) notes on the creation and reception of art quoted from Serner, Hausmann, Baader, Schwitters, and Nietzsche; 3) declarations about life experience and morality from Friedlaender, Huelsenbeck, and Goethe; and 4) statements concerning time from Arp and "Gerturd."[24] Although reminiscent of *L'Oeil cacodylate,* Francis Picabia's autograph painting with collage elements, in that it documents the names and words of artists involved in an avant-garde manifestation in a particular location, *Meine Haussprüche* is a much more refined and crafted piece of art.

Before evaluating the influence of the piece, one should consider whether or not the *Meine Haussprüche* is a mere chronicle of Dada or a critique of the movement. It is possible that the textual collage tells more about Höch than it does about the Dada movement. The piece takes on the role of an autobiographical statement on the artist's personal themes. But what did Höch reveal about herself through her collage choices and assembly and through the citations she chose? How did she show her ownership of the various *Sprüche*? How do the images complement or interpret the "sayings" and vice versa?

Clearly Höch constructed images of time: an actual clock face at the top center becomes the abstraction of a clock in the next image through the evenly distributed points suggesting a circle with a man's arm approximating a clock hand. Then the collage leads a step further toward an abstraction of time at the bottom right as metal ball bearings mirror the clock form in a mechanical symbolic representation. A quotation from Arp, "Ever more time, but no way to show what time it is," is linked with the clock motif, showing the futility of measuring time.

Images seem assembled to invite a diagonal reading. There is a photograph of a stone crucifix anchored near the center of the collage by Huelsenbeck's overlapping text on death: "Death is absolutely a Dada matter." A baby's portrait (labeled "Armin") appears at the top left of the canvas. It seems to be balanced by a photographic self-portrait of the artist (minus the right eye) near the bottom right frame and is accompanied by Nietzsche's *Ecce homo* text on deception. The eye of the viewer, like the eye of a reader, is drawn across and down the collage, from the

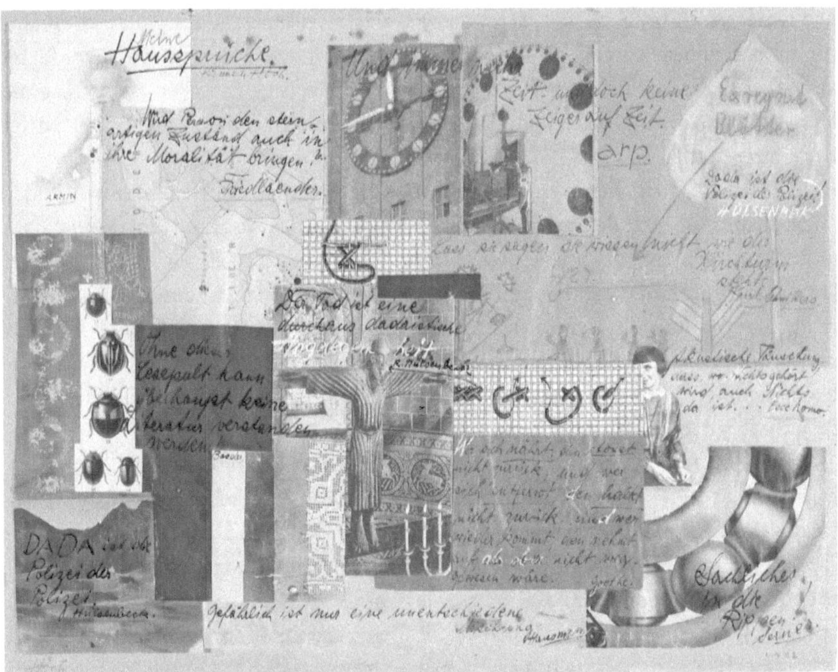

Meine Haussprüche, by Hannah Höch. Courtesy of the Berlinische Galerie Museum für Moderne Kunst.

child to the cross to the artist's photograph. The diagonal line takes the reader through texts on morality, death, and life paths.

Juxtaposed with these human, photographic figures are images of nature: delicately drawn flowers, colorful beetles, a landscape of mountains set behind a valley (resembling photographs she collected in her *Album* or postcards she received from friends), and a large white leaf that forms part of a child's drawing of trees losing their leaves. The banal statement "It's raining leaves," contrasts with a declaration from Huelsenbeck immediately below it: "DADA is the police of the police," which ties the white leaves in the upper right corner to the darkened landscape in the lower left corner by the unprecedented repetition of this *Spruch* in the collage.

Surrounding the central cross and uniting the figures and natural elements are a piece of conventional lace and two cross-stitch pattern instruction grids symbolizing traditionally female artisan handiwork in much the same way as *Schnitt mit dem Küchenmesser* foregrounds feminine work in the use of a kitchen knife to cut and organize the sociopolitical chaos. To complete the universe she has created—of time, nature, art, personal relationships, and religion—there are the zodiac figures of Taurus and Aries, negotiating the space between the baby and the crucifix, or between birth and death. Höch, as a follower of astrological signs, seems to suggest that they can help the viewer choose the correct paths from birth to death.

The fact that Höch employed quotations from many of the well-known Dadaists but did not include any of her own words or those of other female Dadaists is understandable. Berlin Dada was for the most part a male activity, and Höch gave a faithful rendering through the chosen texts of what she might have heard, read, or reproduced in her journals. Nevertheless her composite view—what she did with the "sayings"—reveals a strictly female perspective of 1922 Dada. Her textual choices, collage pieces, and their positioning are finely orchestrated and recontextualized to make a point.

Examination of the work reveals that the artist altered the title appearing in the upper left corner from simply *Haussprüche* to *Meine Haussprüche* with the word "Haussprüche" clearly written in ink and the added possessive adjective "Meine" in pencil. The addition of her signature immediately below the title further implies her ownership of the *Sprüche* as a collection, rather than as individual messages, for which she gives clear credit to each speaker. In the piece as a whole, however, the words belong to her; they are her sayings when they enter into communion with each other and with the images of the collage.

Unlike Picabia who invited a random collection of colorful autographs and comments on the cacodylic eye, Höch appropriated and sublimated the words to her arrangement and thus her interpretation. This borrowing and infusing with new meaning is a statement of her independence within a male-dominated Berlin Dada movement that might have at times during the previous five years of her life effectively silenced her. *Meine Haussprüche* is Höch's self-empowering message to the Dadaists whom she quoted. The work seems to warn them, "I can assemble and arrange you as I please. I can manipulate your words with my choice of juxtaposed images." The male Dadaists' ability to relay meaning is therefore subjected to her will. As Berlin Dada began to lose momentum, it seemed that Höch was finally getting her say, and perhaps the last word. *Meine Haussprüche* is tinged with criticism, like Juliette Roche's critique of the New York Dadaists in her satirical *Minéralisation de Dudley Craving Mac Adam.*

When he described *Meine Haussprüche* as a piece self-reflection during a transition from Höch's Dada to post-Dada phase, Schulz implied that Höch had abandoned Dada. In an interview on May 23, 2000, at the Berlinische Galerie, Ralf Burmeister suggested the same, saying she "went on to other styles." Yet, when asked what she would describe as "the Berlin Dada movement's most original and lasting contribution to modern art," Höch answered that the discovery and development of photomontage defined the movement and that, though she experimented with other styles, she returned in 1928 to photomontage, a Dadaist technique that she "never really abandoned since 1917."[25] Thus, although Höch officially left the Berlin Dada group in 1922, when she ended her relationship with Hausmann, her work and her thought, by her own admission, nonetheless demonstrates a marked Dada influence in the development of her photomontages and paintings. In fact she later remarked that after 1925, when "our Berlin Dadaism . . . ceased to be of much significance as a movement, . . . only [Kurt] Schwitters [and I] continued, for a while, to pursue more or less the same objectives."[26] In addition her enduring friendships and prolific correspondence with others who were intimately involved in Dada events demonstrate a continued interest in and devotion to the propagation of the movement, even beyond Berlin. Finally her courageous preservation of many Dada artifacts during the Nazi years shows that she never abandoned the avant-garde group that she helped to cultivate and spread.

Letters of Love and Friendship

As she became closer to Kurt and Helma Schwitters and formed friendships with Theo and Nelly van Doesburg, Höch moved away from her relationship with Hausmann until they broke all ties in 1922. The correspondence Kurt Schwitters sustained with Höch during this time shows his genuine attachment to his "Liebes Höchlein," "Liebe Hannah," "Liebes Hannahlein," or "Liebes Hannchen Höch," to whom he often sent MERZ collage postcards full of news about his current projects and their common friends. By 1923 Schwitters had begun working in a technique requiring the recycling of the refuse of daily urban life: tram tickets, jar lids, labels, pieces of wood and iron, cardboard, lost buttons, and string. With these elements he constructed *Merzbau*, including a column that grew to be taller than his studio.

Around the same time Höch also became friends with Arp, Täuber, Lucia Moholy, and László Moholy-Nagy. Arp, one of the earlier members of the Zurich Dada group, had illustrated Huelsenbeck's 1917 *Phantastische Gebete* (Fantastic Prayers). Through his work with Huelsenbeck and his acquaintance with Richter, Arp had come into contact with German Dadaists Hausmann, Höch, and Schwitters. Like Höch, Arp was a frequent visitor at the Schwitters' home in Hannover. In August 1923 the Schwitters family, Täuber, Arp, and Höch traveled together to Sellin on the island of Rügen in the Baltic Sea. Afterward Täuber and Arp visited with Höch in Berlin, but Täuber soon had to return to work in Switzerland, and her husband stayed on in Berlin with Höch in her studio at Büsingstrasse. According to Höch, she and Arp became close during this time. In her 1975 interview with Pagé, Höch revealed that Arp fascinated her with his gift for fantasy and his elocution. She described Täuber as a good person whom she first knew as a dancer, but later, Höch said, she found Täuber to be independently gifted in the plastic arts as well.

In March 1924 Arp wrote a card from Heidelberg announcing his plans to come to Berlin and his hope that Höch would again offer him a place to stay. On

December 12, 1925, he playfully wrote to his "liebe haha." Höch subsequently composed a long poem about Arp. A draft version was titled "AN HANS ARP," but the final version became "Hans Arp." One section of the poem portrays him as a true Dada associate:

> He describes his sun-drenched letter paper
> With DADA:
> "the swallow is a good luck bird"
> On the left he is dada
> And on the right dada
> Above and below he is dada
> And it meets in the middle. [27]

> Er beschreibt sein durchsonntes Briefpapier
> Mit DADA:
> "die Schwalbe ist ein glückbringender Vogel"
> Er ist links dada
> Und ist rechts dada
> Er ist oben und unten dada
> Und in der Mitte trifft es sich.

In 1926 Arp wrote to Höch from Paris on a picture postcard of the Pont Alexandre III and the Tour Eiffel, inviting her to come visit him and Täuber in Ascona. He suggestively wrote: "I lust after the flowing lines of your body."[28] On yet another card (from Strasbourg) he thanked Hannah for the publicity she had given his book, and he gave her the address of his studio in Paris. Arp and Höch sustained a lifelong friendship, as evidenced by their continued correspondence. Arp even wrote to the municipal authorities in Berlin on February 14, 1954, suggesting that his friend receive some kind of recognition on her sixty-fifth birthday for her contributions to German culture.[29]

Arp's letters to Höch are at times playful, poetic, and intimate, but some are businesslike and task-oriented. When the van Doesburgs sent Hannah a postcard dated May 25, 1926, inviting her to Paris, Arp teasingly added to the card: "you you you oh come na-naturally 'naked' in my little room." In a letter dated December 4, 1952, Arp wrote more seriously to "Liebe Hanna Höch" about the Dada-Expo in New York and the coming exhibition at the Galerie Maeght in Paris. He asked her to send two of her works and four of Hausmann's photomontages to the Basel Kunstmuseum for the exhibit. He signed it with nostalgia: "I embrace you warmly, in the old True-Dada and send you greetings from there [von Da] to there [zu Da]."[30] The second letter confirms Höch's status as rescuer and curator of the Dadaist works left behind when National Socialism threatened their destruction.

In 1924 Höch accompanied her new friends Nelly and Theo van Doesburg on her first trip to Paris, where she met Dada instigator Tzara and De Stijl cofounder Piet Mondrian. In 1925 she made a second trip to Paris, where she renewed her acquaintance with Tzara. Later he sent her one of his publications. In the French capital, Höch and the van Doesburgs visited artists' studios. The two women got along well. Höch preserved many photographs of her and Nelly on the beach at Belle-Ile, off the Breton coast, where the two posed like twins in 1925. That same year, a photograph taken by Theo at Höch's residence in Berlin-Friedenau captures the women sitting close together, their backs to the light-filled window. The intimacy of the setting, enhanced by the pose and the light, suggests the familiarity of the subjects and their comfort with one another. It was during this time that the van Doesburgs stayed with Höch in Büsingstrasse for two months. Höch was particularly fond of the couple and often acknowledged the meaningful role they played in her life.

She was equally devoted to Schwitters, whom she described as an artist through and through, a man obsessed with art. He published one of her drawings in the first issue of *MERZ* (1923), alongside works by Arp, van Doesburg, Lissitzky, Kasimir Malewitsch, Moholy-Nagy, and Mondrian. The following year, Höch was, as she described it in 1958, "conscripted" to work with her MERZ friend on his (never staged) "Anti-Revue," inspired by their evening at the Berlin Metropol-Theatre's *Halloh die große Revue* (Hello the Big Revue). Her humorous retelling of their middle-of-the-night preparations and before-dawn train ride to Hannover has been printed as "Die Revue: Eine der Reisen mit Kurt Schwitters" (The Revue: One of Trips with Kurt Schwitters).[31] The story reveals his persuasive and impetuous personality and her allegiance to him. Höch recreated the scene as Schwitters awakened her at two in the morning, convinced her to pack everything—including her large Angora cat—and join him in dragging luggage, a typewriter, a package of pictures (of colossal proportions), a portfolio of drawings, packets of publications, and a potted cactus down flights of stairs and across town by streetcar to the Potsdamer train station. The account is comic and full of imagery. Even though it pokes fun at Schwitters for his eccentric behavior, it is nonetheless an endearing portrait of her colleague and friend.

Through Höch's travels and her close lifelong friendships with Arp, Schwitters, and the van Doesburgs, she became one of Dada's most significant networking artists, one who connected members of various points of the avant-garde with each other, thereby helping to facilitate the crosspollination of styles and establish for scholars a traceable line of artistic and literary influence. Her home served as a guesthouse and collection point for artists and writers, as well as for their paintings and publications. Fortunately Höch diligently safeguarded much of the correspondence from these now celebrated members of the European avant-garde, providing a rare glimpse of their ongoing projects, interactions, and aspirations in their own words.

At the invitation of the Schwitters, Höch went to the Netherlands in 1926 to the home of Lajos and Nell d'Ebneth at Kijkduin (near Scheveningen), a meeting place of the international avant-garde in Den Haag. There Höch came into contact with members of the De Stijl group and met the poet Til Brugman, who had been invited by either Schwitters or the van Doesburgs. Höch was impressed by Brugman and estimated that the writer "was friends with half the world, and known by the other half."[32] The women soon formed an inseparable bond and became lovers. From 1926 to 1929 Höch lived with Brugman in Den Haag. There she worked with the art group De Onafhankelijken (The Independents), an association of visual artists, and exhibited with them in 1928 and 1929.

Schwitters easily acknowledged the lesbian relationship between Brugman and Höch, even addressing cards and letters to them as an interchangeable couple: "Fraulein Hannah Brugman und Fraulein Tillit Höch." On one such postcard from 1926, preserved in the Berlinische Galerie Archives, he continued to blend their names in playful ways, addressing them as "Liebe Hannah, liebe Tillet, Liebe Hanlit, liebe Tilhan, Liebe Höchman, liebe Brug." On this same card, Schwitters inscribed in pencil on a view of a church in Oberbärenburg a message to Brugman: "TILIT SEI BRAV" (Tilit be good). In 1927 he wrote again from Norway to "Hannah Brugman and Tilli Hoech" who were living at that time in Berlin-Friedenau.

The van Doesburgs also remained good friends with Höch for many years, traveling and corresponding often with her; however, Theo van Doesburg was less accepting of Höch's involvement with Brugman than was his wife. According to Ohff, "Does" did not object to Hannah's relationship with Til on moral grounds, but he simply did not like Brugman or her poetry. As Theo wrote to J. J. P. Oud, his coeditor of *De Stijl:* "In the Haag there lives a little impetuous one that pretends to be homosexual but she is as feminine as a newborn wet nurse, and its name is Brugman. It makes a daily routine of smearing me with filth, shit, and perfumed spermatozoon. It writes me volumes about crowing chickens and spinning mountains—squabble. Its trashy verses found no place in *De Stijl.*"[33]

As she traveled, Nelly van Doesburg sent cards to Hannah, often signed "Does & Pétro." In a card sent from Hannover on January 20, 1923, Nelly wrote about the couple's most recent Dada accomplishment: "Dear Hanna Höch!—we're having such success with Dada in Holland! Never have the newspapers written so much about something. As a result, we're getting invitations from various cities. Very nice!"[34] From Carnac on July 1, 1925, Nelly wrote to "Liebes Hännchen," lovingly playing with Hannah's name. In a letter from Clamart, August 6, 1925, she kept Höch up to date, describing an evening with Arp, Tzara, Friedrich Kiesler, and others. In a 1925 note written during her train voyage from Rome to Florence, Nelly described to Hannah the couple's meeting with Italian Futurist Marinetti: "we now have a clearer image of Fascism, and Does has written an aggressive manifesto which should appear in the French paper *Vouloir.*"[35] On October 4, 1928, she sent a note from Paris to "Hännchen Höch" at Ligusterstraat 20 Den Haag, c/o

"Tilly Brugman," sending greetings from Does, Dada, and Pétro. As late as 1967 Nelly still sent news, this time from Perpignan, about the Dada-Expo in Spain (where she saw one of Höch's paintings), Gabrielle Picabia-Buffet's poor health, and her frequent visits with Marguerite Arp at Meudon. The letters and cards that Höch preserved from the many years of her friendship with Nelly prove that these two avant-garde women shared an intellectual curiosity about and engagement in art, literature, and world affairs. Their correspondence also attests to a strong emotional devotion.

When Brugman and Höch separated for a short time in 1932 and Til returned to Holland, Nelly wrote a consoling letter to her German friend, offering her help. She added that "Til was so changed by you; she always said that herself."[36] In her letter Nelly lamented the distance that separated them and expressed her wish for sharing a conversation soon. She noted how letters are inadequate substitutes for a tête-à-tête between friends. There was no one in Meudon, she said, to whom she could talk as she did to Hannah. Thirty years later, in a sisterly letter from Meudon, Nelly revisited memories from those earlier Dada years, reminding Höch of "Huelsenbeck-Dada," Hannah's trip with Kurt and Helma Schwitters, Lissitsky, De Stijl, and Tzara.

It is easy to envision how Höch's extensive correspondence with Schwitters, the van Doesburgs, Arp, and other artists caused her to serve at times as a central switchboard through which information and support flowed. The van Doesburgs were her link to the Parisian art world, the exhibitions there, the painters, and modernist ideas. She was their link to Berlin, and through Schwitters, to Hannover. It was not uncommon for her to receive a packet of printed materials from Theo in Paris, who would ask her to send a hundred copies to Schwitters or to Moholy (as in a letter of January 26, 1925). The van Doesburgs sent her an issue of Picabia's *391* in 1924. They reported that they had already seen Tzara's tragedy *Mouchoir de nuages* (Handkerchief of Clouds) twice and that they were planning on seeing it again.

With some errors in his French spelling, Theo wrote on December 13, 1924: "In Paris it's still lively. Picabia's 'Relache' in the Théatre des Champs Elysses is refreshing. You would like it! When are you coming back to Paris? The latest movement is 'Le mouvement accéléré,' and all the Dadaists have joined. I will send you the flyer."[37] From the content of their frequently exchanged letters, it is clear that Höch's correspondents were all closely involved with the Parisian Dada scene. While keeping each other current on international manifestations of the avant-garde, the correspondence serves as a record of impressions of new encounters with Dada events. The friends felt such a comfortable level of mutual trust that they were able to be candid in revealing their reflections, and so their words are all the more valuable.

Although Höch saved volumes of letters from her friends, her archives hold few copies of her own letters. There is, however, one ingeniously creative example of her writing, a letter/poem she wrote to Schwitters, dated June 1923. Her unorthodox style, shown by sentence fragments, nonsense words, indentations, and onomatopoeic word choices, illustrates her adoption of certain playful Dada characteristics that were the basis of the sound poems performed in Zurich's Cabaret Voltaire. A brief excerpt demonstrates her form and attitude with its repetitions of nonsensical sound words, such as variations on *zwitschern* (to twitter or chirp), *lausen* (to delouse), and *aasen* (to be wasteful):

> Dear Merz—I
> What's going on? Why don't I hear your forget-me-not-colored Merz organ on all the gramophones of the world
> zwitsch
> zwitsch
> zwiwitsch
> lauseaaasen?[38]

The entire letter/poem reveals Höch's Dada spirit and her literary imagination as she recorded non sequitur messages and observations, interspersed with references to her contemporaries (Arp, Paul Klee, Wassily Kandinsky, Mynona, and Helma Schwitters) and to "the immortals" (Richard Wagner, Leonardo da Vinci, Leo Tolstoy, and a poet from Weimar [Goethe] whose name she pretended to have forgotten).

Surprisingly, among the many surviving letters and postcards, there are none between Til and Hannah. Perhaps the women spent so little time apart that there was no need for them to communicate by letter. Still there were certainly reasons and opportunities to exchange correspondence. It is possible that Höch's heirs have kept such letters from public view in an effort to ignore or forget the artist's nine years with Brugman. Although society is probably more open-minded and tolerant toward Höch's lesbian relationship now than it was in 1978, when her papers would have become property of her beneficiaries, still there is the question of whether any intimate correspondence has survived these last thirty-nine years. Based on Höch's inclination to preserve letters from those dear to her, there is a good chance she saved some from Brugman.[39]

The Brugman Years

Although Höch's years with Til Brugman were significant to her life and her art, there is less primary documentation of their relationship than researchers would wish. Fortunately in 1988 the Dutch periodical *Lust & Gratie* (Desire & Grace) daringly printed a poem that Brugman wrote to Höch in 1936. Information about the personality or lifestyle of this influential Dutch poet can shed light on Höch, her post-1926 work, and her continued networking with other artists.

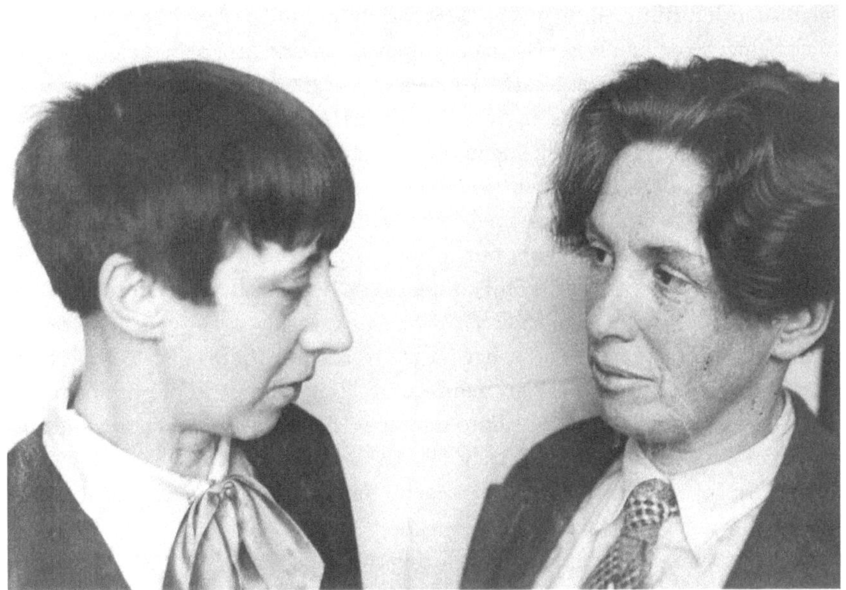

Hannah Höch and Til Brugman, 1931. Unknown photographer. Courtesy of the Berlinische Galerie Museum für Moderne Kunst.

Til Brugmann was born Mathilde Maria Petronella Brugman on September 16, 1888, in Amsterdam and died in Gouda on July 24, 1958. She was the eldest of nine children in a Catholic family. Around 1908 she met Mondrian, and between 1911 and 1917 she lived on her own in Amsterdam after a dispute with her family. Brugman worked as a business correspondent in French, English, and German.

In 1917 she moved to Den Haag with concert singer Sienna Masthoff, and between 1917 and 1929 she traveled to Paris and London, where she studied Greek, Latin, Russian, and possibly Japanese. She is said to have been a gifted linguist. Ohff mentioned that she probably mastered twenty languages, including Malaysian.[40]

From 1917 to 1922 Brugman wrote a series of *Lautgedichte* (sound poems), publishing one titled "R" in the sixth issue of *De Stijl* (May/June 1923) and another, titled "Weg," in the Dadaist periodical *MERZ* (October 1923). Her work was also published in France. Because of her relationship with Schwitters through Höch, she undertook to translate his periodical *MERZ* into Dutch.

In 1926, when she met Höch, Brugman ended her relationship with Masthoff. Soon afterward, Höch moved to Ligusterstraat in Den Haag to live with Brugman, whose home was decorated by Hungarian-born De Stijl painter and designer Vilmos Huszár (who contributed his *Dancing Mechanical Doll* to 1920s Dada events), with furniture designed by De Stijl architect and designer Gerrit Rietveld. Höch helped Brugman in her German compositions, and Brugman introduced her new partner to Dutch avant-garde artists and designers. The couple also traveled extensively for four months, to Antwerp, Gotha, Milan, Verona, Lago Maggiore, Holland, and Paris, before settling in Berlin in 1929.

Not only did the sojourn in Holland offer Höch the stability of a close and devoted intimacy with a fellow modernist, a kind of partnership she had sought unsuccessfully with Hausmann, but it opened new doors to architectural, geometric, Constructivist, and De Stijl influences on her art, allowing her to diversify as an artist. Höch's first solo exhibition was in 1929 at the avant-garde Galerie De Bron in Den Haag. Shortly after her return to Berlin with Brugman, Höch took part in the Internationalen Werkbund-Ausstellung Film und Foto in Stuttgart, where she exhibited her latest photomontages. Between 1930 and 1932 she and Brugman traveled extensively in Italy, France, Switzerland, Norway, Belgium, and Austria. In 1932 Höch's work was to be exhibited in a solo show in Bauhaus Dessau, but the new National Socialist government prevented the opening. Her work, however, was often exhibited abroad during the Nazi years.

In 1933 Höch provided the illustrations for Brugman's "Von Hollands Blumenfelder," which appeared in volume 5 of *Atlantis: Länder/Reisen/Völker.* This publication serves as but one example of the collaborative work of these two modernists. The women benefited intellectually, artistically, and emotionally from their liaison. In one rare instance, Höch wrote of her relationship with Brugman: "Til Brugman was an Eulenspiegel of our days who did not play her tricks in public, but took one's breath away day and night with her witty jokes. These never-ending, somersaulting, sarcastic, crazy attacks that 'danced' upon a profound intelligence, made the years with Til the most amusing of my life."[41]

In Berlin Brugman wrote *Grotesken,* which was published in 1935. That same year Höch's drawings illustrated Brugman's first German publication, *Scheingehacktes* (Chopped Light), a collection of poems. The cover of this volume, a pen-and-ink drawing of a cow eating dandelions while weeping, could possibly hold the key to the purpose of one of Höch's more controversial projects: her 1933 "album" or scrapbook, as Maud Lavin named it in her *Cut with the Kitchen Knife: The Weimar Photomontages of Hannah Höch.* According to Gunda Luyken, editor of the published version, *Hannah Höch Album,* the full-page photograph of a cow in the album is directly linked to the drawing on the cover of *Scheingehacktes.*[42] Close inspection of the original photograph in the Berlinische Galerie Archives reveals a pencil outline on the cow's snout and right eye that Höch borrowed from the photograph and highlighted in her final sketch. In this case an image in Höch's scrapbook metamorphosed into one of her drawings.

Brugman and Höch separated in 1936, and it is likely that the Brugman wrote the French poem "tu ne m'a rien laissé" (you've left me nothing) on May 4, the day she left Höch's home:

one night
you took back
little by little

your hands
that caressed me
and that I loved so much . . .

your breasts
that you offered me
as loving mother . . .

your feet
always ready to do something
to take better care of me . . .

your thighs
delicious, elongated basin
that I lasciviously adored . . .

your temples
innocently unwrinkled
that I religiously respected . . .

your eyes
that often scrutinized me
and whose tenderness made me cry . . .

your arms
that fervently embraced me
silent promise to never leave me

your armpits
painfully folded
from my cruel kisses . . .

your mouth
mixing laughter and caress
that day closed to my distress . . .

the perfume of your body
that nervously excited me
and that I must inhale to live . . .

the nicknames
that you found for me
that I must whisper to myself at night . . .

your heart
enclosing me with infinite tenderness
that cannot leave without tearing me apart

your dear face
covered with my kisses
that this day you turn away

one night
little by little
you withdrew everything

but agonizing pain you left me
come, come save me!!!!![43]

une nuit
tu repris
petit à petit

tes mains
qui m'ont caressée
et que j'ai tant aimées . . .

tes seins
que tu m'as offerts
en amoureuse mère . . .

tes pieds
toujours prêts à s'engager
pour me mieux soigner . . .

tes cuisses
délicieuse vasque allongée
que j'ai lascivement adorée . . .

tes tempes
innocemment non-ridées
que j'ai réligieusement respectées . . .

tes yeux
qui m'ont souvent scrutiné
et dont la tendresse m'a fait pleurer . . .

tes bras
qui m'ont fervemment embrassé
promesse silencieuse de ne jamais me quitter

tes aisselles
douloureusement pliées
de mes cruels baisers . . .

ta bouche
mêlant rire et caresse
ce jour close à ma détresse . . .

ton parfum de corps
qui m'a nerveusement excité
et qu'il me faut pour vivre inhaler . . .

les petits noms
que tu m'as trouvés
que je dois tout bas la nuit me répéter . . .

ton coeur
infiniment tendre à m'enfermer
qui ne peut s'éloigner sans me déchirer . . .

ton cher visage
couvert de mes baisers
que ce jour tu tournes à côté . . .

une nuit
petit à petit
tu as tout repris

mais une douleur d'agonie tu m'as laissée
viens, viens me sauver!!!!!

Intimacy, regret, and emotional devastation permeate the poem. It reads like a note left behind after a quarrel in which things were left unsaid. It is also a strong appeal to a lover who has the power to save the writer from the misery she has caused by the withdrawal of her intoxicating body. The most curious thing about the poem, however, is not its content—which is predictable considering the circumstances—but rather the poet's choice of language. Brugman wrote her poem to Höch in French, not the native tongue of either woman. Based on what little remains of their correspondence, it cannot be claimed that they chose French as their lingua franca; in fact, it is questionable whether Höch had a strong command of the language. There is no evidence of her writing in any language but German. One wonders if Brugman intended Höch to be the designated recipient of the poem. It is entirely possible that she wrote about her pain only for herself and did not write directly to her lover.

In 1939, at the outbreak of war, Brugman finally left Berlin to return to Holland, where she lived and worked with Hans Mertineit-Schnabel until her death in Gouda of a debilitating nerve disease in 1958. During her lifetime she published two novels, four children's books, two novellas, and a cultural study on cats. She won the prestigious Manianne-Philips-Prijs in 1952.

The Grande Dame of Dada

In 1935 Höch met Kurt Matthies, whom she married on September 16, 1938 (Brugman's fiftieth birthday). Höch and Matthies lived together in her small house in Berlin-Heiligensee (An der Wildbahn 33), until their marriage broke up in 1942, after he began a relationship with Nell d'Ebneth (at whose home Höch had met Brugman in 1926). Höch continued to live in the cottage, blocks from the Nieder Neuendorfer Lake, during and after the difficult war years.

In postwar Germany Höch reemerged through her art. She took part in the 1948 Dada-Retrospective at the Museum of Modern Art in New York, and the 1958 Düsseldorf exhibition, which decidedly established Dada as a movement of historical significance. In his 1966 London exhibition catalog, Will Grohmann described Höch as "still working with the same élan as in the years after the first world war. Although her basic concepts and perceptions date from this period she still affirms the value of the ever changing present and in her work is able to come to terms with it. Her work is not tied to the ideas of her group of friends, which has long since broken up. For her Dada was a school, a better one than an academy, where she was both pupil and teacher, where she learnt, not simply how to do things, but, more important, to formulate standards and to keep to them."[44] Grohmann pointed out Höch's underlying Dada roots, both thematic and stylistic, in her later works. More surprisingly he credited the Dada years for establishing her strong work ethic.

Höch remained an innovative and active artist until her death in Berlin in 1978. Her legacy is found in her extant paintings and photomontages, as well as in her correspondence. Her creative vision and innovation in photomontage alone is enough to guarantee her renown as a significant member of the twentieth-century avant-garde. Her choices and methods of assembling various images and words, taken meticulously from their original context in newspapers, magazines, or other printed materials, do more than shock or provoke viewers. In each case Höch crafted a not-yet-imagined universe that, by its careful composition, immediately relays a message in a way that a manifesto, literary text, or stage performance cannot.

A written text relies on the receiver's attention over time to gather and process information linearly; at any moment during exposure to the material, the reader or spectator can lose interest or be drawn away before reaching understanding or constructing meaning. A photomontage piece, on the other hand, is experienced differently. It takes advantage of the eye's ability to pan and zoom. The immediacy of the photomontage—the collected and meaningfully placed figures and words in an overall visual experience—has the advantage of reaching its audience quickly to shape a first reaction. It has a general appeal in its quickly glimpsed totality that can lead the viewer to approach and examine specific intriguing elements individually. In this manner the photomontage holds and communicates with its audience in a nonsequential way, unlike a written or performed text.

Höch preferred such a direct visual communication with her viewers, even though she experimented with poetry and storytelling. She interacted with Dadaists through visual arts (painting, puppet making, photomontage, montage/sculpture, collage, and drawing), through poetry, and, to a lesser degree, through Dada performance. In this Höch resembled other Dadaists, who routinely tried their hand at various art forms. Above all she pledged her loyalty and friendship to an expansive and divergent group of international Dada artists, and thereby facilitated their interactions. In these many ways, she cultivated the avant-garde movement during its early years in Berlin and, through her protective harboring of Dadaist works during the 1930s and beyond, she furthered its survival.

6. The Woman Dadaist

The Advantages of Being a Female Dadaist

In the mid-1980s an anonymous group of women artists who professed to serve as the "conscience of the art world" began posting messages in Manhattan's Soho district. The posters of these "Guerrilla Girls" protested sexism and racism in New York galleries and museums. One such poster from 1988, provided as "a public service message," included a list of "The Advantages of Being a Woman Artist," which is applicable to female artists and writers of most eras:

> Working without the pressure of success.
> Not having to be in shows with men.
> Having an escape from the art world in your 4 free-lance jobs.
> Knowing your career might pick up after you're eighty.
> Being reassured that whatever kind of art you make it will be labeled feminine.
> Not being stuck in a tenured teaching position.
> Seeing your ideas live on in the work of others.
> Having the opportunity to choose between career and motherhood.
> Not having to choke on those big cigars or paint in Italian suits.
> Having more time to work after your mate dumps you for someone younger.
> Being included in revised versions of art history.

Not having to undergo the embarrassment of being called a genius.
Getting your picture in the art magazines wearing a gorilla suit.[1]

Although items on this list seem to be specific to the cause of women artists in New York in the 1980s, on further inspection they can be applied to the women of the European avant-garde and Dada quite easily. For example most of the female Dadaists were not "burdened" with the level of success that their male counterparts enjoyed during their lifetimes. Picabia's celebrity greatly outweighed that of his wife (Buffet) and that of his mistress (Everling). Similarly Arp's name and works are more readily recognized than those of his wife (Täuber). For many years Ball was credited with founding Dada with the help of Tzara and Huelsenbeck, but there is no refuting the evidence of Hennings's initial and continued contributions to the movement's Zurich birth and success.

The reasons for this discrepancy in standing have much to do with other items suggested by the list, namely choosing between career and motherhood; having less access to financial or domestic support, and thus fewer opportunities or less free time to create prolifically; and being labeled an outsider or marginalized contributor, resulting in being less published in male-edited journals, less exhibited in male-dominated shows, or even having one's ideas co-opted and accredited to other, better known (male) artists. Additionally the either passive-aggressive or merely careless misspellings of several female artists' or writers' names by publications and galleries represent a dismissive attitude toward women who dare to be creative.

Now that Dada has become a part of art and literary history and most of its male members are well-known, accepted, or even canonized (such as Picabia, Tzara, Breton, Arp, and Duchamp), it is time to break open the canon and fully include those who live along the boundaries. There, barely seen and hardly heard, reside the marginalized participants who actively contributed to this manifestation of the avant-garde. In the cases of the few women considered so far, it has been shown that they serve as significant and indisputable sources for understanding Dada. More women remain to be studied.

What Was Dada?

Now that readers have heard directly from some female artists and writers who left behind significant texts on Dada (Hennings, Buffet, Everling, Arnauld, Roche, and Höch), one can begin to realize a fuller story of what is in actuality a dual-gendered expression of the avant-garde. The voices of these articulate women in memoirs, poetry, letters, fiction, mixed-media art, and essays substantiate the claim that they were indeed influential women leaving behind written evidence of their roles in the formation and dissemination of Dada in Europe. Despite societal obstacles and frustrations because of their sex, they managed nonetheless to produce works of visual and literary art that display their talent and prove their interaction with the male members of the movement.

As a result of meeting and listening to the testimonies of these women, previously held conceptions of Dada are challenged. The definition of Dada and the trajectory of the movement have expanded. Zurich Dada was neither a whimsical pastime during the war nor a calculated and structured school with rules and a ringleader. It was instead an all-consuming project by which an itinerant performance artist could find the lifesaving means of releasing her talents in music, dance, and writing, as in the case of Hennings. Dada was not an isolated accident of the early twentieth century, but a necessary and unavoidable response in the development of that century's progression of modernisms, as documented by the insightful analyses of Buffet. Dada was not an inconsequential and unrelated phase of the avant-garde that was carried out by nameless and faceless actors. It was a well-integrated explosion of energy that linked previous artistic and literary articulations with those that followed and was peopled by a wide range of individual personalities and talents, as recorded by Everling. Dada produced more than nihilistic verses attacking the status quo. It also generated poetry rich in imagery and evocative language, when written by Arnauld, or typographically innovative poems that ingeniously record the spirit of the times, when composed by Roche. Dada was not static, hermetic, or solidified in one place with a hierarchical supporting structure. Instead it traveled without restriction from one culture to another, its influence carried by friends and lovers across national and linguistic boundaries, as seen in the case of Höch.

Who Was Dada?

Although it is immensely beneficial to study the cases of these six women who left behind written testimonies about their participation in and impact on Dada, the importance of women's contributions to Dada can be enhanced by noticing connections to some of the other avant-garde women from the original list.[2] Though these women often did not record their perceptions of Dada and its participants in published words, they documented their interaction with the avant-garde through their dance, paintings, sculpture, textile work, and music, or through their support of Dada via salons or publications. Because of their interrelationships, their transnational networking, and their adherence to the goals of Dada, their artistic production helped further the spread of this controversial manifestation of the avant-garde from Zurich and New York to significant sites in Germany, the Netherlands, Paris, southern France, Rome, and Czechoslovakia.

Where Was Dada?

Zurich Dada is defined by its international scope, its pacifist stance, and its spontaneous and experimental performance-oriented products. Among the women who were influential in Zurich Dada soirees, was the audacious cabaret singer

Maria Kirndörfer, better known as Marietta di Monaco (1893–1981). Like Hennings, she began her career in Munich at the Café Simplicissimus. In February 1915 she immigrated to Zurich, where she met Christian Schad, for whom she modeled, and Walter Serner, who became her partner. Like Hennings, Kirndörfer performed in the Cabaret Voltaire, joining Tzara, Janco, and Hennings, in Ball's May 31, 1916, "Simultan Krippenspiel" (Simultaneous Nativity Play). Her 1962 *Ich kam—ich geh; Reisebilder, Erinnerungen, Porträts* (I Came—I Went: Travel Pictures, Memories, Portraits) describes the bohemian and Dada atmosphere of 1913–20 Zurich, emphasizing her involvement in the avant-garde events. She also included a poem, "Emmy Hennings," about the singer's release from prison and their subsequent participation in cabaret performances, saying: "Nachts tanzten wir. // Jemand spielte Flöte" (At night we danced. // Someone played flute).[3] In her "Entstehung des Dadaismus" (Origins of Dadaism), Kirndörfer narrated the story of how she, Ball, and Hennings found, cleaned, and opened the Cabaret Voltaire.[4]

Another friend from the Munich bohemian days, the literary scholar Käthe Brodnitz (Käthe Brodnitz-Fröhlich, 1884–1971), was performing alongside Hennings and Ball in Zurich's Modernen Autoren-Abend and Abend deutscher Autoren events in 1915 and 1916. In 1914 she had written the academic study "Die futuristische Geistesrichtung in Deutschland" (The Futurist Direction of the Spirit in Germany), but she went beyond a mere outsider's analysis of the period when she decided to give financial backing to Dada projects early in the movement's history. According to Raimund Meyer's chronology of events in *Dada in Zürich*, Brodnitz was responsible for the monetary support that led to the opening of the Künstlerkneipe Voltaire on February 5, 1916.

Also in the Cabaret Voltaire were the members of the Laban dance group: Mary Wigman, Maya Chrusecz, Suzanne Perrottet, Jeanne Rigaud, Käthe Wulf, and Claire Walter, who were often joined by Täuber and Hennings. Their contributions via dance were vital to the performance orientation of Zurich Dada, which professed its version of the avant-garde by means of provocative stage productions. Drumming accompanied by bold dance movements highlighted many Dada soirees.

Born in Hanover in 1886, Mary Wigman (born Marie Wiegmann) began dance studies in Geneva under Jacques Dalcroze. Her friendship with the Expressionist painter Emil Nolde led to her 1913 enrollment in a summer course in dance given by Rudolf von Laban at Lago Maggiore, Switzerland.

Wigman served as Laban's assistant in Munich and Zurich between 1913 and 1919. She applied his concepts (reveal what is hidden in your being) to her original choreography: *Dance of the Sorceress* (1914), and *Dance of the Dead* (1917). During this time she became acquainted with activities of the Zurich Dadaists and took part in some of their evening cabarets with Perrottet and other dancers of the Laban School. Most of the dancing was accompanied by rhythmic drumming. Influenced by the Laban method as practiced by Wigman, Dadaists Hennings and

Täuber danced in these productions, often in cardboard costumes of their own design or wearing Marcel Janco's masks.

Wigman's most important contribution to dance was the liberation of expression from the strict academic codes of her time, specifically freeing dance movement from the confining influence of musical support. Wigman preferred to work with silences interspersed with percussion. This particular style of dance found its roots in the spontaneous movements by Laban dancers during the early years of Dada cabaret in Zurich, as documented by Tzara in his "Zurich Chronicle 1915–1919."[5]

Dancing alongside Wigman in Zurich was Maya Chrusecz. Born in Germany in 1890 as Maria Josefa Deodata, Chrusecz studied at the Laban Dance School in Zürich. In 1917 she met Tzara, who by July 1920 was sharing her address at Seefeldstrasse 106 in Zurich. During her five-year relationship with the Romanian Dadaist, they also lived in Paris and traveled to Tarrenz bei Imst in the Tyrol to join Max Ernst and Luise Straus-Ernst. Immediately following his marriage to Simone Kahn, Breton (on his honeymoon in Austria) met up with the group, which also included Arp and Täuber. During their holiday in the Tyrol in 1921, Ernst, Tzara, and Arp decided to collaborate on a publication that they named *Dada au grand air* (Dada Outdoors), which Chrusecz humorously called "Der Sängerkrieg in Tirol" (The Battle of the Voices [Singers] in Tyrol). Little is known about her later life, but, according to one source, Chrusecz was associated with the Free Academy of Arts, founded by the writer Hans Henny Jahnn after World War II.[6]

Another dancer, Suzanne Perrottet (1889–1983), whose name was often misspelled by Huelsenbeck, was a Swiss pianist, violinist, and dance teacher who studied with Laban and later became head of the Zurich Laban School. In 1918 she founded her own school of movement in Zurich, where she played compositions by Arnold Schoenberg and Erik Satie at the Eighth Dada Evening. She also took part in the ballet *Noir Kakadu,* sponsored by the Dadaists. The title of her unpublished memoir, "Ich war auch dabei" (I Was Also Around), ironically underlines the often dismissed role of women in the avant-garde and in all periods of literary and artistic production. Her theories of free rhythmic movement may be found in her *Ein bewegtes Leben* (A Moved Life), published in Berlin in 1995.

As an innovative dancer, abstract painter, textile artist, marionette maker, and sculptor, Sophie Täuber influenced many Zurich Dadaists. She was born in Davos, Switzerland in 1889 and attended the Ecole d'Arts Appliqués at St. Gall in 1908–10. After living in Munich and Hamburg, Täuber began teaching at the Kunstgewerbeschule (School of Applied Arts) in Zurich. Along with Arp, Täuber was one of the most original and most devoted members of the Cabaret Voltaire group. Her active participation in their controversial soirées threatened her teaching position, which was one reason why she elected to wear masks during her performances. Through her study of dance between 1916 and 1920, she became close friends with Wigman. Täuber is best known for her abstract paintings (which she called "concrete"), her wooden "dada-heads" sculptures, her marionettes for Carlo Gozzi's Konig Hirsch, her paper-and-cloth pictures, her Laban-influenced dancing, and her innovations in weaving, silk art, and embroidery. Embroidery was a skill she taught to Arp, whom she married in 1922.

Despite her dynamic support for Zurich Dada, Täuber does not figure prominently in this study of the women who wrote eyewitness testimonies of the movement and its participants. This is because her contributions were confined to the visual arts and dance and because her role has been studied by other scholars. Täuber stands as the principle example of a woman artist who had a far-reaching influence on Dada, but whose performances and artisan-based works are not easily documented.

When many of their Dadaists friends moved to Paris or Berlin after World War I, financial restraints forced Täuber and Arp to stay in Zurich. She could not afford to abandon her teaching professorship in textile design. Nevertheless there is evidence that the couple traveled to meet their avant-garde friends in the Tyrol in 1921. During this time Täuber and Arp also kept in touch with and eventually visited Hennings and Ball when their former Dada colleagues were living in Italy in 1925.

In 1926 Täuber received a prestigious commission to design and execute murals for the Café de l'Aubette in Strasbourg. In this project she was assisted by De Stijl founder van Doesburg and by Arp. Unfortunately the murals were removed from the café twelve years later and then destroyed by the Nazis as degenerate art. As a result of this important commission, however, Täuber was finally given some economic independence to live where she wished. When she and her husband moved to Clamart, near Paris, in 1928, she designed and directed the building of the house with local materials. She also designed all the furniture for the home, where the couple entertained many supporters of Dada, including Ernst, the van Doesburgs, Richter, Schwitters, Tzara, Duchamp, Picabia, Buffet, Breton, Hugnet, Soupault, Eluard, the Delaunays, Alberto and Susie Magnelli, and Satie.

In 1930 Täuber joined the Cercle et Carré group, of which Sonia Delaunay and Florence Henri were members. In 1937 she founded the revue *Plastique,* which ran for two years. Former Dadaist Gabrielle Buffet contributed an article about Picabia's 391 to Täuber's periodical.

During World War II, when the Nazis invaded Paris, Täuber and Arp took refuge in southern France, where they joined Sonia Delaunay and other exiles. According to Christoph Kühn's award-winning 1993 film, *Sophie Täuber-Arp,* Täuber had intended to immigrate to the United States in 1941, but she fell in love with the area around Grasse and stayed there nearly two years with Arp, Magnelli, and Delaunay. While in the Alpes-Maritimes the group of former Dadaists worked on a series of collaborative projects and exhibited them. Delaunay guarded these works during the war years. Täuber and Arp returned to Zurich in late 1942.

After Sophie's accidental asphyxiation by a faulty room heater at the home of Max Bill in 1943, Arp immortalized her in poetry and exhibited her final works (*les neuf dernières constructions*, 1942), a series of abstract bronze pieces. These constructions appear in Arp's book *Sophie Taeuber-Arp* (1962), in which photographs of the bronze reliefs are juxtaposed with "Le rêve," a text written by Sophie in Ascona on June 10, 1939.

According to Michel Seuphor, Täuber's timid and humble nature hid her talent at first glance, but, based on the work she produced in 1916 alone, she should be considered one of the great pioneers of abstract art.[7] Her presence in the proliferation and dissemination of Dada proved to be essential. She united various versions of the avant-garde: the Laban School of dance, the textile orientation of the School of Applied Arts, and purely abstract forms in painting. Täuber also served as a conduit for uniting artists of diverse backgrounds and mediums through her networking travels and her multimedia, collaborative projects.

Besides Sophie Täuber, there were other painters and textile artists who drew inspiration from Zurich Dada and in turn influenced the production of artists from other nations. These women include Adja van Rees Dutilh and Alice Bailly.

Adrienne Catherine Dutilh (Adya van Rees-Dutilh) was born in 1876 in Rotterdam. She and her husband, Otto van Rees, were Dutch painters who arrived in Zurich on September 2, 1915, at the invitation of Arp, who had met the pair in Ascona in 1912. Adya and Otto, who had been residing and working in Paris under the influence of Cubism, participated in early Zurich Dada through the Cabaret Voltaire. Adya created abstract designs in wall hangings and tapestries. Her silk embroidery features rich tones of amber and russet with a smooth shimmering texture. As early as 1912, her work appeared in the Moderne Kunstkring (Modern Art Circle) in Amsterdam.

Dutilh's work was also exhibited at the Galerie Dada in shows organized by Tzara and Ball. In November 1915 she exhibited at the Galerie Tanner with her husband and Arp. She also took part in the first Dada-Ausstellung at the Galerie Corray in Zurich (January–February 1917), and Tzara praised her work in his "Conférences sur l'Art Moderne" (1917). He especially emphasized the "mathematical purity of the embroideries," "inner harmony of colors," and "control of form."[8]

Dutilh's needlework was again featured in the May show of the Galerie Dada alongside work by Arp, Giorgio de Chirico, Janco, Klee, Amedeo Modigliani, Richter, and Tzara. A photograph of one such silk embroidery appears in the 1919 volume 4/5 of the *Anthologie Dada*, an issue that features a cover designed by Arp, a frontispiece by Picabia, text by Breton, and the poem "Gambit de la Reine" by Buffet. Dutilh died in 1959.

Another painter and tapestry artist who came into contact with the Dadaists was Alice Bailly. Born in Geneva in 1872, she studied at the Ecole de Beaux-Arts from 1890 to 1895 under Denise Sarkissoff-Gillet and Hugues Bovy. Convinced of Geneva's artistic provincialism, Bailly decided to move to Paris in 1904. She stayed in the French capital for the next ten years, during a period of copious avant-garde immigration. There she came to know many artists, among them Raoul Dufy, Jean Metzinger, Sonia Lewitska, Gleizes, and Picabia, as well as Léger and Laurencin, who both influenced her painting. Beginning in 1906, Bailly exhibited every year in the Salon d'Automne. In the exhibition of 1908 her works were shown alongside those of the Fauves because of her rich and highly keyed palette. During this time Bailly also produced many wood engravings, and she exhibited in the Salon des Tuileries and the Salon des Indépendants. By 1910 her work showed the influence of Picasso and Braque, but she continued to use bright colors instead of their palettes of brown, grey, and ocher.

In 1912 Bailly was chosen to represent Switzerland in an international touring exhibition. At the same time she came under the influence of Futurism. Her studies of rhythm and movement resemble those of Giacomo Balla and Duchamp, but her subject matter is urban life.

Bailly spent the war years in Switzerland, where she began to explore the use of collage combined with painting, a technique employed by Picasso in his 1912 *Nature morte à la chaise cannée* (Still Life with Cane-work Chair) and later expanded by Höch and Hausmann in photomontage works. By 1917 Bailly had come into contact with the Dada group, and she spent 1918 in Zurich. Tzara mentioned her in a letter of that period to Picabia: "Mademoiselle Alice Bailly was here Saturday, very lively and full of hope, believes in a sort of victory of modern painting, but she's very nice."[9] According to one source, Picabia met Bailly in Paris before the war, and she collaborated on his journal *391*.[10] A pencil drawing by Bailly appears in the Zurich-published volume 8, February 1919, issue Picabia's journal, sharing the page with Arp's *Fleur marteau* (Hammer Flower) and poems by Picabia and Tzara. This is the same issue to which Buffet contributed her "Petit Manifeste." In his "Chronique zürichoise, 1915–1919," Tzara documented Bailly's participation in the April 9, 1919, Dada soiree, directed by Serner in the Salle Kaufleuten. He reported that "in the ammonia storm a scarf was brought to the author by Alice Bailly and Augusto Giacometti."[11]

Influenced by the Dada artists working in Zurich, Bailly created *tableaux laine* (wool pictures) in which colored or metallic yarns of wool or silk, interwoven with beads or gold paper, replace paint and brushstrokes. When looking at the tapestry work of such artists as Bailly and Dutilh, one sees an obvious connection between their experiments with materials beyond paint and canvas. According to Vergine, Bailly produced at least twenty-seven of these *tableaux laine,* which include the 1918 wool tapestry entitled *La Procession.*

From 1919 to1922 Bailly alternated residence between Paris and Lausanne, finally settling in Lausanne, where she lived until her death in 1938. Her work was often exhibited during her lifetime in such galleries as the Kunsthaus in Zurich, the Jeu de Paume (Exposition de l'Art suisse contemporain, 1934) in Paris, the

Gallery Moos of Geneva, and the Kunsthalle in Bern. Her native city granted her an exhibition in 1928. One of her last projects was two wall murals of four parts each for the foyer of the Lausanne theater. Before her death she established a foundation to create scholarships for young Swiss artists.[12]

The Berlin version of Dada is best known for the antinationalist, antibourgeois, political, and satiric tone of its drawings, posters, and photomontage pieces. Huelsenbeck brought Dada from Zurich to Berliner artists Grosz, Heartfield, Hausmann, and Baader. Few women were involved in Berlin Dada. Höch is usually identified as the only female contributor. There were, however, at least two other women who made contact with the Berlin Dadaists and contributed to Dada events.

The first was the dancer Valeska Gert, born Valeska Gertrud Samosch of a Berlin Jewish family on January 11, 1892. In her *Verrück nach Leben: Berlin Szenen in den zwanziger Jahren* (Crazy for Life: Berlin Scenes from the 1920s), published in 2000, Ute Scheub included Gert's account of her participation in a Dada evening when she was put on stage to dance in a smoke-filled room as Huelsenbeck and Hausmann recited. She confided that she made her own costume, constructed of newspaper and two pounds of asparagus bought at the local market.[13] Gert was a founder of the modern "satire dance," and as such, she strove to break through the societal boundaries of Weimar Germany. Her association with the Dadaists provided an ideal outlet.

There was yet another woman who worked closely alongside the Berlin Dadaists. Painter and photographer Florence Henri was born in New York in 1893. Her father was French, her mother German. After her mother's death in 1895, her father took her to Europe. They settled in Silesia near family, and in time she began to study piano. After her father's death in 1909, she moved to Rome, where she came into contact with the Futurist Marinetti. By 1912 she was giving concerts in Berlin and eventually settled there, frequenting circles of musicians and artists. In a drastic change of career, Henri abandoned music for painting in 1914, but she continued to play piano for a movie theater.

While in Berlin in 1918, Henri came into contact with artists associated with Dada, namely Arp, Richter, Moholy-Nagy, and Heartfield. She became friends with the van Doesburgs, who were frequently involved in international Dada activities.

As a painter in the 1920s, Henri participated in the most important manifestations of the avant-garde of the period. In 1922–24 she lived in Berlin and Munich. Then she moved to Paris, where she studied at the Académie d'André Lhote and the Académie Moderne, directed by Léger and Amédée Ozenfant, who exercised a considerable influence on the content and form of Henri's paintings. In 1925 Henri participated with Sonia Delaunay, Crotti (Suzanne Duchamp's husband and cofounder of the Dada off-shoot TABU), Janco, and Arp in the exhibition L'Art d'aujourd'hui, the first international exposition that united all avant-garde styles:

Cubism, Purism, Dada, Surrealism, and Constructivism, among others. At this time she became friends with the Delaunays and Mondrian.

The following year Henri exhibited her works at the Galerie d'Art Contemporain as a student of Léger. In 1927 she was accepted into a Bauhaus preparatory course at Dessau. There, influenced by the ideas of Moholy-Nagy, Henri again changed her career, turning to photography and employing the techniques of photomontage, superposition, and "sur-impression," showing the influence of her earlier associations with Berlin Dada. By 1929, after her return to Paris, Henri's experiments in photography were so well known that she was being invited to participate in major international expositions. She frequented the Cercle et Carré group, and her studio (after 1931) became one of Paris's most popular. However, with the onset of World War II, her work was interrupted. She left Paris and eventually abandoned photography for painting after the war. Her best-known photographic portraits, which serve as records of the period, are of such Dadaists and Dada supporters as Arp, Soupault, Robert and Sonia Delaunay, Kandinsky, and Léger. Her works, including paintings, abstracts, and commercial advertisements, were exhibited at the Musée d'art moderne de la ville de Paris in October and November 1978.

Angelika Fick Hoerle, born in 1899, participated in the Cologne Dada group as a painter and collage artist. The Cologne version of Dada was strongly influenced by Max Ernst, who was allied with the Parisian Dadaists and then the former Zurich Dadaists Arp and Täuber. Hoerle's name appears on the "DADA-METER" in the single Dada publication of *Die Schammade* in February 1920. She is the only woman listed alongside stalwart Dadaists Aragon, Arp, Tzara, Breton, Ernst, Huelsenbeck, Picabia, Ribemont-Dessaignes, Serner, Soupault, Johannes Baargeld, and her husband, Heinrich Hoerle.

Combining her art with political activism, Hoerle created linocuts and collages that appear in the Dada publications *Bulletin D* (founded in 1919 and edited by Ernst and Baargeld), *Die Schammade* (begun in 1920 and edited by Ernst and Baargeld), and *Stupid* (catalog of the Cologne Dada-Abspaltung in November 1920). At least three of her works were purchased by Katherine Dreier for the Société Anonyme Collection and are now held by the Yale University Art Gallery. Hoerle died of tuberculosis on September 9, 1923, at the age of twenty-three.

Examples of Hoerle's work may be found in the *Kölnischer Kunstverein* catalog from 1981, *The Dada Period in Cologne,* published by the Ontario Art Gallery in 1988, and Vergine's *L'alta mèta dell'avanguardia, 1910–1940*. The Art Gallery of Ontario, under the direction of guest curator Angelika Littlefield, the artist's grandniece, presented the exhibit Angelika Hoerle: The Comet of Cologne Dada in 2009.

Because of Schwitters, his development of the Dada offshoot MERZ, and his close alliance with Constructivist Theo van Doesburg, Hannover Dada featured collages and *Merzbilder* (assemblages), MERZ sound poems, and influences from Dutch Stijl. One contributing painter and poet, Käte Traumann Steinitz, was born in Upper Silesia in 1889. After her family settled in Berlin, she studied drawing with Käthe Kollwitz and attended the Malschule für Frauen (Women's Painting School). In 1914, after a trip to Paris, she married Dr. Ernst Steinitz, and they moved to Hannover. There she met Schwitters in 1918 and worked with him and van Doesburg, establishing their own publishing house, APOSS Verlag, an acronym for "Aktiv" (Active), "Paradox," "Ohne Sentimentalität" (Without Sentimentality), and "Sensibel" (Sensitive). Steinitz and Schwitters set out to collaborate on Dadaist stories for children. Their Dada-MERZ book series began with the illustrated volume *Der Hahnepeter* (Peter the Rooster), the first installment of *Märchen vom Paradies* (Paradise Fairytales). According to Steinitz, Schwitters dictated the stories under the direction of children, and she sketched the Expressionist illustrations according to their directions. The first volume appeared in 1925 and featured unusual and innovative typographic styles. In her *Kurt Schwitters: Erinnerungen aus dem Jahren 1918–1930*, Steinitz explains that these typographical experiments are more than optical tricks; they provide orientation for the reader.

For several years Steinitz wrote articles for Hannover and Berlin newspapers. In 1933 Dr. Steinitz lost his hospital position because of the racial laws of National Socialism. When Käte Steinitz was forbidden to publish in 1935, the couple immigrated to the United States. Working as a free-lance journalist, Steinitz supported her family after the death of her husband in 1942 and was granted U.S. citizenship in 1944. She became a Leonardo da Vinci expert and was even invited to give the annual lecture in Vinci, Italy, in 1969. That same year, the Los Angeles County Museum sponsored an exhibition of her works for her eightieth birthday. Steinitz died in 1975.

Schwitters served as the link between Dada and yet another artist. Ella Bergmann, born in 1896, is known for her drawings, collages, paintings, and films. While her pre-1923 abstract works, *Sontag für jedermann (Sunday for Everyone) and Explosion,* show a marked Dada influence, her later works are investigations of mathematical precision and asymmetrically balanced movement. Her artistic career includes various mediums and spans multiple movements, including Dada, Constructivism, and Surrealism. The Dadaists held meetings in her home.

When Bergmann and her husband, Robert Michel, were expelled from the Weimar Art School in 1923, her artistic career took a new turn. The couple was living in Vockenhausen, near Frankfurt, and showing with Lissitzky and Schwitters at the Nassauischen Kunstverein in Wiesbaden. The four artists exhibited together again in 1925. Some of Bergmann's work from this period includes poetry pasted on canvas, words painted on images, or photographs incorporated into paintings. These methods echo the work of fellow avant-garde women such as Suzanne Duchamp and Höch.

In 1927 Bergmann, Michel, and Schwitters traveled to the Netherlands, where they joined Höch and her partner Brugman. Bergmann's growing reputation as a European modernist resulted in Marcel Duchamp and Man Ray's inclusion of her works in the Société Anonyme of the United States traveling exhibition Arts Council 1928, which featured art from European Dadaists.

In the early 1930s Bergmann ceased exhibiting her work because of the unfavorable cultural climate in Germany toward the avant-garde. After making several short documentary films, she and her husband turned all their attention to farming in order to survive the war years. After 1945 Bergmann traveled and lectured on European modernism at various American Houses, established by the Marshall Plan to encourage cultural exchange. These lectures enabled her to influence an entire generation of German youth.

The Louise Noun Collection contains examples of Bergmann's work that demonstrate her fascination with blueprints and her familiarity with Lissitsky's design principles. Lissitsky's notion of the artist as social engineer and creator of a new culture influenced such works as Bergmann's *OB 193* (circa 1924). The lines and shapes of the drawing echo the impeccable, mathematical precision of an architect's sketch. Still the viewer realizes that the pencil-and-ink drawing is not a literal plan for construction. Instead Bergmann applied her distinctive aesthetic sense to a sort of drafting exercise, weaving spirals in movement. Her drawings show considerable similarity to the works of the Dadaists in their mechanical aspect (reminiscent of Picabia's *mamomètres*) and strong drafting line (similar to such works as Suzanne Duchamp's *Un et une brisée*). Bergmann's connection to Dada influence was filtered through her working friendships with Schwitters and Lissitzky.

In the 1960s Bergmann and Michel began to exhibit again in Europe and the United States. After her death in April 1971, Bergmann's work was featured in solo exhibits in Germany (1974), Paris (1984), and New York (1984).

As the most portable and adaptable of avant-garde manifestations, Dada went on tour and merged well with elements of Constructivism and De Stijl. First it traveled to Weimar. Dadaists Richter, Tzara, Hausmann, Schwitters, and Arp met with El Lissitzky, László and Lucia Moholy-Nagy, Theo and Nelly van Doesburg, and other artists in September 1922 at the Dadaïstische Konstruktivisten Congres. This convention in Weimar marked the end of Dada as an official group in Berlin, as artists no longer met there as a bloc, but pursued their individual paths.

The Netherlands became the next site of Dada activity outside Berlin. The pianist Nelly van Moorsel van Doesburg, also known as Madame Pétro (Petronella) van Doesburg–van Moorsel, took part in Dada activities with her husband, Theo, along with Kurt Schwitters and Helma Schwitters during the 1922–23 Dada Holland Tour. Pétro played her repertoire of Arnold Schoenberg, Erik Satie, Francis Poulenc, and Igor Stravinsky.

Nelly had studied piano at the conservatory in Den Haag, and, through her growing interest in modernisms, she met her future husband. On March 17, 1921, she went away with van Doesburg to Weimar against her family's wishes. There, among a group of artists, she played modern compositions by Schoenberg, Bela Bartok, Jakob van Domselaer (the only De Stijl composer), Zottan Kodaky, and Vittorio Rieti. Rieti titled his works in the Dada style: *Funeral March for a Bird* and *Wedding March for a Crocodile.*

At the Generalprobe on January 10, 1923, Pétro van Doesburg played Satie's "Ragtime-Dada" on piano. The evening, complete with recitations from Schwitters and Theo van Doesburg and a mechanical dance by Filmos Huszár, was a huge success. Holland was smitten with Dada.

After the Holland tour, Nelly and Theo went to Paris, meeting with Tzara and Arp, as well as Ray, Eluard, Ernst, and Duchamp. In the last Dada *Soirée du coeur à barbe* (Barbed Heart Soirée) Nelly played van Domselear's *Proeven van Stijlkunst* (Experiments in Artistic Style). She again included his works, alongside those of Riete and Satie, in her February 14, 1924, performance in Potsdam. After her husband's death in 1931, Nelly devoted several years to organizing his works in a De Stijl archive.

Literary works—manifestos, journals, and public readings—characterize Parisian Dada. In addition, one of the most memorable aspects of Dada in the French capital was the clash between two divergent notions of Dada, represented by Tzara and Breton. While most of the conflict found its way into words, there were visual artists in Paris who contributed significantly to the mission of Dada, and they managed to do so without taking the road to Surrealism.

Though not professed Dadaists, Sonia Terk Delaunay (1885–1979) and her husband, Robert, were associated with Dada members and began to participate in their activities not long after their Paris meeting with Arp in May 1914. When Tzara brought Dada to Paris in 1920, the Delaunays were ready to lend their support. Sonia designed costumes for one of Tzara's plays; Robert contributed to Tzara's journal *Dada.*

Sonia Delaunay was born in the Ukraine in 1885 as Sofia Ilinitchna Terk. At age five she was adopted by her uncle Henri Terk and educated in St. Petersburg. Her uncle's financial support allowed her to study in Karlsruhe, Germany, and from 1905 at the Académie de la Palette in Paris. During this time she met Wilhelm Uhde, a German art dealer and critic, and Robert Delaunay. In 1908 her work was exhibited in Uhde's gallery in rue Notre-Dame-des-Champs. She married Uhde but divorced him in 1910 to marry Delaunay.

She collaborated with Delaunay on developing a method of rhythmical colors. Together they worked out theories of color and rhythm that Apollinaire baptized Orphism in 1912. According to some accounts, these theories might owe their origin to a simple Ukranian-style patchwork blanket that Sonia made for her baby's crib in 1912. The quilt demonstrates her modern experiments with color.

After the 1912 abstract quilt, Sonia began to design book covers in needlework for Apollinaire, Blaise Cendrars, Jules Laforgue, and Ricciotto Canudo. These prewar works are made of paper, leather, and cloth. She returned to this medium in the early 1920s to create book bindings for Tzara's collection of poems *De nos oiseaux* (Of Our Birds) and Illiazd (Il'ia Zdanevich)'s 1923 *Lidantiu Faram* (Ledantiu as a Beacon).

Beginning in 1913 she turned her imagination to the fabrication of "simultaneous clothing," which inspired Cendrars to write the poem "Sur la robe elle a un corps" (On the Dress She Has a Body) in 1914. Similtaneism was meant to express all aspects of reality concurrently. After spending part of World War I in Spain, Sonia began an extensive production of simultaneous fabrics for coats, scarves, hats, purses, shirts, and children's clothes. Her designs helped support her family.

Because of her work in clothing design, Delaunay was invited to design costumes for Serge Diaghilev's ballet *Cléopâtre,* presented in London in 1918. She also created costumes for Massine's *Quatre Saisons* (Four Seasons) and for Dada performances such as the *Soirée du coeur à barbe* and for Tzara's 1923 play *Le Coeur à gaz* (The Gas Heart). According to Whitney Chadwick, the costumes for Tzara's play "exhibited the same frontal abstract and geometric conception soon to be displayed on the backs of fashionable society women in Paris who bought [Delaunay's] appliquéd coats."[14] Such designs were so successful that celebrities such as Gloria Swanson purchased them. Even Tzara is pictured wearing a patterned and colorful Delaunay scarf in a 1923 portrait of the Dada leader by Robert Delaunay.

By 1923 Sonia Delaunay had begun designing fabrics commercially and working in wool tapestry, much like Täuber, Bailly, and Dutilh. In the 1920s and 1930s she again designed covers for books, but this time for those that featured her art.[15] In 1935 she designed the cover for the review *La Devanture* (The Front).

Her artistic production suffered after the death of her life companion and collaborator in 1941. In fact, after her husband's death, she did not exhibit again until 1958. She spent many years cataloging and exhibiting Robert's paintings and drawings. As is the case with most women artists, Sonia's work appears less often in museums and galleries than Robert's paintings. But Karen Petersen and J. J. Wilson suggest that her artistic influence is not to be overlooked: "Sonia Delaunay's creative and expansive energy undoubtedly influenced her husband's artistic development in ways not always acknowledged. Jacques Damase, in his deeply appreciative book on Sonia Delaunay, states that she was always 'a collaborator rather than a disciple.' This may be something of an understatement."[16] This description is emblematic of the relationship held by other female artists with their mates: Hennings with Ball, Buffet with Picabia, Roche with Gleizes, Höch with Hausmann.

Perhaps Delaunay's most significant contribution to the avant-garde is in her creation of an abstract art that penetrates everyday life. Like her close friend Sophie Täuber, Sonia Delaunay did not hesitate to experiment in the so-called minor (decorative or applied) arts, and expanded from there to create furniture, tapestries, books, murals, handbags, and even painted cars. In addition to her prolific creation of paintings and graphics, she designed and sold simultaneous fabrics and clothing that moved fashion to focus on simple forms and primary colors.

Her other extensive projects include her 1913 collaboration with Cendrars on the first simultaneous book, the two-meter-long poem *La Prose du Transsibérien et de la petite Jehanne de France* (The Prose of the Transsiberian and the little Jehanne of France), the vast decorative compositions for the air and train pavilions at the 1937 Exposition intérnationale, and the interior decoration of the Sans Pareil bookstore at Neuilly.

Delaunay's brief association with the Dada group in Paris led to a lifetime friendship with Täuber and Arp. She also developed a lasting friendship with Nelly and Theo van Doesburg. She spent time with both couples in Grasse during World War II.

When Arp and Täuber left Meudon because of the German occupation and went to Grasse, they found Alberto and Susi Magnelli. The Arps then called the recently widowed Sonia Delaunay to join the circle. This became a period of communal production for all. In an announcement advertising a June 16 to July 15, 1954, exhibition, Buffet explained that the exposition reunited the community of artists from the period around 1941. She further explained their method of work: "One of the four inscribed the initial motif, which was then developed by the other three, each working in turn on the same sheet."[17] These constructions could well have been destroyed during the bombardments along the Mediterranean coast in 1944, but Sonia stayed on in Grasse and preserved the fruits of their collaboration. Her autobiography, *Nous irons jusqu'au soleil* (We'll Go All the Way to the Sun) was published in 1978.

Also based in Paris was Suzanne Duchamp. Born in 1889 in Blainville, Seine-Inférieure, Duchamp was a poet and abstract painter who was involved for five years in Parisian Dada, though her participation came to the attention of the art community only during preparations for the September 5 to October 19, 1958, exhibition at the Düsseldorf Kunsthalle. Duchamp came from an uncommonly artistic family: her grandfather was the painter and engraver Emile Nicolle, and three of her brothers—Marcel Duchamp, Raymond Duchamp-Villon, and Jacques Villon—cultivated successful careers in modern art.

Suzanne Duchamp first studied at the art academy in Rouen, and by 1912 she was already exhibiting in the Section d'or. She served as a nurse during World War I, following the dissolution of her first marriage. When she married the painter Jean Crotti in April 1919, she constructed *Ready-made malheureux*

(Unhappy Ready-Made) by proxy, a gift with instructions from her brother Marcel, then living in Buenos Aires. According to Peggy Dunford, Suzanne Duchamp was actively involved in all Parisian Dada activities. In 1921 alone, the year she and her husband exhibited the works they had created in New York between 1916 and 1920 at the Galerie Montaigne, Duchamp was involved in "signing manifestos, organizing exhibitions and soirees, and in showing her own work in both the Salon d'Automne and the Indépendants."[18] She also signed Picabia's *L'Oeil cacodylate,* and launched, with her husband, the Dada offshoot called TABU.

On page 3 of a four-page ephemeral Dada publication titled *La Pomme de Pins* (The Pinecone), Duchamp contributed "La valeur intrinsique a une densité plus grande que la valeur relative" (The intrinsic value is denser than the relative value). The cryptic line is reminiscent of the sort of text she often included in paintings such as *ArieTte d'oubli de la chapelle étourdie.* Her works were labeled "Dada" by the Dadaists because of their rejection of traditional art and their geometrical-mechanical forms, but her colorful palette, intense imagery, and unusual inscriptions personalize her art.

A final participant in Parisian Dada expositions, Greta Knutson, a Swedish painter and writer, was born in 1899. She studied with painter Carl Wilhelmsson from 1917 before attending the School of Fine Arts in Stockholm. Eventually Knutson moved to Paris in 1922 and studied under Cubist painter and sculptor André Lhote. While in Paris, she met Tzara in 1924, married him the following year, separated from him in 1926, and divorced him in 1942. Despite this unstable relationship, Knutson's 1928 *Portrait de Tristan Tzara* pokes good-natured fun at her former partner. Tzara is sketched in profile with his brain dissected into whimsically numbered sections with descriptive figures, indicating what might be filling his head.

Although Knutson participated actively in the production of Dada art, almost none of her work from this period survives. She went on to contribute to all the Surrealist exhibitions in Paris from 1927 to 1932. In 1933 Knutson contributed to *Le Surréalisme au service de la révolution.* The May 15 issue features two of her poems, one in verse, "Pays étranger" (Foreign Land) and the second in prose, "Passiflore" (Passion Flower). Knutson spent the World War II years in Aix-en-Provence. In 1945 her memoir *L'Age d'or* (The Golden Age) appeared, and in 1985 Flammerion published her *Lunaires* (Lunars).

Dada into the Next Generation

Berlin-born artist Meret Oppenheim might best represent those female artists who carried on the Dada spirit to subsequent generations, conveying some of its personality into the next stage of the avant-garde, Surrealism. Two 1936 multimedia works by Oppenheim illustrate this continuation of the Dada aesthetic: *Déjeuner en fourrure* (Breakfast in Fur) and *Ma gouvernante, ma nurse, mein Kindermädchen* (My Governess, My Nanny, My Nursemaid).

Although Oppenheim, born in 1913, clearly belongs to the post-Dada generation by virtue of her age, the spirit and execution of her gazelle-fur-covered cup, saucer, and spoon in *Déjeuner en fourrure* assign her the appellation "daughter of Dada." The cup assemblage provokes revulsion and amusement, thus displaying both the affronting and the whimsical sides of Dada. The influence of Dada's questioning of traditional art is strong in all Oppenheim's highly imaginative and irreverent multimedia works, while adding an element previously explored in Höch's later collages: the exploitation of women seen through an atypical presentation or arrangement of everyday objects. This vision is clearly stated in *Ma gouvernante, ma nurse, mein Kindermädchen,* which displays a pair of women's shoes, trussed tightly together and presented on a tray like poultry ready for baking. Oppenheim's art moves from the startling humor of juxtaposed objects to the uncomfortable realm of an otherworldly, surreal reality.

It remains the work of future scholars to study further manifestations of Dada and the paths it might have taken through Fluxus, Happenings, Lettrism, Situationist International, and, according to Willard Bohn, to the Theater of the Absurd and Abstract Expressionism.[19] Many of today's artists, especially those who work in collage, cite Dada as an inspirational source. Current French collage and installation artist Béa Aaronson, whose work appears on the cover of this book, should be acknowledged as a granddaughter of Dada. Her residence, studio, and gallery are in San Miguel de Allende, Mexico.

The Glue That Connected Dada

Unlike most artistic movements in literature and especially in the visual and performance arts, Dada found itself firmly and simultaneously implanted in diverse locations. It successfully united artists from New York, Romania, Switzerland, the Netherlands, Barcelona, Paris, and at least three areas of Germany. What linked the various centers were the members and supporters of Dada: like-minded, young, rebellious artists whose yearning for radical social, political, or artistic change tied them together. Additionally the willingness and ability of Dadaists to travel from one Dada center to another or to strike out and infiltrate new locations while on "Dada tours" caused the movement to spread after World War I. Without the eager participants and their networking skills, even a contagious European manifestation such as Dada would have remained localized in Zurich.

Among the men who carried Dada onto new centers were Huelsenbeck, Tzara, Arp, Picabia, and later, Schwitters. However, as mobile as these male Dadaists were, the effects of their forced or voluntary relocations can hardly match the achievements of the collaborative, networking women artists involved in Dada, who were forced to battle societal confinement while working in a man's world. Traveling, cooperative, and sharing artists such as Bailly, Hennings, Täuber, the Laban dancers, Laurencin, Bergmann, Höch, Hoerle, Knutson, Everling, Loy, Arnauld, Buffet, Delaunay, Duchamp, Roche, Brugman, Henri, Dutilh, and van

Doesburg—to name just a few—were just as responsible as their male counterparts for disseminating the avant-garde across Europe between 1914 and 1924. Female Dadaists' groupings and regroupings with each other and with male members of Dada furthered the movement and, just as important, added a gendered depth to this manifestation of the avant-garde that others—such as Cubism, Futurism, or Surrealism—did not have.

How was the perspective of the female participants able to enhance Dada? First through performance. The cabaret origins of Dada opened doors to women through the introduction of dance, song, piano playing, recitations, marionette shows, as well as costume and mask making. Most of these contributions were ephemeral and not easily preserved by history, thus making the women appear less productive. Artistic and literary movements that foreground painting, sculpture, and published works usually leave little room for women, who often have limited time and materials to create the kind of works that end up in museums and anthologies. A performance-based group of artists does not disparage less recordable forms of art. Instead it welcomes artisan creations alongside beaux arts. It encourages experiment in textiles, scenery, sound, rhythm, and movement because of its stage orientation.

Women involved in Dada also confronted traditional, nineteenth-century notions of gender as they challenged established ideas of what art should be and who should produce it. Not only were they fighting to create a new kind of art (as were the men of Dada), but female Dadaists were simultaneously struggling against societal gender oppression for recognition as artists. Some, such as Höch and Hennings, were forced to choose between bearing or caring for children and earning a living through their art. Others, such as Buffet, tried to care for children and a frequently childlike husband, all the while pursuing their writing careers. What they have in common with each other, and with women such as Roche, Täuber, Brugman, and other women, was their need to produce art, singly and in collaboration with other artists. In addition they and the other women involved in Dada questioned the traditional, domestic roles assigned to women. Instead of conforming to the status quo, they explored their bodies through dance, entered into new relationships with colleagues, and took part in artistic activities that took them far from the foyer. They shared, as Sandra Gilbert and Susan Gubar might suggest, "a common female impulse to struggle free from social and literary confinement through strategic redefinitions of self, art, and society."[20]

What the women highlighted in this volume bring to our understanding of Dada is an intimate perspective (Hennings and Everling), a subversive voice (Roche and Höch), a new way to view beauty (Arnauld and Höch), and an insider's critique (Buffet and Roche). They motivated the hesitant Ball, tempered the mechanical Picabia, nurtured the inventive Hausmann, inspired and gave focus to a wandering Tzara, and provided a satiric chastisement of Dadaists in New York, Barcelona, Berlin, and Paris. The men they worked with and alongside were not entirely resistant to their influence and contributions. There were excellent collaborations in painting, acting, music, and publishing. In fact, with perhaps one exception (Picabia), male Dadaists portrayed women in their drawings, paintings, poems, and other writings in a favorable, or at least equal, light—once they got to know them as colleagues. Dadaists more readily allowed women equal access to create or compose than did the virulently antifeminist Futurists. Moreover the women of Surrealism, who followed in the footsteps of their Dadaist sisters, did not enjoy the same level of tolerance. In fact Leonard Koos has pointed out that, though Surrealism was Dada's inheritor, it "reverted to more traditional figurations of women, often with misogynistic overtones."[21] The works of female Surrealist painters often go one step further, recording self-portraits of pain and mistreatment. Referring primarily to the works of Dorothea Tanning, Frida Kahlo, and Oppenheim, Whitney Chadwick has confirmed this tendency: "Now it is violence directed against the self, not projected onto another, violence inseparable from the physiological reality of woman's sexuality and the social construction of her feminine role."[22] The women of Dada, on the other hand, joined with male members of the group, more often than not, in a unified attack on socializing norms.

The women who supported Dada activities across Europe certainly made sacrifices and fought the commonly held perceptions of their generation about women. They had an immense impact on the avant-garde, not in spite of the fact that they were women but because they were women. In contrast to the one-upmanship evidenced in many male-generated paintings and journals, the less competitive nature of female productions and collaborations made possible their linking relationships and transnational networking with each other and with male artists and poets. These personal skills—combined with their talent in painting, writing, dance, music, and textile work, their undaunted persistence, and their individual interpretations of the goals of Dada—make the appreciation of women Dadaists' contributions essential for understanding the development of the entire Dada enterprise.

Notes

Preface

1. See http://en.wikipedia.org/wiki/Dada (accessed January 10, 2012).
2. Harmon, *A Handbook to Literature*, 137.
3. Excellent volumes by Dachy, Faucherau, Hugnet, Sanouillet, Annabelle Melzer, Raoul Schrott, Hanne Bergius, Hans Bolliger, Raimund Meyer, Judith Hossli, Juri Steiner, and Guido Magnaguagno, provide insightful views of Dada and its most publicized manifestations.
4. See Whitney Chadwick, *Women Artists and the Surrealist Movement* (1985) and *Mirror Images: Women, Surrealism, and Self-Representation* (1998); Susan Suleiman, *Subversive Intent: Gender, Politics, and the Avant-garde* (1990); Mary Ann Caws, Rudolf E. Kuenzli, and Gwen Raaberg *Surrealism and Women* (1991); Renée Riese Hubert, *Magnifying Mirrors: Women, Surrealism, and Partnership* (1994); Penelope Rosemont, *Surrealist Women: An International Anthology* (1998); Annette Shandler Levitt, *The Genres and Genders of Surrealism* (2000); and Betty Ann Brown, *Gradiva's Mirror: Reflections on Women, Surrealism, and Art History* (2002).
5. This is nearly the same geographical focus as Francis M. Naumann's pioneering 1994 *New York Dada, 1915–1923*.
6. See for example Carolyn Lanchner, *Sophie Taeuber-Arp* (1981); Barbara Bloemink, *The Life and Art of Florine Stettheimer* (1995); and Amelia Jones, *Irrational Modernism: A Neurasthentic History of New York Dada* (2004).

Introduction

1. Steven C. Foster, review of *New York Dada*.
2. Georges Hugnet, "The Dada Spirit in Painting."
3. Ernst Cohn-Wiener, "Grosse Monster-Dada-Show," *Neue Berliner Zeitung* (noon edition), July 6, 1920, 3.
4. MERZ, begun and spearheaded by Hannover artist Kurt Schwitters (1887–1948), is best known for its use of discarded or found objects to create sculptures and collages. The Dutch De Stijl movement, influenced by some Dada ideas, merged art,

architecture, and design. Its best-known artists are Theo Van Doesburg, Piet Mondrian, Gerrit Rietveld, and Vilmos Huszár.

5. Egyptian Aliaa Magda Elmahdy and Iranian Golshifteh Farahani have both staged feminist protests to their respective regimes by baring their bodies to the public. In comparing early-twentieth-century artistic protest with these manifestations of Islamic women's protest in the twenty-first century, we can see the provocations of Dada as protests against a society and its values. The political climate of World War I and following, with its air of revolution followed by rising fascist activity, finds an echo in the second decade of the twenty-first century with the specter of Islamic revolution being met by religious fundamentalist backlash.
6. Hamid Dabashi, "La Vita Nuda: Baring Bodies, Bearing Witness." *Aljazeera*, January 23, 2012; http://www.aljazeera.com/indepth/opinion/2012/01/201212111238688792.html (accessed January 28, 2012).
7. According to Irmell Hautamäki, German culture was affected by the Nazi persecution and expulsion of avant-garde artists until the 1960s. It was only then that German theoreticians began to refer to the avant-garde, which they had preferred to label as "Modernism." See Hautamäki's *Avantgarden alkuperä, Modernin estetiikkaa Baudelairesta Warholiin* (Origin of Avant-garde: Modern Aesthetics from Baudelaire to Warhol), 2003.
8. Qtd. in Dawn Ades, ed., *The Dada Reader: A Critical Anthology*, 28.
9. I was contacted by a researcher from the University of Southern California who was understandably confused by the error at a now-defunct website: http://members1.chello.nl/~m.woestenburg/dada/alphabet/dermee.html (accessed June 19, 2002). I notified the webmaster of the true identity of Arnauld, after which the site became inactive.

Chapter 1: Emily Hennings

1. Qtd. in Emmy Ball-Hennings, *Briefe an Herman Hesse*, 297. (Unless otherwise indicated, all translations are my own.)
2. Schütt-Hennings, introduction to Emmy Ball-Hennings, *Ruf und Echo: Mein Leben mit Hugo Ball*, 9–10.
3. The poem "Nach dem Kabarett," on page 13 of her 1913 collection *Die Letzte Freude*, is reprinted in its entirety as "Nach dem Cabaret" in *Emmy Ball Hennings 1885–1948, "Ich bin so vielfach . . .": Texte, Bilder, Dokumente*, 70.
4. Reprinted with differing punctuation in *Emmy Ball Hennings 1885–1948*, 67. The poem (without title) appears on page 6 of *Die Letzte Freude*.
5. Elderfield, introduction to Hugo Ball, *Flight Out of Time: A Dada Diary*, xxvii.
6. The poem appears on page 15 of *Die Letzte Freude*.
7. "Ich weiß es im voraus. Es kann für die Rolle niemand sonst in Frage kommen. Nur Sie, Sie sind es." Qtd. in Ball-Hennings, *Ruf und Echo*, 39.
8. "Sie spricht, als habe sie gar keine eigenen Worte, wiederholt auch oft die Worte des Mannes, was aber nicht monoton wirkt. Es ist wie Ruf und Echo. Wäre das Echo nicht da, würde der Mann seine einsame Stimme kaum hören. Es ist, als vernehme er sich erst durch die Frau, und so strömt sein Wort ihm beglückend zurück. Einmal ist es dann wie Musik in stiller Nacht. Das Spiel des Mannes geht in das der Frau über, die Melodie der beiden wesen strömt ineinander, als umarme ein Klang den andern, und der harmonische Ein- und Ausklang des Stückes ist namenlos schön." Ibid., 43.

9. "Weißt Du eigentlich, daß Hardekopf in Paris lebt und französischer Royalist geworden ist? Das ist aber nichts gegen den Fall Emmy Hennings, die aus Liebe für ihn auf den Strich ging und auf seinen Rat die Kunden bestahl." Qtd. in a letter from Siegfried Jacobsohn to Kurt Tucholsky, May 26, 1926. Reprinted from *Siegfried Jacobsohn: Briefe an Kurt Tucholksy 1915–1926*, in *Emmy Ball Hennings 1885–1948*, 88.
10. Journal entry by Erich Mühsam, reprinted in *Emmy Ball Hennings 1885–1948*, 86.
11. "Hugo und ich jedoch träumten bis weilen so eindrucksvoll, daß der eine dem andern oftmals seinen Traum erzählte, wie eben zwei Menschen, die einander nahestehen, sich ihre Erlebnisse mitteilen" Ball-Hennings, *Ruf und Echo*, 75.
12. Huelsenbeck, *Memoirs of a Dada Drummer*, 10.
13. The Laban method of free, expressive dance as an art form in itself was formulated by Austro-Hungarian choreographer Rudolf von Laban. By 1913 one of his many dance schools was located in Monte Verità, overlooking Ascona, Switzerland, and by 1915 he had opened the School of Movement Art in Zurich. The dancers from the school regularly attended and contributed to Dada events. For a further discussion of Laban's role in modern dance, see Partsch-Bergsohn, *Modern Dance in Germany and the United States: Crosscurrents and Influences*.
14. Arp, "Dadaland," in *Arp on Arp: Poems, Essay, Memories*, 234.
15. Zeller, ed., *Hermann Hesse in Selbstzeugnissen und Bilddokumenten*, 90.
16. Huelsenbeck, *Memoirs of a Dada Drummer*, 16.
17. "Ich hatte so etwas noch nie gesehen und war sofort gewonnen für die Dadaisten . . . Emmy Hennings . . . stand da, angekleidet mit einem Rohr aus Karton, über den Kopf bis an die Füße, das Gesicht war eine gräßliche Maske, der Mund offen, die Nase auf die Seite gedrückt, die Arme in dünnen Kartonröhren verlängert, mit stilisierten langen Fingern. Das einzige Lebendige, was man gesehen hat, waren die Füße, nackt, ganz allein für sich da unten, das war so prägnant und eindrucksvoll. So hat sie getanzt. Sie konnte nichts anderes machen als mit den Füßen klappern oder das Ganze wie einen Kamin neigen, und dabei hat sie noch geredet hie und da, aber man hat es nicht verstanden, man hat es gespürt, und manchmal hat sie einen Schrei ausgestoßen, einen Schrei . . . " Qtd. in Schrott, *Dada 15/25*, 51.
18. Huelsensbeck's "Dada Lives" of 1936 is quoted by John Elderfield in his afterword to Ball's *Flight Out of Time*, 246.
19. Ball, *Flight Out of Time*, 112.
20. Ibid., 106.
21. Ball-Hennings, *Helle Nacht*, 21.
22. Ball, *Flight Out of Time*, 95.
23. "Er trug deine Art Ritterrüstung aus blauem Glanzpapier und sein langes, schmales, abgründig ernstes Gesicht war auch sonst dem eines Don Quijote recht ähnlich, wie man sich den Ritter von der traurigen Gestalt vorstellt, und wie ihn etwa Goya gemalt hätte." Ball-Hennings, *Ruf und Echo*, 93.
24. "Ich schreibe keinen Roman, es muß zu sehr mein Leben sein, das ich preisgebe und das mir nachgeht. Je mehr man davon wegzustoßen meint, um so mehr strömt einem zu. Ich bestimme nicht, was ich schreibe, es bleibt mir keine Wahl, und ich möchte gerne einmal wählen dürfen." Ibid., 74.
25. "es gibt keine Perspektiven mehr in der moralischen Welt. Oben ist unten und unten ist oben." Ibid., 95.
26. "Der Künstler, der ohne Ruhe nicht schaffen kann, wenn er ins Zentrum, ans Herz der Dinge dringen will, wird aus seiner Bahn herausgeschleudert, der Raum wird

ihm entzogen. In solch unruhvoller Zeit ist er nicht mehr das Herz der Welt, in der es auf die Zerstörung, die Vernichtung des Geistes abgesehen ist. Wo Kanonen donnern, wo das Chaos herrscht, kann nicht mehr harmonisch gestaltet werden, die Stimme des Dichters muß verstummen. Es war so viel Verzweiflung beim Dadaismus, wenigstens im Beginn, da er noch keine Modeangelegenheit, noch nicht durchgesetzt, also ganz echt gemeint war." Ibid.

27. "Der Dadaismus wurde geschoben und weiter geschoben, nicht nur von den Dadaisten selbst. Er war da und irgendwie auch schon verloren, um nicht zu sagen 'überholt,' sobald er von der Presse und vom Publikum ernsthaft anerkannt wurde. Der Erfolg war unvermeidlich, und gerade vor der Abstempelung, vor dem Erfolg hatte Hugo einem instinktiven Abscheu. Er sträubte sich, begann den Dadaismus als Laune zu bezeichnen, aus dem man keine Kunstrichtung machen dürfe. Alles mußte schwebend bleiben, so schwebend als möglich." Ibid., 98.
28. "Mein geliebtes Emmylein, ich danke Dir so sehr, daß ich hier bin und daß Du mir so gut zur 'Flucht' verholfen hast." Qtd. in ibid., 99.
29. Ball, *Flight Out of Time*, 96.
30. Ibid., 117.
31. Ibid., 118.
32. The March 17, 1917, letter is reprinted in its entirety in Schrott, *Dada 15/25*, 90.
33. "Heute Abend habt ihr Soirée, und aller Erfolg möge mit euch sein, und daß ihr die geliebte Galerie, unser Freuden- und Sorgenkind, recht behandelt und betreut bis zum Schluß, und wenn es sein muß, komme ich." Qtd. in ibid., 137.
34. "Sei herzlich geküßt, mein Liebling, und tausend Dank für deine treue Hilfe, dein Hugo." Qtd. in ibid., 139.
35. "Inzwischen sind drei Monate vergangen." Ball-Hennings, *Gefängnis*, 7.
36. "Ich stehe still . . . ich kann nicht atem. Was ist los? Jetzt weiß ich, weiß für immer: Es gibt keinen Raum, es gibt keine Zeit, es gibt keine Luft." Ibid., 34.
37. "Ich lege meinen Mund in diese kleine Rundung. Kühl ist die Eiseneinfassung. Das Glas, wie glatt und kalt! Meine Lippen berühren das schwarze Glas, das still bleibt. Und ich spreche, flüstere; denn niemand soll uns hören: Bleib mir treu. Du wirst mich nicht enttäuchen. Sei nachgiebig unter meinen Augen. Schmiege dich meinem Willen. Sei barmherzig und laß dich verführen, bis ich dich beherrsche. Immer spiegele das Bild, das meine Seele erträumt. Dein Echo brauche ich. Halle nach, lange: ich liebe dich . . . Leise . . . leise . . . liebe dich . . .

    Was sprach? Sprach ich?" Ibid., 47.
38. "Ich stehe vor einem hohen eisernen Tor, das ich zu öffnen versuche." Ibid., 115.
39. "Je länger ich gehe, desto freier fühle ich mich." Ibid., 178.
40. "Langsam wird es dunkler. Ich fürchte mich nicht. Der Schnee leuchtet. Ich bin so allein. Und niemand begegnet mir. Niemand sieht mich. Ich breite meine Arme aus vor Glück. Ich habe die Stadt noch nicht erreicht und die Menschen." Ibid., 178.
41. Ball, *Flight Out of Time*, 167.
42. Ibid., 159.
43. Ibid., 160.
44. Ibid., 162.
45. Ibid., 163.
46. Ibid., 167.
47. Ball-Hennings. *Ruf und Echo*, 132.

48. Ball, *Flight Out of Time,* 196.
49. "Wir wollten einmal versuchen, unabhängig voneinander zu arbeiten. Hier muß ich freilich für mein klein Teil zugeben, daß ich in jener Zeit nicht allzusehr ans Arbeiten gedacht habe, nicht immer restlos davon überzeugt war, daß die Arbeit die Hauptaufgabe oder das nahezu Wichtigste in unserem Leben ist." Ball-Hennings, *Ruf und Echo,* 173.
50. "Müde bin ich, sehr müde, und ich möchte nach Hause. Ob ich den Brief fortschicke, weiß ich noch nicht. Vielleicht werfe ich ihn in den Arno und dann nehmen die Wellen meine Worte auf, die sachten, trägen Wellen." Ibid., 193.
51. "Ich möchte ungesehen zu den Menschen sprechen. Ich liebe sie und will sie nicht sehen. Eine Dunkel Glut is oft in Deinen Worten, Hugo, ein versengend Schönes und ist wie ein Brand, von dem ich nie genug bekommen kann. Ich bin wort- und flammensüchtig nach Dir." Ibid., 194.
52. "Vielleicht suchten wir in Rom nicht den Frieden, nicht den letzten Frieden, nur eine kleine Rast, eine Ruhe in der Dunkelheit der Tage." Ibid., 216.
53. "Wir müssen wissen, Emmy, daß das Kind in Gottes Hand ist. Dann kannst Du auch ruhig bleiben." Qtd. in ibid., 258.
54. "Schon vor vielen Jahren trug ich mich mit dem Plan, ein Schriftliches Bekenntnis meines Lebens abzulegen." Ibid., 9.

Chapter 2: Gabrielle Buffet and Germaine Everling

1. *L'oeil cacodylate* translates literally as "the cacodylic eye," or the eye affected by a poison of the organo-arsenic family that causes respiratory tract, skin, and eye irritation. The unusual use of the word *cacodylate* in the title of the painting is clarified in part by Germaine Everling's use of the same term to describe Dada in her chapter "Dada périclite" in *L'Anneau de Saturne:* "Pourtant convenons qu'il servit de piqûre de cacodylate à une époque anémiée par une assimilation difficile. . . ." (As long as it served as an injection of cacodylate to an era made anemic by its difficult assimilation. . . , 137). The painting and Dada itself were both intended to shock and awaken the viewing public. In addition Dan Franck mentions that at the time Picabia created *L'oeil cacodylate,* the artist was suffering from an eye infection that was being treated with sodium cacodylate. See Franck, *Bohemian Paris,* 338.
2. "Ses dons bien français sont l'intellect, l'esprit, le jugement, la compréhension, la finesse." Arp, "Gabrielle Buffet-Picabia," in *Rencontres,* 25.
3. "On demande: Pourquoi *391*? Qu'est-ce que *391*?" was published in Zurich Dadaist Sophie Täuber's periodical *Plastique* in 1937.
4. "Nous voulions nous libérer et nous dégager de toute la technique traditionnelle, de toutes les vieilles syntaxes et grammaires, pour explorer ce que nous appelions la musique pure." Qtd. in Borràs, "Une Jeune femme appelée Gabrielle Buffet," *Rencontres,* 16.
5. "Il les disait avec une certaine pompe, d'une voix contenue, appuyant sur les rimes. Son profil romain était éclairé par la flamme et toute cette ambiance romantique lui seyait à merveille je l'avoue. Il dit ainsi plusieurs poèmes du recueil Alcools qui n'était pas encore paru à cette époque, et l'un d'eux qui retrace sa vie, son enfance et ses déboires fit à ma mère une grande impression. . . . Ma mère lui demanda le titre de ce poème. 'Il n'est pas encore terminé, répondit-il et n'a pas encore de nom. . . .' Puis tout à coup, gentiment il se tourna vers elle et lui dit: 'je l'appellerai zone', ce qui fut fait." Gabrielle Buffet, "Rencontre avec Apollinaire," 194.

6. "Combien nous étions loin ce soir de l'Esprit Nouveau, des différenciations entre le Cubisme et l'Orphisme!" Ibid., 194. This statement refers to l'Esprit Nouveau (the New Spirit) movement, begun in 1918 by Le Corbusier and Amedée Ozenfant, which emphasized an urbanized geometric order and clarity. Apollinaire used the term *orphisme* as early as 1912 to describe the technique of Sonia and Robert Delaunay. Orphism is also known as Orphic Cubism.
7. "entre un attachement certain à la tradition romantique et conservatrice et un désir non moins impératif qui le poussait aux avant-gardes du surréalisme naissant. . . ." Ibid., 194.
8. "Pour moi, l'époque dada a commencé le jour où j'ai rencontré Picabia." Buffet, "Dada," *Rencontres*, 213.
9. "Introduction de l'art moderne aux Etats-Unis," ibid., 177–78.
10. Ibid., 178.
11. Ibid., 182–83.
12. "Nous fûmes dès notre arrivée incorporés dans une bande hétéroclite et internationale où l'on faisait de la nuit le jour, où se côtoyaient des objecteurs de conscience de toute condition et de toute nationalité, dans un déchaînement inimaginable de sexualité, de jazz et d'alcool." Buffet, "L'Epoque 'pré-dada' à New York," *Rencontres*, 194.
13. "Introduction de l'art moderne aux Etats-Unis," 183.
14. "Une jeune fille appelée Gabrielle Buffet," *Rencontres*, 20–21. Borràs reports that Buffet published a series of articles in American newspapers but accorded them no significance. No one has yet collected information on most of these curious writings. In one case, in the Bibliothèque Jacques Doucet, there is an incomplete and undated clipping with the author's photograph—taken by Man Ray. Borràs estimates that the article dates from 1920, but she cannot be sure because whoever clipped the article did not imagine it would one day have scholarly worth.
15. "Une jeune fille appelée Gabrielle Buffet," *Rencontres*, 21.
16. Ibid.
17. "On demande: 'Pourquoi *391*? Qu'est-ce que *391*?'" 2.
18. "Introduction de l'art moderne aux Etats-Unis," 186.
19. Buffet-Picabia, "Arthur Cravan and American Dada," *Four Dada Suicides*, 86.
20. Buffet, "Marie Laurencin," *Rencontres*, 85.
21. "On demande," 6.
22. Ibid.
23. Ibid.
24. "Cinématographe."
25. "Très amusé par le nom de 'dada' que nous n'avions jamais entendu et le ton enthousiaste de la lettre, il répond à l'invitation, et nous irons à Zurich au début de 1919." Buffet, "Francis Picabia," *Rencontres*, 50.
26. "l'une des meilleures étapes de toutes nos peregrinations." Ibid.
27. "Leurs flèches empoisonnées sont des flèches pour rire et avec eux l'on joue plus qu'on ne massacre." Ibid., 50–51.
28. "On demande," 8.
29. "une eminence rayonnant de toutes les couleurs de l'arc-en-ciel" and "une femme fantasque and séduisante." Arp, "Gabrielle Buffet-Picabia," *Rencontres*, 25–26.
30. Ades, ed., *The Dada Reader*, 106.
31. "Mais n'ayez pas peur: ce qui vous affole en ce moment c'est l'ombre de votre nombril—il ne peut contenir qu'une goutte d'eau—ce bruit effrayant ce sont les

battements de votre coeur. Approchez-vous du monstre il ne mord pas—son pelage est comme de la peluche de soie et a les reflets des pigeons ses yeux roulent à droite et à gauche en avant en arrière comme ceux des caméléons dans son ventre ronronne un bruit de moteur, voyez ses pattes, elles bougent. . . . il va sauter. . . . . il saute ah! ah! ah! ah!—

"Mais oui—c'est un joujou tout simplement." Reprinted in Hans Bollinger, Guido Magnaguagno, and Raimund Meyer, *Dada in Zürich,* 234.

32. "langage anarchique mais non pas hermétique, où les mots perdent leur sens immediat et échangent les exigences de la syntaxe contre celles d'un rythme ou d'une image, et deviennent eux-mêmes plastiques." Buffet, "L'Epoque 'pré-dada' à New York," *Rencontres,* 199.
33. The poem is reprinted in *Rencontres,* 157–58.
34. The poem is reprinted in ibid., 155.
35. "Elle définissait avec une grande sensibilité la philosophie de Picabia et ce qu'il gardait de solide dans le jeu de ses paradoxes." Everling, "C'était hier: DADA," 161.
36. "Preface pour Jésus-Christ Rastaquouère." Reprinted in *Rencontres,* 163–65.
37. "l'épanouissement de ses dons de poète et de polémiste et celui de ses ambitions." Buffet, "Francis Picabia," *Rencontres,* 51.
38. "On demande," Reprinted in *Rencontres,* 211.
39. See James Knowlson, *Damned to Fame: The Life of Samuel Beckett,* 279–84.
40. Reprinted under the same title in *Rencontres,* 257–71.
41. "Je pus revoir Picabia; en le racontant je l'avais accepté. J'avais compris que le génie déséquilibre celui qui en porte le poids. . . ." Everling, *L'Anneau de Saturne,* 12.
42. "En 1921 éclatait à Paris la bombe 'Dada'; Tristan Tzara l'avait amenée de Zurich mais c'est Picabia qui en fournit le détonateur" (cover of *L'Anneau*).
43. "Rien ne se croyait moins vu que nous, mais l'oeil cacodylate n'était pas le seul à nous observer. Un oeil de femme s'en chargeait avec une gentillesse implacable." Qtd. in the preface to Everling, *L'Anneau,* 9.
44. "mais vous-même n'êtes-vous pas marié et père de trois enfants?" Everling, *L'Anneau,* 22.
45. "qui peignait des cubes auxquels on ne comprenait rien!" Ibid., 24.
46. "comprendra parfaitement la situation. Elle ne tient nullement à moi; elle est d'une loyauté absolue; elle acceptera de me rendre ma liberté." Ibid., 39.
47. "J'avais devant moi une femme petite, légèrement voûtée, très brune, avec un visage mobile dont le caractère résidait en un menton extraordinairement long et carré du bas, signe de volonté et d'obstination; une bouche aux lèvres minces et légèrement rentrées, des yeux noirs, dont le regard d'une acuité extraordinaire semblait véritablement déshabiller ceux qu'il observait. Mais la voix, déjà entendue au téléphone, était si merveilleuse et prenante qu'elle déroutait les reserves qu'on aurait pu faire sur l'expression de son visage. . . . C'était là, en tout cas, un être très au-dessus de la moyenne—une personnalité indiscutable." Ibid., 40.
48. "C'est affreux. . . . Je crois que je n'aurai jamais le courage de quitter ma femme et mes enfants." Ibid., 54.
49. Qtd. in ibid., 42.
50. "Gabrielle ne cessait de me mettre en garde contre le caractère 'despotique' de Picabia, 'son effrayant égoïsme, veritable chancre mortel qui le rongeait.'" Ibid., 67.
51. "ce pays inexistant où l'amour et l'art ressemblent à des albums d'estampes intellectuelles." Ibid., 80.
52. "C'était pour Noël" and "ça lui a fait tant plaisir." Ibid., 81.

53. "Je vous donne ma parole que, d'ici peu, le mot 'cubisme' sera périmé et remplacé par un autre qui fera plus de bruit dans le monde que le cubisme n'en a jamais fait." Ibid., 88.
54. "moindain par éducation et par goûts inavouées. Il fit figure de gracieux papillon, qui ne dédaigne aucune fleur, mais qui a ses préférences—et il montra bientôt quel avait été son meilleur butin." Ibid., 101.
55. "Ainsi que tous les marins, aussi différents soient-ils de nationalité, ont une démarche commune, les collaborateurs de la revue avait emprunté à Breton sa façon lente et détachée de prononcer chaque syllabe et semblaient parler du bout des dents. Par la suite, tous les jeunes intellectuels qui avaient approché le groupe affectèrent un ton semblable." Ibid.
56. "le plus sincèrement révolutionnaire des dadaïstes!" Ibid.
57. "il y avait en lui la finesse de Verlaine, alliée à des complexes très personnels." Ibid., 102.
58. "Au rez-de-chaussée, dans un baignoire, en compagnie de Marthe Chenal qui s'amusait beaucoup, Picabia applaudissait de tout son coeur en criant: 'Vive Dada!'

    "A ce moment, un spectateur de l'orchestre, poussé au paroxysme de la colère et reconnaissant en Picabia un des promoteurs du mouvement, quitta sa place et, s'avançant jusqu'à la loge, se mit en devoir de l'escalader. Il brandissait une canne menaçante et criait, au nom de la Légion d'honneur dont il était décoré. . . :

    "'Vous êtes tous des salauds! . . . Vous n'êtes pas des Français! . . . A bas les métèques! . . . ,' etc.

    "Picabia l'attendait, impassible, les bras croisés. Mais Marthe Chenal, inquiète sans doute pour son élégante toilette, s'interposa entre eux deux:

    > "'—Vous n'allez pas vous battre ici, devant une femme? C'est insensé et . . . inconvenant! . . . Attendez donc la sortie!'

    "—Eh bien, c'est entendu, dit à Picabia le champion de l'Ordre des Braves. Je vous attends à la sortie." (Ibid., 125)
59. Schwarz, *The Complete Works of Marcel Duchamp*, 693.
60. "l'esprit qui avait soufflé si durement et ardemment dégénérait sous le climat parisien d'après-guerre en polémique de clan, voire même d'individu." Buffet, "On demande," *Rencontres*, 206.
61. "Dada agissait sur les esprits comme une boisson pétillante et stimulante, et ne pouvait se fixer sans perdre irrémédiablement ses vertus fugaces, imponderables, sa raison d'être." Ibid., 211.
62. "En réalité, le Surréalisme n'était qu'un petit moyen de continuer Dada." Everling, "C'était hier: DADA," 178.
63. "Dada avait été un jeu; le 'Surréalisme' serait une école." Ibid.

Chapter 3: Céline Arnauld

1. Antonin Artaud's review appears on page 7 of "La Critique et Céline Arnauld," an undated supplement to Arnauld's *Heures intactes* in the Bibliothèque de l'Arsenal, Paris.
2. Clipping from an unidentified newspaper at the Bibliothèque Marguerite Durand, Paris, and the website of the University of Iowa Dada Archive, www.lib.uiowa.edu/dada/ARNAULD.htm (accessed February 9, 2004).
3. Hemus, *Dada's Women*, 194.

4. Rousselot, *Dictionnaire de la poésie française contemporaine,* 19.
5. "Je suis venue à la poésie par l'intermédiare de mon compagnon Paul Dermée. Il fit ma connaissance, au Collège de France, au cours de Pierre Janet, et m'initia par la suite à la nouvelle poésie surréaliste." Qtd. in Lacaze-Duthiers, *Anthologie des écrivains du V*[e] *Paris,* 38.
6. "Nous avons conscience d'appartenir à une magnifique époque de renaissance lyrique!" "Mais la poésie doit redevenir un peu plus humaine." Qtd. in Fernand Lot, "A Belle union, belle difference."
7. Paul Dermée's review appears in "La Critique et Céline Arnauld," a supplement to Arnauld's *Heures intactes* in the Bibliothèque de l'Arsenal, Paris.
8. "deux vagues dont tour à tour chacune va recouvrir l'autre." Breton, *Entretiens: 1913–1952,* 62.
9. Arnauld, "Farandole," *Anthologie Céline Arnauld: Morceaux choisis de 1919 à 1935,* 21.
10. Arnauld, "Cinéma," ibid., 19.
11. Tzara, *Dada est Tatou. Tout est Dada,* 83.
12. The December 1919 letter may be found in Sanouillet (1993 edition), *Dada à Paris,* 591, piece no. 175: "J'y joins un poème de Mme Céline Arnauld." And "Vous avez dû recevoir *Tournevire* de Mme Céline Arnauld . . ." (I attach a poem by Mrs. Céline Arnauld. You must have received *Tournevire* by Mrs. Céline Arnauld . . .).
13. For more on the relationship between Dada and cinema, see Elsaesser "Dada/Cinema."
14. Reprinted in Bohn, ed., *The Dada Market: An Anthology of Poetry,* 18–19, his translation. I would have translated "sentiments" as "feelings," and "descentes de lit" as "bedside rugs" (later suggesting "stepped on feelings" by the phrase "les sentiments en descente de lit"). I would also render "matin en papillotes" as "morning in curlers." "Avertisseur" originally appeared on page 4 in the March 1920 issue of *Z.*
15. The original text was published in issue 12 of *391* (March 1920). The translation by Susan de Muth appears in Ades, ed., *The Dada Reader,* 126–29.
16. Qtd. in ibid., 128.
17. Qtd. in ibid., 127.
18. Sanouillet, *Dada à Paris* (1993 ed.), 219.
19. Bettina Knapp, *French Theatre 1918–1939,* n27.
20. "Céline Arnauld, coiffée navire et perroquet, les cils en vers luisants." Eluard, "Présentations de circonstance" appeared in *Cannibale* 1 (April 25, 1920) and is reprinted in Sanouillet (1993 edition), *Dada à Paris,* 219.
21. Qtd. in ibid.
22. "Pour mettre fin à la stupide comédie de ceux qui se croient les défenseurs d'une nation qu'ils empoisonnent avec leur art fait de commérages, j'ai inventé une chanson filmée, une chanson qui tue, une chanson qui étrangle et qui désinfecte les regards en épluchures d'oignon; c'est le dernier film-fusée insecticide, visible au Cinéma Céline Arnauld, à Montmartre." Arnauld, "Dangereux."
23. Arnauld, "Mes Trois Péchés Dada," 12. Reprinted in Hemus, *Dada's Women,* 174.
24. "Dada aime sonner aux portes, frotter les allumettes pour enflammer les cheveux et les barbes. Il met de la moutarde dans les ciboires, de l'urine dans les bénitiers, et de la margarine dans les tubes de couleur des peintres." Ribemont-Dessaignes, "Manifeste," 11.
25. "Dada tue-Dieu. Le plus ancien et le plus redoutable ennemi de Dada s'appelle DIEU!" Paul Dermée, "Manifeste."

26. Céline Arnauld, "Ombrelle Dada." Reprinted in Hemus, *Dada's Women*, 184.
27. This was probably not the first time, and it certainly was not the last, that Céline Arnauld's name was misspelled. In Leonard R. Koos's encyclopedic entry on "Dada" to the 1999 *Feminist Encyclopedia of French Literature*, edited by Eva Martin Sartori, he gives her name as Céline Arnaud. Even her contemporary Germaine Everling referred to Arnauld as "Cécile."
28. In Tzara, *Dada est Tatou. Tout est Dada*, 357.
29. "*Projecteur* est une lanterne pour aveugles. Il ne marchande pas ses lumières, elles sont gratuites. *Projecteur* se moque de tout: argent, gloire et réclame—il inonde de soleil ceux qui vivent dans le froid, dans l'obscurité et dans l'ennui. D'ailleurs, la lumière est aussi produite par une pullulation madréporique dans les espaces célestes." Arnauld, *Projecteur* 1 (May 21, 1920): 1. Reprinted in Hemus, *Dada's Women*, 189.
30. "Les Ronge-Bois" appears on page 11 of *Projecteur* and is reprinted and translated in Bohn, ed., *The Dada Market*, 16–17.
31. Arnauld, *Projecteur* 1 (May 21, 1920): 6. Reprinted in Hemus, *Dada's Women*, 191.
32. "Tous les Dadas se feront tondre les cheveux sur la scène" and "Chacun de vous a dans le coeur un comptable, une montre et un petit paquet de merde." Reprinted in Sanouillet (1965 edition), *Dada à Paris*, 226. In *French Theatre 1918–1939*, 29, Bettina Knapp remarks that meat—bought during the intermission—was hurled at the actors on stage.
33. According to Everling, Breton, "qui avait les nerfs à fleur de peau, ne pouvait supporter plus de cinq minutes la repetition de ces onomatopées. Il passait dans la pièce voisine en grinçant les dents!" (who had nerves like flower petals, could not put up with more than five minutes of the onomatopic repetitions. He fled to the adjoining room, gnashing his teeth!). "C'était hier: DADA," 146.
34. Dachy, *The Dada Movement, 1915–1923*, 136.
35. Moroy's comments appear on page 4 of "La Critique et Céline Arnauld," a supplement to Arnauld's *Heures intactes*, which can be found in the Bibliothèque de l'Arsenal, Paris.
36. Faucherau, *Expressionnisme, Dada, Surréalisme et autres ismes*, 22.
37. Artaud, review in "La Critique et Céline Arnauld," supplement to Céline Arnauld's *Heures intactes*, 7.
38. Qtd. in Lacaze-Duthiers, *Anthologie des écrivains du V*[e] *Paris*, 38.
39. "Eprise de musique et de philosophie, les outrances surréalistes s'accordaient mal avec mon lyrisme. J'ai préféré m'en tenir à ce domaine silencieux de la vie intérieure où tout est amour et connaissance. Il y a dans ce que j'écris un désir angoissant d'étreindre l'Univers, de vivre toute la vie. De l'amertune aussi, cette amertune de quiconque n'est point dupe des palinodies. J'ai tracé ma route comme un enivrement, ma vie de nomade ne m'a donné qu'une religion, celle du merveilleux. Je suis fière de mon indépendance dans le mouvement poétique moderne et n'ai suivi personne, ne m'abaissant à aucun compromis et dédaignant la réclame. Je suis restée Poète." Qtd. in ibid., 38.
40. "LUI

"——— Je connais un pays où les fossoyeurs enterrent les vivants, les morts s'enterrent eux-mêmes, c'est pour cela qu'il y a là-bas tant de morts célèbres.

"elle

"———¡ Le maléfice s'est écrasé contre les tombes indociles à tout orage; la levée d'écrou a été faite à travers une pluie de diamants et les salutations cuivrées du soleil toujours plus superbe, et plus candidement suspendu à son Eldorado d'estampe. Capricieuse et entrelacée de soupirs, la porte du tonnelier s'est ouverte aux lianes et aux antilopes pures de toute trahison et ennoblies de charme et de grâce enfantine . . ." (Arnauld, *Anthologie*, 73).

41. Sanouillet (1993 edition), *Dada à Paris*, 225n39.
42. Rémy, review in "La Critique et Céline Arnauld," supplement to Céline Arnauld's *Heures intactes*, 16.
43. Arnauld, "Extrait de Saturne," *391* 15 (July 1921): 5.
44. Makward and Cottenet-Hage, eds., *Dictionnaire littéraire des femmes de la langue française*, 29. This source also identifies Arnauld merely as a Surrealist poet and does not mention Dada. At least her name is spelled correctly.
45. Huelsenbeck, *Dada Almanac*, 167.
46. Speculations on the date of Arnauld's death by Lacaze-Duthiers, *Anthologie des écrivains du Ve Paris*, 106; Moulin, *La Poésie feminine*, 251; and Rousselot, *Dictionnaire de la Poésie française contemporaine*, 19.
47. University of Iowa Dada Archive, www.lib.uiowa.edu/dada/ARNAULD.htm. (accessed February 9, 2004). The archive spelled her name "Arnaud."
48. Hemus, *Dada's Women*, 194.
49. Moulin, *La Poésie feminine*, 16.

Chapter 4: Juliette Roche

1. Here is another female contributor to Dada whose dates are in question. Although the Fondation Albert Gleizes lists Roche's year of death as 1982, her gravestone in the Cimetière de Serrières lists the date of her death as November 23, 1980.
2. Besides Burke's in-depth essay of 1998, there exist few sources of information on the life and works of Juliette Roche. Vergine's *L'altra metà dell'avanguardia 1910–1940* devotes two and a half pages to Roche. Schwarz's *Almanacco dada* and Naumann's *New York Dada* and *Making Mischief* provide additional data. Other useful facts about Roche may be collected from Alibert's *Gleizes: Biographie*, Brooke's *Albert Gleizes: For and Against the Twentieth Century*, Blanc's "Avant-propos" for the 1962 exhibition of Roche's works at the Galerie Miroir, and Ernoult's "Juliette Roche, notice du catalogue de l'exposition Dada."
3. Roche, unpublished memoir.
4. Ibid.
5. "Le dessin est quelque chose que tu penses et auquel tu mets une ligne autour." Qtd. in Vergine, *L'autre moitié de l'avant-garde*, 181.
6. http://www.fondationgleizes.fr/fr/gleize/page/juliette-roche/ses-ecrits. (accessed June 30, 2014).
7. "Hôtel Astoria entièrement remis à neuf" and "Rome Elysée Palace / 400 Chambres ouvert toute l'année." Juliette Roche, "Toulon-Cannes," *Demi cercle*, n.pag.
8. Alibert, *Gleizes*, 94.
9. Brooke, *Albert Gleizes*, 52.
10. Alibert, *Gleizes*, 94.
11. Vergine, *L'autre moitié de l'avant-garde*, 181.
12. "—La ville contenait déjà ses bruits de guerre." "Jardin Public" was published in her 1920 collection, *Demi Cercle*, n.pag.
13. "J'avais eu l'imprudence de commencer un portrait de Cocteau. Pendant les vacances de Pâques dans mon atelier je fais le portrait ou j'essaye de la faire. Son agitation continuelle et ses propos trop amusants m'empêchent de travailler. . . . Un coup de

sonnette imprévu m'inquiète. C'était Albert Gleizes que je n'attendais pas. C'est une catastrophe. . . . Depuis un an Cocteau se moque agréablement de 'mes' cubistes et aussi de ceux de Roger de la Fresnaye et nous lui répondons gentiment qu'il est mûr pour l'Académie. Il va se passer des choses atroces. Je prononce les deux noms aussi mal que possible et d'une voie [*sic*] étranglée, avec le faible espoir qu'ils ne les comprendront pas, et pour ne pas assister à ce qui est probable, je disparais dans mes coulisses pour faire le thé. Lorsque je reviens avec ma théière, ils sont assis tout près l'un de l'autre, l'air ravi, échangeant des cartes, des numéros de téléphone et prenant un rendez-vous. Huit jours plus tard Cocteau ne parlait plus que de Jacques Villon, de Duchamp-Villon, d'Albert Gleizes et Missia Godebska [*sic*] me faisait des scènes de reproches: 'Pourquoi avez-vous mis Jean en contact avec les cubistes? C'est un homme de droite, ce n'est pas un homme de gauche . . . Il va se perdre dans ces milieux. . . .'" Qtd. in Alibert, *Gleizes*, 63–64, translated in Brooke, *Albert Gleizes*, 43–44. A belle epoque pianist and host of a Parisian literary-artistic salon, Misia Godebska was painted by Pierre Auguste Renoir, Henri de Toulouse-Lautrec, Edouard Vuillard, and Pierre Bonnard.

14. According to Alibert, Roche's marriage came about because Gleizes was mobilized and stationed at Toul.
15. Qtd. in Alibert, *Gleizes*, 96.
16. Jules Roche had acquired La République Française in 1906.
17. Brooke, *Albert Gleizes*, 52.
18. Qtd. in Addington, "New York Is More Alive and Stimulating than France Ever Was, Say Two French Painters."
19. Qtd. in ibid.
20. Qtd. in ibid.
21. Qtd. in ibid.
22. Qtd. in ibid.
23. Qtd. in ibid.
24. Roche, unpublished memoir.
25. ibid.
26. See http://www.fondationgleizes.fr/aaa-GB/ag-mf-lyon-gb.html
27. Burke, "Recollecting Dada: Juliette Roche," 554.
28. Roche, unpublished memoir.
29. See http://www.fondationgleizes.fr/fr/gleize/page/juliette-roche/sa-vie-son-uvre (accessed June 30, 2014.
30. Roche, unpublished memoir.
31. *Demi Cercle*, n.pag.
32. Ibid.
33. Roche, unpublished memoir.
34. Ibid.
35. Burke, "Recollecting Dada," 556.
36. The *Auto-portrait à l'estampe japonaise* is featured on the cover of the catalog from the Galerie Miroir for the solo exposition of Juliette Roche's works on December 15–28, 1962.
37. *Francis Picabia: Singulier ideal*, exhibition catalog 16, November 16–March 16, 2003.
38. Roche, unpublished memoir.
39. *La Minéralisation de Dudley Craving Mac Adam* (1924 edition), 1.
40. "un gros philosphe, un peu guatémalien, les doigts raidis de bagues." Juliette Roche, "La Minéralisation de Dudley Craving Mac Adam" (1922): 28.

41. Burke, "Recollecting Dada," 570. Burke also offers an in depth analysis of the novella on 564–70.
42. André Benedetto, "Productions des oeuvres par autres auteurs." *Forum du théâtre des carmes*, http://perso.wanadoo.fr/forum.theatre/historique.htm (accessed November 12, 2002).
43. Qtd. in Brooke, *Albert Gleizes*, 63. In 1941 Gleizes officially returned to the Catholic faith.
44. Qtd. in ibid.
45. Qtd. in ibid.
46. The attack was published in *Cannibale* 2 (May 1920) during the dispute begun by Gleizes's "L'Affaire Dada," which alludes to the Dadaists' sexual exploits. Picabia, who fathered at least five children, did not overlook that Gleizes was childless. One of the reasons for Picabia's bitter resentment could have been because he felt betrayed by Gleizes, whose 1912 publication of *Du "Cubisme"* was possibly financed by Picabia.
47. The letter appears in Sanouillet (1993 edition), *Dada à Paris*, 513–14.
48. Roche, preface to *Albert Gleizes, Paintings, Gouaches, Drawings*, 4.
49. "Au point de vue pathologique, le cas des leaders-dadistes est facilement saisissable. C'est leur manque absolu de volonté directrice qui les a voués à l'anarchie spirituelle dans laquelle ils cherchent une justification de leur individualité" Gleizes, "L'Affaire Dada," 30.
50. "J'avais pardonné à Albert Gleizes sa rupture brutale avec Cocteau après la guerre de 1914." Qtd. in Alibert, *Albert Gleizes*, 134.
51. Brooke, *Albert Gleizes*, 78.
52. Roche, preface, 6.
53. Brooke, *Albert Gleizes*, 136.
54. Qtd. in Brooke, *Albert Gleizes*, 165.
55. "Au creux de sa paume lourde viennent aboutir des gerbes de voûtes. Cette main est tout ce qu'on peut apercevoir d'une vorace et dangereuse créature emmurée. [. . .] Les peintures écaillées dans les chapelles à la Chaise-Dieu, les figures des vitraux et des tapisseries racontent aussi de singulières histories . . . " Roche, "Christophle de Gamon, honnête homme," 14.
56. "Gamon porte en lui cette bonne humeur un peu goguenarde, ce bon sens robuste et jovial des vieux imagiers." Ibid.
57. "On retrouve dans ses poèmes le fumet de ces grands plateaux âpres, couverts de cultures maigres et cernés de volcans éteints, aux villages pauvres, roussis par des étés brutaux et terrés tout l'hiver sous la menace des 'burles', mais d'où l'on sent pourtant la Provence si proche, avec la poussière somptueuse de ses villes chaudes, avec ses platanes somnolents et tout son plaisir de vivre méditerranéen." Ibid., 16.
58. "Christophle de Gamon, vous auriez été un charmant voisin de campagne. Ibid., 20.
59. "Dans le recueillemment de Gamon, dans son acceptation tranquille et polie de l'existence, peut-être pourrait-on retrouver le sourire aigu de quelque lointain grand-père aux yeux bridés?" Ibid.
60. "Le monde est une usine de stupidité" and "La mort n'est qu'un phénomène physico-chimique sans aucune importance: c'est seulement après ma mort que je commencerai à m'amuser sérieusement." Roche, "Charles Henry," 31.
61. "Son esprit était un clavier de mille octaves, contenant les intervalles les plus imperceptibles et capable de rendre tous les sons." Ibid., 27.

62. See http://designethistoires.lecoledesign.com/2011/07/de-lidee-a-la-forme-exposition-porza-musee-galliera-1939/ (accessed September 12, 2012).
63. Roche, preface, 7–8.
64. Ibid., 8.
65. I am currently engaged in further research on Roche through her novella and memoirs.
66. Alibert, *Gleizes*, 95.
67. Since her death in 1980, Roche's paintings have been included in the following exhibitions: Making Mischief: Dada Invades New York (Whitney Museum of American Art, 1996–97), the Paris-Barcelona exhibition at the Grand Palais in Paris and the Picasso Museum in Barcelona (2001–2), and the Dada exhibit at the Centre Georges Pompidou (2005–6). A wide variety of her pictorial works, including many mentioned in this text, can be viewed at http://www.fondationgleizes.fr/fr/gleize/page/juliette-roche/sa-vie-son-uvre (accessed June 20, 2014).

Chapter 5: Hannah Höch

1. Krieger, "Hannah Höch, son oeuvre et Dada," *Hannah Höch: collages, peintures, aquarelles, gouaches, dessins*. 7.
2. Qtd. in Roditi, "Hannah Höch," 68.
3. Hille, *Hannah Höch und Raoul Hausmann: Eine Berliner Dada-Geschichte*, 81.
4. Reprinted in Thater-Schulz, ed., *Hannah Höch: Eine Lebenscollage. 1889–1918*, 194.
5. Qtd. in ibid., 101–2.
6. Qtd. in Roditi, "Hannah Höch," 66.
7. Pagé, "Interview with Hannah Höch," *Hannah Höch Collages, Peintures, Aquarelles, Gouaches, Dessins*, 23–31.
8. Qtd. in Mehring, *Berlin Dada*, 91. "The Malik group" that Höch mentions, refers to Malik-Verlags, founded by brothers Wieland Herzfelde and John Heartfield in 1917. The name was borrowed from the novel *Der Malik* by Else Lasker-Schuler.
9. "Sind die Schablonen der Stiche die ich für Orlik gemacht habe. . . ." Qtd. from a handwritten note on back of photograph in Berlinische Galerie, Landesmuseum für Moderne Kunst, Fotografie und Architektur, Künstler-Archive, hereafter referred to as Berlinische Galerie Archives.
10. Pagé, "Interview with Hannah Höch," 25. The Spartakus movement mobilized Berlin's working masses at Potsdamer Platz in May 1916. The demonstration, led by Rosa Luxemburg and Karl Liebknecht, was famously repressed with violent arrests.
11. Qtd. in Adriani, "Biography-Documentation," 19.
12. Qtd. in Roditi, "Hannah Höch," 74.
13. Hille, *Hannah Höch und Raoul Hausmann: Eine Berliner Dada-Geschichte*, 81.
14. Ibid., 82. The names "Hannchen" and "Hanna Hösch" might further be suggestive of "Haschen" (bunny), "Hänschen" (little Johnny), and "Höschen" (knickers).
15. Bergius, *Das Lachen Dadas: Die Berliner Dadaisten und ihre Aktionen*, 372.
16. "Zu Wort kam ich erst später, in der 'Kameradschaftszeit.'" Qtd. in Pagé, "Interview with Hannah Höch," 26.
17. Qtd. in Ohff, *Hannah Höch*, 23.
18. Qtd. in Roditi, "Hannah Höch," 70.
19. Bergius, "Hannah Höch: Künstlerin im Berliner Dadaismus," 38. See also Hausmann's 1919 essay "Zur Auflösung des bürgerlichen Frauentyps."
20. "einen ganzen Menschen auch für mich—und nicht einen Teil eines Menschen" Qtd. in Hille, *Hannah Höch und Raoul Hausmann*, 82.

21. "denn ich hätte die Verpflichtung gehabt, Hanna soviel halt zu bieten und so sehr unser Kind zu wünschen, dass es ihr auch möglich geworden ware, es zu bekommen." "Meine Unklarheit und meine Selbsttüaschung über meine wahren Antriebe sind die Ursache, dass unsere Kinder nicht geboren wurden." Qtd. in Züchner, ed., *Scharfrichter der bürgerlichen Seelen: Raoul Hausmann in Berlin 1900–1933*, 50–52.
22. "Ich brauchte ein Kind, er brauchte eine Mutter" Qtd. in Ohff, *Hannah Höch*, 21.
23. "Aber Helma u. Hausmann wollten nicht mitaufsteigen." Qtd. from a picture postcard in the Berlinische Galerie Archives.
24. Schulz, "Bild- und Vokabelmischungen sind Weltanschauungen zu Hannah Höchs Collage 'Meine Haussprüche,'" 134. Huelsenbeck: "Dada ist die Polizei der Polizei!" (twice) and "Der Tod ist eine durchaus dadaistische Angelegenheit"; Serner: "Sachliches in die Rippen!," Hausmann: "gefährlich ist nur eine unentschiedene Mischung," Baader: "Ohne dieses Lesepult kann uberhaupt keine Literatur werden," Schwitters: "Lass sie sagen, sie wissen nich wieder Kirchturm steht," and Nietzsche from Ecco homo: "Akustische Täuschung dass, wo Nichts gehört wird, auch Nichts da ist . . . "; Friedlaender: "Wird Person der Stern artigen Zustand auch in ihre Moralität bringen?" and Goethe: "Wer sich nähert, den stoset nicht zurück, und wer sich entfernt, den haltet nicht zurück, und wer wieder kommt, den nehmt auf als ob er nicht Weg gewesen wäre"; Arp: "Und immer mehr Zeit—und doch keine Zeiger auf Zeit" and Gerturd: "Es regent Blätter." Friedrich Nietzsche and Goethe, though certainly not Dadaists, find a place among the Berlin Dada group: Nietzsche because Raoul Hausmann the Dadasoph often spoke of this influential thinker and Goethe because every German-educated child can quote from this key figure in German literature.
25. Qtd. in Roditi, "Hannah Höch," 69, 71.
26. Qtd. in ibid., 70.
27. This undated poem and its hand-corrected draft may be found in the Berlinische Galerie Archives. It is reprinted in full in Remmert and Barth, eds., *Hannah Höch: Werke und Worte*, 41.
28. "ich giere nach dem linienfluss ihres körpers." Qtd. from a picture postcard in the Berlinische Galerie Archives.
29. The complete letter is in the Berlinische Galerie Archives.
30. "dein dein dein o komme na-natürlich nakischt in mein kämmerlein. ARP" and "Ich unarme Sie herzlich, in alter Dada-Treue und grüsse Sie von Da zu Da." Qtd. from personal correspondence in the Berlinische Galerie Archives.
31. In Remmert and Barth, eds., *Hannah Höch: Werke und Worte*, 36–38.
32. "Sie war mit der halben Welt befreundet, und mit der anderen Hälfte bekannt." Qtd. in Ohff, *Hannah Höch*, 25.
33. "In Den Haag wohnt ein kleines Ungetüm, das vorgibt, homosexuell zu sein, doch die so weiblich ist wie eine frischgeborene Amme, es heisst Brugman. Es macht es sich zur täglichen Gewohnheit, mich mit Dreck, Scheisse und parfümierten Spermatozoen einzuschmieren. Es schreibt mir Bände über krähende Hühner und kreisende Berge—Zank. Ihre Schundverse fanden keinen Platz in De Stijl." Qtd. in Ohff, Heinz "Holland," 263.
34. "Liebe Hanna Höch!—Wir haben in Holland sehr viel success mit Dada! Nie ist hier über etwas so viel in die Zeitungen geschrieben. Dabei bekommen wir aus verschiedene Städte Einladungen. Sehr schön!" Personal correspondence in the Berlinische Galerie Archives.

35. "Wir haben jetzt auch ein klarer Blick in der Fascismus, und Does hat ein agressives Manifest geschieben, welcher in den französoschen Zeitscrift Vouloir veröffentlich werden soll." Personal correspondence in the Berlinische Galerie Archives.
36. "Til war so geändert durch dir, daß hat sie doch selber auch immer gesagt." Personal correspondence in the Berlinische Galerie Archives.
37. "In Paris wird es wieder lebendig. Picabia's 'Relache' [*sic*] in Théatre [*sic*] des Champs Elysses [*sic*] ist erfrisschend. Das würde Ihnen Spaß machen! Wann kommen Sie wieder nach Paris? Die neueste Bewegung ist "Le mouvement accéléré," woher alle dadaïsten angeschlossen sind. Ich werde Ihnen das Flugblatt schicken." Personal correspondence in the Berlinische Galerie Archives.
38. "Lieber Merz—I / Was ist das? Warum höre ich nich Dein Vergissmeinnichtfarbenes Merzorgan in allen Grammophönen der Welt / zwitsch / zwitsch / zwiwitsch / lauseaaasen?" The letter, found in the Berlinische Galerie Archive, is reprinted in its entirety in Remmert and Barth, eds., *Hannah Höch: Werke und Worte*, 32–33.
39. See "Dadaïstische Brief van Til Brugman aan Hannah Höch, Den Haag 12–13 September 1926" in *Dames in Dada: Het Aandet van vrouwen in de Dadabeweging*, ed. Gioia Smid (Amsterdam: Amazone, 1989), 112.
40. Ohff, *Hannah Höch*, 25.
41. "Til Brugman war ein Eulenspiegel unserer Tage, der seine Possen zwar nicht auf den Straßen trieb, aber mit den Drolerien auf hoher Ebene ihre Umgebung Tag und Nacht in Atem hielt. . . . Diese nie endenden, purzelnden, sarkastischen, verrückten Einfälle, die auf einem riesigen Wissen 'tanzten', machten die Jahre mit Til zu den amüsantesten meines Lebens." Qtd. in Ohff, *Hannah Höch*, 25. Höch makes reference to the Low German folkloric trickster Till Eulenspiegel.
42. Luyken, "Das Album von Hannah Höch. Materialsammlung, Skizzenbuch oder Konzeptkunst?" in Luyken, ed., *Hannah Höch Album*.
43. Brugman, Til. "tu ne m'a rien laissé." *Lust & Gratie* 19 (1988), 57.
44. Grohmann, *The Dada-World of Hannah Höch*, 5.

Chapter 6: The Woman Dadaist

1. Courtesy of Guerrilla Girls, 1988.
2. Alice Bailly, Käthe Wulff, Marietta di Monaco, Ella Bergmann, Greta Knutson, Käte Steinitz, Maria d'Arezzo, Suzanne Duchamp, Katherine Dreier, Gala Eluard, Jane Heap, Mabel Dodge, Renée Dunan, Isadora Duncan, Valeska Gert, Juliette Roche, Adya van Rees Dutilh, Agnes Ernst Meyer, Margaret Anderson, Louise Stevens Arensberg, Germaine Albert-Birot, Alexandra Exter, Erika Deetjen, Sophie Täuber, Maya Chrusecz, Marie Laurencin, Angelika Hoerle, Mary Wigman, Meret Oppenheim, Gabrielle Buffet, Til Brugman, Marthe Tour-Donas, Liubov Popova, Bernice Abbott, Louise Norton, Adrienne Monnier, Marguerite Buffet, Clara Tice, Florence Henri, Nelly van Doesburg, Natalia Goncharova, Djuna Barnes, Edith Olivié, Beatrice Wood, Olga Rosanowa, Claire Goll, Else Von Freytag-Loringhoven.
3. The poem is reprinted in *Emmy Ball Hennings 1885–1948*, 88.
4. See ibid., 113.
5. Reprinted in Huelsenbeck, *Dada Almanac*, 15–36.
6. "Biographies," in Huelsenbeck, *Dada Almanac*, 168. Jahnn (1894–1959) was a German novelist, dramatist, pacifist, music publisher, and renovator of organs. He won the Kleist Prize for his 1919 drama *Pastor Ephraim Magnus*.

7. Seuphor, *Arp + Sophie Taeuber*. This brochure/guide was designed for an exposition sponsored by l'Association pour le progrès intellectuel et artistique de la Wallonie (Liège), September 19–October 1, 1953.
8. Tzara's critique, as translated from French to German by Hugo Ball, appears in Bollinger, Magnaguagno, and Meyer, *Dada in Zürich*, 259. "Die mathematische Reinheit der Stickereien von Frau van Rees: innere Harmonie der Farbe, religiös gedacht, Leitung der Formen und deren friedfreudiges Nebeneinander; leuchtende Weisheit. –Die mathematische Reinheit der Stickereinen von Frau van Rees ruft die Seele in einen Springbrunnen der Unendlichkeit. Ihre klaren Farben haben den sonoren Schwung der Nacht, die Milchstrassen kreist."
9. "Mlle Alice Bailly était ici, samedi, très vivante et pleine d'espoir, croit à une sorte de victoire de la peinture moderne, mais elle est très sympathique." Qtd. in Sanouillet, *Dada à Paris* (1965), 479.
10. "Biographies," Huelsenbeck, *Dada Almanac*, 167.
11. "Dans l'orage amoniaque une écharpe est apportée à l'auteur par Alice Bailly et Augusto Giacometti." Qtd. in Tzara, *Dada est Tatou. Tout est Dada*, 331.
12. Her work may be viewed in Geneva (where the Musée d'art et d'histoire owns eighteen of her works), Lausanne, and in Washington, D.C., at the National Museum of Women in the Arts, where her colorful 1917 self-portrait graces the museum's 2000 catalog and is part of the permanent collection.
13. Qtd. in Scheub, *Verrück nach Leben: Berlin Szenen in den zwanziger Jahren*, 60–61.
14. Chadwick, *Women, Art, and Society*, 256.
15. *Sonia Delaunay, ses peintures, ses objets, ses tissus simultanés, ses modes* (Sonia Delaunay, Her Paintings, Her Objects, Her Simultaneous Fabrics, Her Fashions), 1925; *Tapis et Tissus* (Rugs and Fabrics), 1929; and *Sonia Delaunay: compositions, couleurs, idées* (Sonia Delaunay: Compostions, Colors, Ideas), 1930.
16. Qtd. in Petersen and Wilson, *Women Artists: Recognition and Reappraisal from the Early Middle Ages to the Twentieth Century*, 111–12.
17. "L'un des quatre inscrivait le motif initial, développé ensuite par les trois autres, chacun travaillant à tour de rôle sur la même feuille." Qtd. in a one-page exhibit announcement for Galerie Bing, 174 rue du Faubourg St-Honoré, June 16–July 15, 1954.
18. Dunford, *A Biographical Dictionary of Women Artists in Europe and America Since 1850*, 86.
19. Fluxus was a 1960s antiart network of musicians and visual artists, influenced by the works of John Cage and George Maciunas. Allan Kaprow first used the term *happenings* to describe art pieces at pop artist George Segal's 1957 farm picnic. Happenings usually included simultaneous performances of music, dance, recitations, and so forth, all amid the audience rather than on stage. Yayoi Kusama used human bodies as canvas in her Body Festival Happenings of the mid- to late-1960s. Isidore Isou arranged letters without regard to meaning in lettrism, while the situational internationalists through Guy Debord called for radical gestures in art and society and have been recently linked to the Occupy (Wall Street) Movements.
20. Gilbert and Gubar, *The Madwoman in the Attic: The Woman Writer and the Nineteenth Literary Imagination*, xii.
21. Koos, "Dada," 138.
22. Chadwick, *Women, Art, and Society*, 296.

Bibliography

Primary Sources

Arnauld, Céline. *Anthologie Céline Arnauld: Morceaux choisis de 1919 à 1935*. Brussels: Les Cahiers du Journal des poètes, 1936.

———. "Extrait de Saturne." *391* 15 (July 1921): 5.

La Nuit rêve tout haut. Paris: Librairie Paul Magné, 1939.

Le Clavier secret. Paris: Collection des D.I. de l'Esprit Nouveau, 1934.

Les Réseaux du Réveil. Paris: G.L.M., 1937.

Rien qu'une Étoile, suivi de plain-chants sauvages. Paris: Montbrun, 1948.

———. *L'Apaisement de l'*éclipse: Passion en deux actes; précédée de Diorama. Paris: Ecrivains réunis, 1925.

———. "Avertisseur." *Z* 1 (March 1920): 6.

———. "Dangereux." *Cannibale* 1 (April 25, 1920): 2.

———. *Heures intactes: Poèmes*. Brussels: Les Cahiers du Journal des poètes, 1936.

———. "Luna Park." *Projecteur* (May 21, 1920): 6.

———. "Mes Trois Péchés Dada." *Cannibale* 2 (May 25, 1920): 12.

———. "Ombrelle Dada." *Littérature* 13 (May 1920): 19.

———. *Poèmes à claires-voies*. Paris: Editions et librairie de l'Esprit nouveau, 1920.

———. "Prospectus Projecteur." *Projecteur* 1 (May 21, 1920): 1.

Arp, Hans. *Arp on Arp: Poems, Essay, Memories*. Edited by Marcel Jean. Translated by Joachim Neugroschel. New York: Viking, 1972.

———. *Sophie Taeuber-Arp*. Paris: Denise René, 1962.

Arp, Jean. "Gabrielle Buffet-Picabia." In Buffet-Picabia, *Rencontres*, 25–28.

Ball, Hugo. *Flight Out of Time: A Dada Diary*. Translated by Ann Raimes. Edited by John Elderfield. New York: Viking, 1974.

Ball, Hugo, and Emmy Hennings. *Damals in Zurich: Briefe aus den Jahren 1915–1917*. Zurich: Arche, 1978.

Ball-Hennings, Emmy. *Briefe an Hermann Hesse*. Frankfurt: Suhrkamp, 1956.

———. *Emmy Ball Hennings 1885–1948. "Ich bin so vielfach . . .": Texte, Bilder, Dokumente*. Frankfurt am Main: Stroemfeld, 1999.

———. *Das Flüchtige Spiel: Wege und Umwege einer Frau*. Einsiedeln: Benziger, 1940.

———. *Die Letzte Freude*. Leipzig: Kurt Wolff, 1913.

———. *Gefängnis*. Berlin: Erich Reiß, 1919.

———. *Helle Nacht*. Berlin: Erich Reiß, 1922.

———. *Ruf und Echo: Mein Leben mit Hugo Ball*. Einsiedeln: Benziger, 1953.

Breton, André. *Entretiens: 1913–1952*. Paris: Gallimard, 1973.

Brugman, Til. "tu ne m'as rien laissée." *Lust & Gratie* 19 (Fall 1988): 57.

Buffet-Picabia, Gabrielle. *Aires Abstraites*. Geneva: P. Cailler, 1957.

———. "Arthur Cravan and American Dada." *transition* (April-May 1938): 314–21. Reprinted in *The Dada Painters and Poets: An Anthology*, edited by Robert Motherwell, 13–17. Cambridge, Mass.: Harvard University Press, 1988; and *Four Dada Suicides*, 81–88. London: Atlas Press, 1995.

———. "Cinématographe." In *391: revue publiée de 1917 à 1924 par Francis Picabia*, edited by Michel Sanouillet. Vol. 1. Paris: Terrain vague, 1960. 28.

———. "On demande: 'Pourquoi 391? Qu'est-ce que 391?'" *Plastique* 2 (June 1937): 2–8.

———. "Rencontre avec Apollinaire." *Le Point* 5 (November 1937): 184–99.

———. *Rencontres avec Picabia, Apollinaire, Cravan, Duchamp, Arp, Calder*. Paris: Belfond, 1977.

Dermée, Paul. "Manifeste." *Littérature* 13 (May 1920): 19.

Everling, Germaine. *L'Anneau de Saturne*. Paris: Fayard, 1970.

Everling Picabia, Germaine. "C'était hier: DADA." *Les Oeuvres libres* 109 (June 1955): 119–78.

Francis Picabia: Singulier ideal. Exhibition catalog 16, November 16–March 16, 2003. Paris: Adagp/Panthé international, 2002.

Gleizes, Albert. "L'Affaire Dada." *Action* (April 3, 1920): 26–32.

Höch, Hannah. *Hannah Höch: collages, peintures, aquarelles, gouaches, dessins*. Parallel text with *Collagen, Gemälde, Aquarelle, Gouachen, Zeichnungen*. Berlin: Gebr. Mann, 1976

———. *Hannah Höch Album*, edited by Gunda Luyken. Berlin: Hatje Cantz, 2004.

———. *Hannah Höch: Werke und Worte*, edited by Herbert Remmert and Peter Barth. Berlin: Frölich und Kaufmann, 1982.

———. *Hannah Höch 1889–1978: Collages*. Stuttgart-Bad Cannstatt: Cantz'sche, 1985.

Hausmann, Raoul. *Am Anfang War Dada*. Gießen: Anabas, 1972.

Huelsenbeck, Richard. *Dada Almanach*. Berlin: Erich Reiss, 1920. Translated by Malcolm Green as *Dada Almanac*. London: Atlas, 1993.

———. *En Avant Dada*. 1920. Reprint, Hamburg: Nautilus, 1978.

———. *Memoirs of a Dada Drummer*. Edited by Hans J. Kleinschmidt. New York: Viking, 1974.

Knutson, Greta. *Lunaires*. Paris: Flammarion, 1985.

Mehring, Walter. *Berlin Dada*. Zurich: Peter Schifferli, 1959.

Monaco, Marietta di. *Ich kam—ich geh; Reisebilder, Erinnerungen, Porträts*. Munich: Süddeutscher, 1962. Munich: Allitera, 2002.

Perrottet, Suzanne. *Ein bewegtes Leben*. Berlin: Quadriga, 1995.

Ribemont-Dessaignes, Georges. *Déjà jadis, ou du mouvement Dada à l'espace abstrait*. Paris: Julliard, 1958.

———. "Manifeste." *Littérature* 13 (May 1920): 11.

Richter, Hans. *Begegnungen von Dada bis heute; Briefe, Dokumente, Erinnerungen*. Cologne: Schauberg, 1973.

———. *Dada, Art and Anti-Art*. Trans. David Britt. London: Thames & Hudson, 1965.

———. *Dada, Kunst und Antikunst*. Cologne: Schauberg, 1964.

———. *Dada Profile*. Zurich: Arche, 1961.

Roche-Gleizes, Juliette. "Albert Gleizes et son temps." *Zodiaque* 100 (April 1974): 2–14.

———. "Belle journée est passée." *Dernier hommage à Anne G. Dangar et Albert Gleizes.* Saint-Léger-Vauban, Yonne: les Presses Monastiques, 1955.
———. "Charles Henry." *Cahiers de l'Etoile* 13 (January-February 1930): 25–31.
———. "Christophle de Gamon, honnête homme." *Excerpta.* Paris: La Connaissance, 1927.
———. *Demi Cercle.* Paris: Editions d'Art La "Cible," 1920.
———. "La Minéralisation de Dudley Craving Mac Adam." *La Vie des Lettres et des Arts* 8 (1922): 22–271. Separately published as *La Minéralisation de Dudley Craving Mac Adam.* Paris: Croutzet et Depost, 1924.
———. "Mémoires." Undated typescript. Musée National d'Art Moderne, Paris.
———. Preface to *Albert Gleizes, Paintings, Gouaches, Drawings.* Exhibition catalog. London: Marlborough Fine Art, 1956.
Steinitz, Käte. *Kurt Schwitters: A Portrait from Life.* Berkeley: University of California Press, 1968.
———. Kurt Schwitters: *Erinnerungen aus dem Jahren 1918–1930.* Zurich: Arche, 1987.
Tzara, Tristan. *Dada est Tatou. Tout est Dada.* Ed. Henri Béhar. Paris: Flammarion, 1996.
Wigman, Mary. *Le langage de la danse.* Paris: Chiron, 1990. French edition of *Die Sprache des Tanzes,* 1963, translated from the German by Jacqueline Robinson. Translated into English by Walter Sorell as *The Language of the Dance.* Middleton, Conn.: Wesleyan University Press, 1966.

Secondary Sources

Addington, Sarah. "New York Is More Alive and Stimulating than France Ever Was, Say Two French Painters" *New York Tribune,* October 9, 1915: 9.
Ades, Dawn, ed. *The Dada Reader: A Critical Anthology.* Chicago: University of Chicago Press, 2006.
Adriani, Götz. "Biography-Documentation." In Höch, *Hannah Höch 1889–1978: Collages,* 8–63.
Alibert, Pierre. *Albert Gleizes, naissance et avenir du cubisme.* Saint-Etienne: Aubin Visconti, 1982.
———. *Gleizes: Biographie.* Paris: Michèle Heyraud, 1990.
Altshuler, Bruce. *The Avant-garde in Exhibition.* New York: Abrams, 1994.
Artaud, Antonin. Review in "La Critique et Céline Arnauld." Supplement to Arnauld, *Heures intactes,* 7.
Béhar, Henri, and Michel Carassou. *Dada, histoire d'une subversion.* Paris: Fayard, 1990.
Behr, Shulamith. *Women Expressionists.* Oxford: Phaidon, 1988.
Benstock, Shari. *Women of the Left Bank: Paris, 1900–1940.* Austin: University of Texas Press, 1986.
Bergius, Hanne. *Dada: Dada in Europa: Werke und Dokumente.* Berlin: D. Reimer, 1977.
———. *Das Lachen Dadas: Die Berliner Dadaisten und ihre Aktionen.* Gießen: Anabas, 1989.
———. "Hannah Höch: Künstlerin im Berliner Dadaismus." In *Hannah Höch: collages, peintures, aquarelles, gouaches, dessins.* Berlin: Gebr. Mann, 1976.
Bergius, Hanne, and Karl Riha. *Dada Berlin: Texte, Manifeste, Aktionen.* Stuttgart: Reclam, 1977.
Berlinische Galerie. *Hannah Höch 1889–1978. Ihr Werk, ihr Leben, ihre Freunde.* Berlin: Argon, 1989.
Berlinische Galerie. *Profession ohne Tradition:125 Jahre Verein der Berliner Künstlerinnen.* Exhibition catalog, Berlin, 1992.
Billeter, Erika, and José Pierre. *La Femme et le surréalisme.* Lausanne: Musée cantonal des beaux-arts Lausanne, 1987.

Blanc, Lucien. "Avant-propos." *Juliette Roche: Galerie Miroir.* Montpellier: Galerie Miroir, 1962.

Bloemink, Barbara. *The Life and Art of Florine Stettheimer.* New Haven: Yale University Press, 1995.

Bohn, Willard, ed. *The Dada Market: An Anthology of Poetry.* Carbondale: Southern Illinois University Press, 1993.

Bollinger, Hans, Guido Magnaguagno, and Raimund Meyer. *Dada in Zürich.* Zurich: Arche, 1985.

Borràs, Maria Lluïsa, "Une Jeune femme appelée Gabrielle Buffet." In Buffet-Picabia, *Rencontres,* 13–24.

Brinker-Gabler, Gisela. *Deutsche Literatur von Frauen.* Vol. 2. Munich: C. H. Beck, 1988.

Brooke, Peter. *Albert Gleizes: For and Against the Twentieth Century.* New Haven: Yale University Press, 2001.

Brown, Betty Ann. *Gradiva's Mirror: Reflections on Women, Surrealism, and Art History.* New York: Midmarch Arts Press, 2002.

Bucher, Regina, and Berhard Echte, eds. *Emmy Ball-Hennings: Musa, Diseuse, Poetessa.* Wäldenswil: Fondazione Hermann Hesse Montagnola, 2006.

Burke, Carolyn. *Becoming Modern: The Life of Mina Loy.* New York: Farrar, Straus & Giroux, 1996.

———. "Recollecting Dada: Juliette Roche." In *Women in Dada: Essays on Sex, Gender, and Identity,* edited by Naomi Sawelson-Gorse, 546–77. Cambridge: MIT Press, 1998.

Burmeister, Ralf and Eckhard Fürlus, eds. *Hannah Höch: Eine Lebenscollage. 1921–1945.* Vol. 2, parts 1–2. Berlin: Hatje, 1995.

Burmeister, Ralf, Eckhard Fürlus, and Karin Hoerstel, eds. *Hannah Höch: Eine Lebenscollage. 1946–1978.* Archiv-edition. Vol. 3, parts 1–2. Berlin: Künstler-Archive der Berlinischen Galerie, Ladesmuseum für Moderne Kunst, Photographie und Architektur, 2001.

Camfield, William. *Tabu Dada: Jean Crotti and Suzanne Duchamp.* Edited by William Camfield and Jean-Hubert Martin. Bern: Die Kunsthalle, 1983.

Caws, Mary Ann. *The Poetry of Dada and Surrealism: Aragon, Breton, Tzara, Eluard, Desnos.* Princeton: Princeton University Press, 1970.

Caws, Mary Ann, Rudolf E. Kuenzli, and Gwen Raaberg, eds. *Surrealism and Women.* Cambridge, Mass.: MIT Press, 1991.

Chadwick, Whitney. *Mirror Images: Women, Surrealism, and Self-Representation.* Cambridge, Mass.: MIT Press, 1998.

———. *Women, Art, and Society.* New York: Thames & Hudson, 1990.

———. *Women Artists and the Surrealist Movement.* Boston: Little, Brown, 1985.

Chadwick, Whitney, and Isabelle de Courtivron, eds. *Significant Others: Creativity and Intimate Partnership.* New York: Thames & Hudson, 1993.

Crespelle, J-P. *La Vie quotidienne à Montparnasse à la Grande Époque, 1905–1930.* Paris: Hachette, 1976.

Dachy, Marc. *Journal du Mouvement Dada 1915–1923.* Geneva: Skira, 1989.

———. *The Dada Movement, 1915–1923.* New York: Editions d'Art Albert Skira, 1990.

———. *Tristan Tzara: dompteur des acrobates: Dada Zurich.* Paris: L'Echoppe, 1992.

Daval, Jean-Luc. *Journal des avant-gardes: les années vingt, les années trente.* Geneva: Skira, 1980.

Dermée, Paul. "Opinions sur 'La Nuit rêve tout haut' suivie de 'Le Clavier secret'—1934." Supplement to Arnauld, *Heures intactes.*

Dunford, Peggy. *A Biographical Dictionary of Women Artists in Europe and America Since 1850.* New York: Harvester Wheatsheaf, 1990.

Eiger, Dietmar and Dr. Elger Dietmar. *Dadaism*. Cologne: Taschen, 2004.

Elderfield, John. Introduction to *Flight Out of Time: A Dada Diary*, by Hugo Ball. Translated by Ann Raimes. Edited by John Elderfield. New York: Viking, 1974.

Elsaesser, Thomas. "Dada/Cinema" *Dada Surrrealism* 15 (1956): 13–27.

Ernoult, Natalie. "Juliette Roche, notice du catalogue de l'exposition *Dada*." Paris: Centre George Pompidou, 2005. 852–53.

Fauchereau, Serge. *Expressionnisme, Dada, Surréalisme et autres ismes*. Paris: Denoël, 1976.

Fine, Elsa Honig. *Women and Art: A History of Women Painters and Sculptors from the Renaissance to the 20th Century*. Montclair, N.J.: Allenheld & Schram, 1978.

Fleisser, Marieluise. *Avant-garde*. Frankfurt am Main: Suhrkamp, 1972.

Florenne, Yves. "Picabia et son témoin passionné: *L'Anneau de Saturne* de Germaine Everling." *Le Monde*, August 1, 1970.

Flouquet, Pierre-Louis. "Opinions sur 'La Nuit rêve tout haut' suivie de 'Le Clavier secret' —1934." Supplement to Arnauld, *Heures intactes*.

Foster, Stephen C. Review of *New York Dada, 1915–1923*, by Francis M. Naumann. *Art Journal* 54 (Summer 1995): 93–97.

Francis Picabia: Singulier idéal. Exhibition catalog 16, November 16–March 16, 2003. Paris: Adagp/Panthé international, 2002.

Franck, Dan. *Bohemian Paris*. Translated by Cynthia Hope Liebow. New York: Grove, 2001.

Gammel, Irene. *Baroness Elsa: Gender, Dada, and Everyday Modernity. A Cultural Biography*. Cambridge, Mass.: MIT Press, 2002.

Gass, René. *Emmy Ball-Hennings. Wege und Umwege zum Paradies*. Zurich: Pendo, 1998.

Gilbert, Sandra, and Susan Gubar. *The Madwoman in the Attic: The Woman Writer and the Nineteenth Literary Imagination*. New Haven: Yale University Press, 2000.

Grohmann, Will. *The Dada-World of Hannah Höch*. Exhibition catalog. London, 1966.

Harmon, William. *A Handbook to Literature*. Ninth ed. Upper Saddle River, N.J.: Prentice Hall, 2003.

Hautamäki, Irmell. *Avantgarden alkuperä, Modernin estetiikkaa Baudelairesta Warholiin*. Helsinki: Gaudeamus, 2003.

Hedges, Inez. *Languages of Revolt: Dada and Surrealist Literature and Film*. Durham: Duke University Press, 1983.

Heller, Nancy G. *Women Artists: Works from the National Museum of Women in the Arts*. Washington, D.C.: National Museum of Women in the Arts, 2000.

Hemus, Ruth. *Dada's Women*. New Haven: Yale University Press, 2009.

Hille, Karoline. *Hannah Höch und Raoul Hausmann: Eine Berliner Dada-Geschichte*. Berlin: Rowohlt, 2000.

Hubert, Renée Riese. *Magnifying Mirrors: Women, Surrealism, and Partnership*. Lincoln: University of Nebraska Press, 1994.

Hugnet, Georges. *Fantastic Art, Dada, Surrealism*. Edited by Alfred H. Barr Jr. New York: Museum of Modern Art, 1947.

———. *L'Aventure Dada, 1916–1922*. Paris: Galerie de l'Institut, 1957.

———. *Dictionnaire du Dadaïsme, 1916–1922*. Paris: Simoën, 1976.

———. "The Dada Spirit in Painting." In *The Dada Painters and Poets: An Anthology*, edited by Robert Motherwell, 125–41. Boston: G.K. Hall, 1981.

Jones, Amelia. *Irrational Modernism: A Neurasthenic History of New York Dada*. Cambridge, Mass.: MIT Press, 2004.

Jürgs, Britta, ed. *Etwas Wasser in der Seife: Portraits dadaistischer Künstlerinnen und Schriftstellerinnen*. Berlin: Aviva, 1999.

Just, Ward S. *Ambition and Love*. Boston: Houghton Mifflin, 1994.

Katalog der Austellung Dada. Dokumente einer Bewegung. Düsseldorf: Kunsthalle Düsseldorf, 1958.

Klüver, Billy, and Julie Martin. *Kiki's Paris: Artists and Lovers 1900–1930.* New York: Abrams, 1989.

Knapp, Bettina. *French Theatre 1918–1939.* New York: Grove Press, 1985.

Knowlson, James. *Damned to Fame: The Life of Samuel Beckett.* New York: Touchstone, 1997.

Koos, Leonard R. "Dada." In *The Feminist Encyclopedia of French Literature,* edited by Eva Martin Satori, 138. Westport, Conn.: Greenwood Press, 1999.

Krieger, Peter. "Hannah Höch, son oeuvre et Dada." In *Hannah Höch:* collages, peintures, aquarelles, gouaches, dessins : A.R.C. 2, Musée d'art moderne de la ville de Paris, 30 janvier-7 mars 1976, Nationalgalerie Berlin, Staatl. Museen Preuss. Kulturbesitz, 24. März-9. Mai 1976. [Katalog, Barbara Dieterich, Peter Krieger ; Übers., Jean-Claude Walfisz, Genoveva Dieterich]. Berlin: Mann [in Komm.], 1976. 7–21.

———. "Paradox and Poetry in Hannah Höch's Collages" In Höch, *Hannah Höch 1889–1978 Collages,* 84–94.

Lacaze-Duthiers, Gérard, ed. *Anthologie des écrivains du Ve Paris et le quartier latin.* Paris: Bibliothèque de l'Aristocratie, 1953.

La Charité, Virginia A. *Twentieth-Century French Avant-garde Poetry, 1907–1990.* Lexington: French Forum, 1992.

Lanchner, Carolyn. *Sophie Taeuber-Arp.* New York: Museum of Modern Art, 1981.

Lavin, Maud. *Cut with the Kitchen Knife: The Weimar Photomontages of Hannah Höch.* New Haven: Yale University Press, 1993.

Levitt, Annette Shandler. *The Genres and Genders of Surrealism.* New York: Palgrave Macmillan, 2000.

Lot, Fernand. "A Belle union, belle différence." *Les Nouvelles littéraires,* December 11, 1937, 3.

Luyken, Gunda. "Das Album von Hannah Höch. Materialsammlung, Skizzenbuch oder Konzeptkunst?" In *Hannah Höch Album,* edited by Gunda Luyken. Berlin: Hatje Cantz, 2004.

Makward, Christiane P., and Madeleine Cottenet-Hage, eds. *Dictionnaire littéraire des femmes de la langue française.* Paris: Editions Karthala, 1996.

Melzer, Annabelle. *Latest Rage the Big Drum.* Ann Arbor: UMI Research Press, 1980.

Meyer, Raimund, et al. *Dada Global.* Zurich: Limmat, 1994.

Moroy, Elie. Review in "La Critique et Céline Arnauld." Supplement to Arnauld, *Heures intactes.*

Motherwell, Robert, ed. *The Dada Painters and Poets: An Anthology.* Boston: G. K. Hall, 1981.

Moulin, Jeanine. *La Poésie feminine: Epoque Moderne.* Paris: Seghers, 1963.

———. *Huit siècles de poésie féminine.* Paris: Seghers, 1975.

Naumann, Francis M. *Making Mischief: Dada Invades New York.* New York: Whitney Museum, 1996.

———. *New York Dada, 1915–1923.* New York: Abrams, 1994.

Nochlin, Linda. *Women, Art, and Power and Other Essays.* New York: Harper Collins, 1989.

Ohff, Heinz. *Hannah Höch.* Berlin: Gebr. Mann, 1968.

Pagé, Suzanne. "Interview avec Hannah Höch." In *Hannah Höch: collages, peintures, aquarelles, gouaches, dessins,* 23–31.

Partsch-Bergsohn, Isa. *Modern Dance in Germany and the United States: Crosscurrents and Influences.* Oxford: Routledge, 1994.

Petersen, Karen, and Inge Schumacher, eds. *Künstlerinnen International, 1877–1977.* Berlin: Neue Gesellschaft für Bildende Kunst, 1977.

Petersen, Karen, and J. J. Wilson, eds. *Women Artists: Recognition and Reappraisal from the Early Middle Ages to the Twentieth Century*. New York: New York University Press, 1976.

Reetz, Bärbel. *Emmy Ball-Hennings: Leben im Vielleicht*. Frankfurt: Suhrkamp, 2001.

Remmert, Herbert, and Peter Barth. "Vorwart" to *Hannah Höch: Eine Lebenscollage. 1889–1918*, edited by Thater-Schulz, 11–42.

Riese Hubert, Renee. *Magnifying Mirrors: Women, Surrealism, and Partnership*. University of Nebraska Press, 1994.

Riha, Karl. *Da Dada War, Ist Dada da: Aufsätze und Dokumente*. Munich: Hanser, 1980.

Robbins, Daniel. "The Formation and Maturity of Albert Gleizes: A Biographical and Critical Study, 1881–1920. Diss., New York University, Institute of Fine Arts, 1975.

Roditi, Edouard. "Hannah Höch." In *Dialogues: Conversations with European Artists at Mid-Century*, edited by Edouard Roditi. San Francisco: Bedford Arts, 1990.

Roters, Eberhard. "Pictorial Symbolism in Hannah Höch's Work." In Höch, *Hannah Höch 1889–1978 Collages*. 64–69.

Rosemont, Penelope, ed. *Surrealist Women: An International Anthology*. Austin: University of Texas Press, 1998.

Rousselot, Jean. *Dictionnaire de la poésie française contemporaine*. Paris: Larousse, 1968.

Rubin, William S. *Dada and Surrealist Art*. New York: Abrams, 1968.

Rugh, Thomas F. "Emmy Hennings and Zurich Dada." *Dada / Surrealism*. 10/11 (1982): 5–28.

Sanouillet, Michel. *Dada à Paris*. Paris: Pauvert, 1965. New ed. Revised and expanded by Anne Sanouillet. Paris: Flammarion, 1993.

Sawelson-Gorse, Naomi, ed. *Women in Dada: Essays on Sex, Gender, and Identity*. Cambridge, Mass.: MIT Press, 1998.

Scheub, Ute. *Verrückt nach Leben: Berliner Szenen in dem zwanzinger Jahren*. Hamburg: Rowohlt, 2000.

Schippers, K. *Holland Dada*. Amsterdam: Querido, 1974.

Schmid, Gioia. *Dames in Dada: Het aandeel van vrou wen in de DADA-Beweging*. Amsterdam: Amazone, 1989.

Schrott, Raoul. *Dada 15/25*. Innsbruck: Haymon, 1992.

Schulz, Armin. "Bild- und Vokabelmischungen sind Weltanschauungen zu Hannah Höchs Collage 'Meine Haussprüche.'" In *Hannah Höch 1889–1978: Ihr Werk, ihr Leben, ihre Freunde*, 133–45.

Schütt-Hennings, Annemarie. Introduction to *Ruf und Echo: Mein Leben mit Hugo Ball*, by Emmy Ball-Hennings. Einsiedeln: Benziger, 1953.

Schwarz, Arturo. *Almanacco dada: antologia letteraria-artistica, cronologia, repertorio delle riviste*. Milan: Feltrinelli, 1976.

———. *The Complete Works of Marcel Duchamp*. New York: Abrams, 1969.

Seuphor, Michel. *Arp + Sophie Täuber*. Paris: Union, 1953.

Silver, Kenneth E. *Esprit de Corps: The Art of the Parisian Avant-garde and the First World War, 1914–1925*. Princeton: Princeton University Press, 1989.

Smid, Gioia, ed. *Dames in Dada: Het Aandet van vrouwen in de Dadabeweging*. Amsterdam: Amazone, 1989.

Staber, Margit. *Sophie-Taeuber Arp*. Translated by Eric Schaer Lausanne: Editions Rencontre, 1970.

Suleiman, Susan Rubin. *Subversive Intent: Gender, Politics, and the Avant-garde*. Cambridge, Mass.: Harvard University Press, 1990.

Thater-Schulz, Cornelia, ed. *Hannah Höch: Eine Lebenscollage. 1889–1918*. Band I, 1. Abteilung. Berlin: Argon, 1989.

———. *Hannah Höch: Eine Lebenscollage. 1919–1920.* Band I, 2. Abteilung. Berlin: Argon, 1989.

Thomas, Karin. "Hannah Höch—the 'good girl' who works hard. The Feminist Question-Mark." In *Hannah Höch 1889–1978 Collages*, 70–83.

Van den Berg, Hubert, ed. *Das Ding an Sich und das Ding an ihr: Dada Erotiken.* Berlin: Nautilus, 2003.

Vergine, Lea. *L'autre moitié de l'avant-garde 1910–1940.* Paris: Des femmes, 1982.

Wheeler, Kenneth W., and Virginia Lee Lussier, eds. *Women, the Arts, and the 1920s in Paris and New York.* New Brunswick, N.J.: Transaction, 1982.

Zeller, Bernhard, ed. *Hermann Hesse in Selbstzeugnissen und Bilddokumenten.* Hamburg: Rowohlt, 1977.

Züchner, Eva, ed. *Scharfrichter der bürgerlichen Seelen: Raoul Hausmann in Berlin 1900–1933.* Berlin: Berlinische Galerie, 1998.

Index

About the author

PAULA K. KAMENISH is an associate professor of English at the University of North Carolina Wilmington. She received her university's Board of Trustees Award for Teaching Excellence and has published articles on Bertolt Brecht, Jean Genet, Eugène Ionesco, Quebecois novelist Roch Carrier, the fate of South Slavic poetry, and best practices in teaching.

www.ingramcontent.com/pod-product-compliance
Lightning Source LLC
LaVergne TN
LVHW050152080826
844660LV00002B/185

* 9 7 8 1 6 1 1 1 7 4 6 8 7 *